The Transformation of Cities

Also by David C. Thorns:

Suburbia

Quest for Community

New Directions in Sociology (ed.)

Cities Unlimited (with L. Kilmartin)

Eclipse of Equality (with D. Pearson)

Social Theory and the Australian City (with L. Kilmartin)

Fragmenting Societies: A Comparative Analysis of Regional and Urban Development

Understanding Aotearoa/New Zealand: A Historical Statistical Base for Social Scientists (with C. Sedgwick)

The Transformation of Cities

Urban Theory and Urban Life

David C. Thorns

First published 2002 by
PALGRAVE MACMILLAN
Houndmills, Basingstoke, Hampshire RG21 6XS and
175 Fifth Avenue, New York, N.Y. 10010
Companies and representatives throughout the world

PALGRAVE MACMILLAN is the global academic imprint of the Palgrave Macmillan division of St. Martin's Press, LLC and of Palgrave Macmillan Ltd. Macmillan® is a registered trademark in the United States, United Kingdom and other countries. Palgrave is a registered trademark in the European Union and other countries.

ISBN 0–333–74596–5 hardcover
ISBN 0–333–74597–3 paperback

This book is printed on paper suitable for recycling and made from fully managed and sustained forest sources.

A catalogue record for this book is available from the British Library.

Library of Congress Cataloging-in-Publication Data

The transformation of cities : urban theory and urban life/David C. Thorns.
    p. cm.
  Includes bibliographical references and index.
  ISBN 0–333–74596–5 (cloth) – ISBN 0–333–74597–3 (paper)
    1. Cities and towns–History–20th century.   2. Sociology, Urban.   I. Title.
Thorns, David C.
307.76–dc21   2002020061

10   9   8   7   6   5   4   3   2   1
11   10   09   08   07   06   05   04   03   02

Printed and bound in Great Britain by Creative Print & Design (Wales), Ebbw Vale.

Contents

List of Figures, Tables and Boxes

Boxes

Preface

In 1996, I attended the United Nations Habitat 2 conference in Istanbul. This amazing multicultural event stimulated and challenged my thinking about the way the city was being changed in the last years of the twentieth century. The next stage in my journey was a sabbatical in 1998 taking me to Los Angeles, New York, Kingston (Jamaica), London, Paris and Geneva where I saw, at first hand, a range of global cities. King's College London and the British Library of Political and Economic Science gave me access to excellent resources and a time to develop plans for the book. On returning to Aotearoa/New Zealand in September, 1998, I undertook a new course on Globalisation and Urban Change which shaped this book. In 1999, I also had the opportunity to visit Shanghai and attend a conference on the Future of Chinese Cities. Seeing the pace and scale of urban development and the juxtaposition of the traditional and ultra modern in the urban landscape confirmed my focus upon urban transfomation as the key theme of the book.

People as well as places have been significant in shaping my ideas over the past three years. I have been fortunate to work amongst colleagues who have provided a supportive and stimulating environment and who have aided, often unwittingly, the development of my research. There are also particular people to whom I would like to express my thanks – Peter Marcuse, Sharon Zukin, Chris Hamnett, Alan Murie, Pat Mullins and Terry Burke. With all, I have had valuable conversations. My honours classes in 1999 and 2000 have also been a valuable sounding board for ideas and a constant source of challenge. So to Alex Broom, Lynne Batty, Lorraine Leonard, Carmelia Chaves, Sarah Meek, Sarah McAlpine, Hazel Ashton and Tobias Geisler I express my appreciation. Lorraine Leonard also ably assisted me in the construction of the bibliography. During the past three years, I have greatly appreciated the support, encouragement and critique of my colleagues on the Foundation for Research Science and Technology research programme – New Zealanders at home, Harvey Perkins and Ann Winstanley. Harvey, in particular, has been particularly significant as a sounding board and critic for my ideas and also provided much appreciated feedback on earlier drafts of this book. Steven Kennedy and Catherine Gray of Palgrave have been most generous with their support and constructive criticism at various stages in the writing of this text. To all these people I say thank you. In the end, the responsibility for the book is mine.

David C. Thorns
Christchurch

Acknowledgements

The author and publishers want to thank the following for their permission to use included materials:

Eolss Publisher for Figures 9.1 and 9.2 taken from *Encyclopaedia of Life Support Systems* 1997.

IMF, for Table 3.1 adapted from Steetal K. Chand and Albert Jaeger, *Ageing Populations and Public Pensin Schemes*, 1996.

United Nations International Crime and Justice Research Institute for Table 7.2 taken for *Criminal Victimisation of the Developing World*, 1995.

United Nations Publications for Figures 3.1, 3.2, 3.3 and 3.4 taken from the United Nations Publications Department of Public Information Website.

United Nations Human Settlements Programme for Table 3.2, 3.3 and Figure 3.5 taken from the UN-Habitat report, 2001.

Every effort has been made to trace all the copyright holders but if any have been inadvertently overlooked the publishers will be pleased to make the necessary arrangements at the first opportunity.

List of Abbreviations

CBOs	Community-based organisations
IMF	International Monetary Fund
NATO	North Atlantic Treaty Organisation
NGOs	Non-governmental organisations
NIMBY	Not-in-my-backyard
PTAs	Parent–teacher associations
OECD	Organisation for Economic Cooperation and Development
TNCs	Transnational Corporations
UN	United Nations
UNCHS	United Nations Centre for Human Settlements
UNCRI	United Nations International Crime and Justice Research Institute
UNESCO	United Nations Educational, Scientific and Cultural Organisation
WCED	World Commission on Environment and Development
WTO	World Trade Organisation

1

Introduction

An Urban Millennium

The twenty-first century is likely to be dominated by urban living in a way that we have not experienced before. Over half the world's populations are now city dwellers. By 2025, according to World Bank estimates, 88 per cent of the world's total population growth will be located in rapidly expanding urban areas and 90 per cent of that urban growth will be absorbed by the developing world (World Bank 1996). Having said this, it is also important to appreciate that cities contain enormous diversity. Crucial in creating these differences have been the pace at which cities have grown, their historical roots and the layers of physical and social structure that have given rise to the present social and physical infrastructures and practices. At the present day, we have the phenomenon of the incredibly fast growth of areas such as Pudong in China, the new economic zone of Shanghai, which has gone from green fields and farming in nine years to an urban area of 1.8 million people (Shanghai: Pudong New Area Press Office 1998). This new area is being promoted as the financial, information, and manufacturing hub of the increasingly market-oriented Chinese economy. At the other end of the spectrum, we have centuries-old cities in Europe where the additions and refurbishment to the urban landscape have occurred much more gradually over time. The urban worlds that we see are more interconnected now than they have ever been before through the new systems of communication that have developed and shaped the present 'information age'. Thus, the underlying theme of this text is that of transformations. Transformations are occurring at every level from the global economic, political and social structures to the ways that we fashion our everyday lives. We now share in a global culture in a way that has not previously been possible yet at the same time we live out our lives in 'local places' – in our houses, neighbourhoods, cities, regions and nations.

Globalisation has been a key transformation of the last two decades of the twentieth century. Globalisation is not a product, something that has now happened but an interrelated set of processes, economic, social, political, cultural and ecological, that are continuing to shape the world

1

in which we live. These globalising processes crucially affect the city as this is the place where most people live. For some, globalisation has brought increased homogeneity, for others the result is difference and heterogeneity. For some, global processes have impacted upon the local in ways that have reduced our ability as individuals, families and communities to shape our lives. For others, resistance is still possible and in fact a very significant part of the global world.

Exploring the dimensions of city transformation from the industrial-modern city to the global city will require an interrogation of these claims. These will be addressed through an examination of the way the city has been reshaped over the second half of the twentieth century. The book will also explore how useful the systems of explanation and analysis are that have grown up in the past and have formed the basis of urban scholarship. Such scholarship has been largely dominated by work based in and around Western Europe and North America and thus is largely centred on Western Europe and North America. Are these ideas and analyses still as relevant in a global world where the 'centre' is no longer as clearly based in these regions of the world?

Exploring the nature of city transformation requires some consideration of what is the city. The definition of what constitutes the city has been somewhat elusive given its multidimensional character. Most definitions have involved some concept of size. For example, one definition of the city by Davis (1973:1) is as 'concentrations of many people located close together for residential and productive purposes'. However, how large an urban area has to be in order for it to qualify as a city is quite variable and relates to the way particular countries have developed their systems of administration. Saunders (1986:7), in addressing this question, points out that 'cities are places where large numbers of people live and work' – but this is problematic as in different countries settlements of the same size may be designated as small towns, suburbs or cities. The attention to how settlements are categorized draws our attention to the fact that cities are not just places of large numbers of people but are also political and legal entities, usually places of local government and economic activity and sites of leisure and recreational activity. As Elliot and McCrone (1982:5) suggest, 'cities are a very special human institution (or if you prefer, a complex of institutions)'. Combining these two ideas of size and a complex set of institutions gives us a starting point to examine the notion of urban transformation.

Transformation also implies changes over time and thus an appreciation of the importance of the history of any particular city's development. The present urban fabric results from successive generations of settlers leaving their mark in both the physical structure and in the political, economic and social institutions. To understand the present thus requires some reflection on the past course of city growth and development. The city has been through a number of transformations since it emerged in human history.

The first cities arose at a time when the capacity of societies had grown such that they could become more settled and permanent. A move from hunting and gathering towards agrarian production occurred leading to surplus production and the emergence of new classes within the population who had greater wealth and a more differentiated set of tasks and lifestyles. There was thus the need for an administrative system to complement the family and clan structures which had provided the basis of social organisation. Cities are relatively recent developments emerging around 3000–4000 BC in the Nile valley and Mesopotamia of the Fertile Crescent (Carter 1983). They first became significant as places of trade and governance – activities, which were to continue to be significant for decades to come. Later, around 2000 BC, cities also emerged in Crete, the Yellow River area of China, Greece, and the Indus valley. In South America, the Mayan Aztec urban settlements date from the first millennium AD.

As the settled parts of the world grew in Europe, urban areas and cities became a feature of the landscape. Over time, they grew from small settlements for trade and fortification into grander political, economic and cultural centres. London, for example, in Roman times was a site of Imperial activity. With the fall of the Roman Empire, its importance waned and it was some centuries later when it started to become again a centre of trade, commerce and political power. The division was sharp between the city of London, a place of trade and merchants and the newer city of Westminster, the site of the court and Government. Early theorising about the city reflected these aspects and thus emphasized the city as a political entity and as a market place for trading and wealth generation. Many cities were city-states and, as such, wielded considerable economic and political power in the centuries before nation-states became the dominant geo-political entities (Weber 1921).

The major transformation, that created the most rapid shift in patterns of settlement from the country to the city, was the rise, in the nineteenth century, of the modern industrial city. The industrial revolution of the eighteenth and nineteenth centuries ushered in the modern world, a world where manufacturing production was the driving force of societies. The new wealthy and powerful were not the aristocrats and landed gentry or the merchants and their guilds, but industrial capitalists making the new commodities of an industrial age. The rise of industry required the harnessing of new resources and new forms of energy to drive machinery in the growing number of factories. New locations thus became significant. Labour was required for the factories and housing developed for workers close to the new sources of employment. Industrial cities grew rapidly providing sharply differentiated residential locations for the new workers and new bosses (Weber 1889). Urbanisation was the dominant spatial process of the nineteenth and early twentieth centuries in the industrialising world. Britain, for example, in 1801 had 85 per cent of the population still living in rural areas. By the middle of the nineteenth century, this had changed and more people lived in urban areas than in the country and almost one third lived in towns with a population over 50,000 (Mellor 1977, Elliott and McCrone 1982). Power and wealth shifted from the older port and merchant cities to the new industrial cities. The discovery of the new world and migration were also to change the population distribution and impact upon city growth. Cities such as New York were cities of migrants, people attracted by the new land of opportunities and pushed by famine, war, and poverty from their homelands. In some cases, this was as a consequence of rapid industrialisation and the shifting national and international patterns of trade.

Just as in the early years of industrialisation major changes took place in the nature of urban life, in the latter part of the twentieth century a further transformation has been taking place. This time it is from the industrialised modern system of cities based around wealth created from large-scale commodity production for a mass market place to a new system based around the generation of wealth from information services which are globally rather than nationally organised. Cities now compete in an international system where there are new hierarchies of power and opportunity from the core global cities of New York, London and Tokyo where the world's information and financial super highway is centred, to regional and local centres. The various centres intersect with the global system in a variety of ways creating the differences and local variations which are visible across the cities of the world (Sassen 1991, Friedman 1995, Knox 1996). Although all cities are increasingly drawn into a system of global relations, local identities have survived and are part of what, in the end, creates their competitive advantage as increasingly the quality, as well as the quantity, of life has become an important global issue.

The shift from the rural to the urban was a dramatic and far-reaching change to people's lives. The rural order integrated work and living, the cycles of the year shaped activity, peasants were tied to the land in ways which limited mobility. Inequality was considerable. The transition to the urban industrial world in the eighteenth and nineteenth centuries produced one of the great transformations in human history (Giddens 1987). Work and residence were separated. Production became factory based. Working-class men and women became wage earners, selling their labour power within the now capitalist-based urban economy. Living became urban based within single-family housing of various kinds. This new structure of work and living, over time, led to a clearer separation of gender roles increasingly leading to women occupying roles separated from the world of paid work in the domestic sphere. In this urban world the dominant discourse was about growth, both in terms of wealth and urban expansion. Growth was seen as the key to the increase in overall social and economic well-being. As the industrial age developed, changes in technology, and the logic and practices of the capitalist form of accumulation, have created de-industrialisation, re-industrialisation and expansion into new 'greenfield' sites – both within the industrialised nations and into other parts of the world. Much of this is shaped by the quest for 'comparative advantage' in terms of labour, the cost of raw materials and proximity to expanding markets.

The latest set of transformations has centred on the shift to the so-called knowledge and information industries. These are less dependent on being physically located within particular regions. Their raw materials are ideas and knowledge and thus require research-centred institutions and access to knowledge flows. Much of these are now information technologies, ones associated with computers on the Internet and the World Wide Web. Web-based search engines can now explore knowledge from remote sites. The old space advantages are thus being reconfigured. The new forms of wealth creation are however not evenly spread across the globe and questions of access and control are still significant.

There are a variety of explanations for these transformations of urban life. We have, for example, explanations seeking to identify the 'causal components of change'. Much of this work is influenced by economic determinism. The logic of capitalist accumulation is seen as one of the key determinants of the urban system. The shift from industrial to information-centered capitalism being a key change in the late twentieth century (Castells 1997, 1998). Much of this analysis has been influenced by economic geographers who have utilised regulation theory to talk about the transition from 'Fordism' – based around mass production and consumption – to 'flexible' forms of accumulation based more around greater variety, choice and flexible rather than mass production techniques (Harvey 1990, Britton, Le Heron and Pawson 1992). Much of this analysis gives relatively little weight to human agency. Where humans are given agency it is often as 'class actors' or as 'wage workers'. This leads to dichotomous views of the world based around struggle over wage relations and the distribution of wealth (Jessop 1990). It also stresses the universal nature of the urban process as the world becomes completely dominated by the logic of capital accumulation and thus tends to downplay the nature of local differences and national variations. Further, because of its concentration upon wage relations it tends to pay less attention to other forms of agency as expressed at the level of social movements constituted around different social bases for example gender, ethnicity, environmentalism, sexuality, or at the level of individual identity (Seidman 1994).

Other theories of the urban transformation tend to rely less on the search for causes and look more to the contextual and contingent aspects of change. They are more likely to be grounded in the study of the local and the everyday life of the urban dwellers. They are less concerned with predicting the pattern of change and more focused upon the meaning attached by individuals and groups to their place – their home, community, neighbourhood and city (Featherstone 1991). A more contingent and contextual approach would lead to a different range of questions requiring exploration. The first would be about how wealth is being created within contemporary cities. Here clearly there are divergences and difference. The overall thrust of change in developed cities has been away from manufacturing production, the original engine of urban growth, towards producer and consumer services. The rise of the new 'consumption spaces' has attracted a lot of attention in the urban literature of the 1980s and 1990s. The creation of new forms of work, the changing balance between full- and part-time work, the work of women and men, the creation of an increasingly varied and unequal workforce and the question of who gets included and excluded in these changes are very important issues. The growth of the urban as spectacle, the greater concentration upon urban place making and inter-urban competition over the new growth agenda of consumption spaces – casinos, malls, towers, sports stadia, convention centres, and so on (Sorkin 1992, Zukin 1995, Dear 2000, Schollmann, Perkins and Moore 2000, Perkins and Thorns 2000b) are placed at the centre of the analysis.

In developing cities the agenda is likely to be different. Some are still passing through the industrialising phase of their development but are doing so at a much greater pace than was the case for western cities. Many of them are also experiencing a faster rate of growth of their population than of their economic capacity leading to many migrants occupying squatter and marginal forms of housing and getting by in the informal economy rather than the formal. The imperative to growth and the need to be part of the 'globalising economy' for many of these cities is just as strong as it is for the older cities of Europe, and the restructuring that has occurred and continues has led to both social and spatial inequalities and new forms social of exclusion.

A second significant question is, how are we governed under these new conditions? A major debate has arisen about the nature and form of local government and whether decentralisation has led to empowerment and changed the nature of representation. What role does the state play here in shaping the lives of the urban citizen? The late twentieth century has seen in many countries a retreat from the welfare state and a refashioning of the state–citizen relationship around a neo-liberal rights and responsibilities model rather than one of universal entitlements. This has led to the restructuring of the relationship between public and private life and the 'reconstitution of civil society'. The politics of representation and identity become part of a changing city governance.

The final question to consider is how our sense of self and identity is created within the contemporary urban world. The impact here of changing place/space relations and the question of whether we need a secure 'place' to create our sense of who we are has been taken up in both academic and policy debates (UNCHS 1996b, Young 1997). The international debate at Habitat 2 was about the right to shelter and access to land. In respect to these 'rights', there was considerable variation of views and experience. Crucially important were the social relations of gender, class, and ethnicity (UNCHS 1996a).

Urban Analysis and Urban Transformation

Having briefly thought about some of the transformations that have occurred, it is also useful at the beginning of our exploration of city change to consider how urban analysts have examined the question of change in city life. The growth of analysis is closely connected to the emergence of the modern world and the development of interpretation and understandings of that world. Sociology, for example, is the exploration of modernity in all its facets.

The earliest writers on the city sought to explain urban growth and how city life differed from country or rural life. Therefore, a strong tradition of 'contrast' theory creating typologies of urban and rural life emerged with writers such as Toennies (1956), and Durkheim (1960) as part of this tradition. They provided a view of urban life often overlain by nostalgia for the 'world we had lost', the rural world of the small-scale, personal 'gemeinschaft' rather than the impersonal, large-scale, heterogeneous world of the city. In the 1920s, Chicago in the USA became the centre of an alternative tradition of urban analysis shaped by ecological analogies, Darwinian competitiveness and market economics. The city was subject to successive waves of migrants and this led to the view that the dominant processes were those of invasion, succession, and domination. Later, Wirth (1938), writing in Chicago, took up the theme of urbanism as a way of life and saw this to be the result of changes to the size, density, and het-

erogeneity of the city. Collectively, these processes created a greater complexity and scale to urban life and changed social relations from those
based upon close knowledge and intimacy to those of an impersonal and
formal nature.

By the 1970s the dominant 'ecological model' came under sustained
attack as it was seen as deficient in its approach and, in the 1970s, new
forms of analysis emerged which were influenced by both Weberian, represented by urban managerialism, and Marxist theory (Pickvance 1976,
Castells 1977a, Harloe 1977, Pahl 1977, Saunders 1981). Much of the earlier
theory was dismissed as 'ideology' and the focus shifted from quasi-
biological metaphors of process to analysis of the power, political
processes and economic determinants of the urban system. Also allied
with this structuralist focus was the growing identification of the role of
agency through social movements. Initially, this was featured in class-
based movements but expanded to recognise the significance of both
gender and ethnicity as bases for mobilisation and struggles over the
shape and direction of the city.

The 1980s and 1990s saw a renewed emphasis upon empirical analysis
of both global and local changes. This resulted in studies of economic
restructuring and de-industrialisation and the changes this brought about
to city spatial and social structure (Smith 1980). For a time the neo-Marxist
regulation school provided much of the framing for urban research exploring the patterns of accumulation and nature of social regulation. These
were consequently written of largely in terms of the transition from
'Fordism' to post-Fordism and identified urban employment and unemployment and the changing profile of the urban labour force (Massey 1984,
Bluestone and Harrison 1986). Later in the 1980s, the role of consumption
rather than production as the key influence on city shape and form
began to be given greater prominence. Diversity rather than convergence
became the dominant theme of urban studies as they embraced a more
postmodernist-influenced analysis (Soja 1989, Johnson 1994a, Watson and
Gibson 1995). The focus of much US postmodernist analysis has been
upon Los Angeles, now seen as the quintessential postmodern city, rather
than Chicago or New York (Dear 2000).

Research and analysis therefore shifted away from grand narratives to
those more reflective of the diversity of urban experience shaped by the
contexts and contingencies of urban development and change. Although
we are living in an increasingly global world the local still retains a powerful influence on the shape of everyday living. Writers such as Simmel
(1969) have therefore been rediscovered, as meanings attached to urban
life and transformations of living patterns have regained centrality in the
urban agenda.

Structure of the Book

The book, over the next eight chapters, explores in more depth the theme of urban transformation beginning with the emergence of the modern industrial city. Chapter 2 will look at the transformations that occurred with the rise of the industrial city. The pre-industrial city was centred on political and administrative activities and, as trade was a key aspect of wealth generation, port location was especially attractive (Sjoberg 1960), for example, as in Amsterdam, London, and Antwerp. Spatial and social structures reflected these dominant economic and political activities. The city-states of Europe were thus more significant in the seventeenth and eighteenth centuries than later when cities became mass cities with a large industrial working class (Weber 1921). The spatial and social structures of modern industrial cities will be explored. However, questions will be raised about the universality of this path of city growth and form. Contemporary post-colonial analysis of the city raises significant questions about how we understand the growth of cities in other parts of the world that owe their existence and form to the colonial expansion of the eighteenth and nineteenth century when large numbers of migrants moved from Europe to 'new lands' (Jacobs 1996). The chapter will also examine explanations developed by urban analysts for the social and spatial structure of the modern industrial city, particularly those arising from the work of the contrast school of urban writers who drew distinctions between rural and urban society, the Chicago schools of urban ecology, and the critiques that emerged later in the writings of those adopting either a urban managerialist or urban political economy perspective.

In order to appreciate the nature of the city transformations that are occurring, it is necessary to have a good understanding of the demographic context within which this is taking place. Chapter 3 therefore explores the likely size and shape of the world's population in the first half of the present century and identifies the main patterns of migration. The size and distribution of the urban population is also examined and the rise of the mega city documented. A significant demographic feature of the contemporary city is ageing, especially within the developed societies of Europe and North America. However, this is also now affecting parts of Asia, particularly Japan, China and Singapore. Singapore, for example, in August 2000 introduced a range of incentives to encourage families to have more children to arrest the decline in population that was predicted due to falling birth rates (*Melbourne Age*, 21 August 2000). In these societies, the proportion of the population over the age of 65 will, on average, in the present century be around 20–25 per cent (Japan is estimated to be at 25 per cent by 2020). Strong growth in the younger 15–24 age group, often as a result of migration, both rural to urban and international, is a further significant factor in the demographic structure of many cities in the developing world.

Chapter 4 takes up the question of how significant is the transformation now taking place. Are we at a defining moment in the history of the world where we are moving through a set of changes as far reaching in their consequences as those encountered in the industrial, political, economic and intellectual transformation at the beginning of the modern era? The chapter looks at the debates about postmodernity and globalisation to explore whether this change challenges the basis of our previous explanation such that we need a new set of tools and concepts to explore cities in the twenty-first century.

Chapters 5 and 6 are concerned with exploring aspects of the contemporary city seen to be emerging from the latest set of transformations. Chapter 5 takes up the theme of everyday life in the city and explores questions surrounding the crafting of identity. The multiple nature of identity within the contemporary city is explored through an analysis that moves from the individual to the household to the community and neighbourhood.

In Chapter 6, how the economic base of the contemporary city is being restructured around consumption activities (entertainment, recreation, leisure, tourism) is explored to show the implications for employment, gender, visual landscape and the utilisation of space. Place promotion and the generation of 'urban identities' through marketing and city enhancement projects is a further aspect of the reconstructing of place that will be examined. This is an area of the global-local intersection that has been strongly influenced by the growth and impact of the global media, through the Internet and World Wide Web (WWW) (for example, e-commerce) travel, migration, and economic activities (through the actions of transglobal companies). At the local level, the preservation of difference has become valued, sometimes as a commodity to sell, through the rediscovery of heritage sites, and conservation and the recreation of the past.

Chapters 7, 8 and 9 explore the key issues of urban inequality, planning and sustainable development that are likely to shape how well cities cope with the changes that have been identified. The other side of the contemporary city is explored in chapter 7, and the questions addressed focus on those who are included/excluded and who are at the city margins. The chapter thus looks at urban spatial and social inequalities, poverty, homelessness, crime and gentrification. The shifting of the boundary between state and market relations has been significant during the period of neoliberal dominance in many regimes in the latter part of the twentieth century. Thus, policies addressing inequality and exclusion have tended to move from direct state intervention to those based more around enhancing individual capacities. Such an emphasis indicates that these policies flow from an analysis rooted in explanations seeking the causes of urban troubles within the lives of the individual citizen.

Chapter 8 examines issues of planning, urban governance and social movements. Planning is about attempts to control the growth and shape of the city. In the 1950s and 1960s, planning drew its legitimation from scientific rationalism and forms of social engineering linked to the state. The 1970s and 1980s saw this form of legitimation undergo critical attack leading to planning becoming less popular and somewhat fragmented. In the 1980s and 1990s, planning, under neo-liberalism becomes detached from the state and privatised encouraging greater reliance upon market signals and promotional activity. Associated with planning changes has been the decentralisation of the state and the growth of new forms of partnerships and debates about the nature of representation and governance.

Chapter 9 takes up the question of the sustainable city that has become a dominant theme in urban debates in the latter stages of the twentieth century. In a global urban world, the 'solutions' to urban problems are seen to lie in the creation of the sustainable city, the green city. This idea permeates debates at all levels from global fora to national and local government and local community groups. The degree to which this is a matter of rhetoric rather than a matter of reality will be addressed. The chapter looks at the way sustainable development has been defined – Bruntland Report (WCED 1987), Agenda 21 and Habitat 2 declaration (UNCHS 1996b). What gets incorporated into policy-making and decision-taking, it is argued, is often 'sustainable management' focused around natural resource preservation but excluding the social equity dimensions of Agenda 21. Consequently, much of the debate downplays or fails to recognise that the city is a social and political construction. The city is often a site of struggle and conflict and thus the role of social movements in shaping the city needs to be recognized.

The sustainable city is linked to the global debate about sustainable development arising from a growing recognition that the resources of the planet are finite and that change is needed in the way that these are consumed. The chapter will provide a critique of the sustainability debate and examine a number of case studies of how the idea of 'sustainability' has become incorporated into the discourse on the city. The concept, in some form or other, is increasingly being placed within legislation shaping city planning and it is therefore useful to try and gauge the effect of this move. The implications of this are examined together with the tensions between the sustainability ideal and economic growth pushed by the greater emphasis on entrepreneurial activity as cities seek to obtain 'global status' and market domination in the new system of global markets and exchange.

The final chapter returns to the theme of the transformation of cities as we move into the twenty-first century. In this review, consideration is given to the theoretical tools available to assist us in understanding the transformations that have both occurred and are continuing as the new millennium unfolds.

2

Industrial-Modern Cities

Origins and Growth of the Pre-industrial City

In order to understand the transformations that occurred with the onset
of the industrial city, it will first be necessary to look at the origin of cities
and the growth of the pre-industrial city. The definition of the city by
Davis (1973:1), used in Chapter 1, sees the city as 'concentrations of many
people located close together for residential and productive purposes'.
This sensitises us to two shifts that were important in the transformation
that created the earliest cities. The most significant was probably the shift
in the productive base of a society. The occupants of the cities were no
longer engaged in agricultural activity and were not self-sufficient. Rather,
they supplied services and commodities to the rural population and in
exchange they gained their food and other requirements. In order for this
new arrangement to occur, productivity had to increase to such an extent
that the farmers were producing more than they and their families could
consume. This required settled agriculture rather than nomadic hunting
and gathering. This is one of the reasons for the earliest cities emerging in
the places where they did. These regions had a benign climate and soil
and water conditions conducive to agriculture – the growing of wheat and
barley. Thus, we see the first cities emerging around 3500 BP in the fertile
crescent area of Mesopotamia (Sjoberg 1973). In this period, the metal
utilized was bronze and the agrarian production was enhanced through
the invention of the plough hauled by oxen. Wheeled vehicles had also
been invented which allowed the transport of produce to the urban
population. Cities were not large. The earliest were home to probably
between 5000–10,000 people. Ur, which has been extensively excavated,
housed around 34,000 people by 2000 BP. Cities spread by diffusion and
the transfer of the technology of agrarian production to the Indus valley
(modern-day Pakistan) by 2500 BP and the Yellow River area of China by
1000 BP (MacNeish 1964, Lamberg-Karlovsky and Lamberg-Karlovsky
1973).

In the newly emerging cities, a new social structure took shape. Cities
are social inventions rather than natural constructions so new forms of

organisation had to evolve to cope with large population concentrations. As Davis noted:

> For some villages to become large enough to approach an urban scale, trade in artefacts and materials had to be available, and technologies of water control, soil management, storage, transport, permanent house building and food preservation had to be developed (Davis 1973:11).

This required new political structures and a different division of labour to ensure the various tasks were accomplished. Further closer settlement meant that land became a resource in demand. Who should own and control land in the city? What form of property rights should develop? What form of governance? Rulers who filled both spiritual and temporal roles mostly governed the earliest cities. The central spaces of the city were the ones where the rulers would be located and the significant buildings, for example the temples, then further out, would be the residences of the artisans and trades. Cities were often walled or fortified as the urban populations were small relative to the surrounding rural and nomadic populations.

The new technologies of production and forms of political and economic organisation required record-keeping, both for levying taxes and recording trading activity, hence the need for written records. Cities were shaped by the broader civilisations in which they were embedded and to which their fate was linked. Under the Roman Empire, for example, the city was diffused through much of Europe following along behind the legions. Urban life was established. With the decline of the Roman Empire, however, many of the cities that existed at that time disappeared. Early cities were open to many problems associated with closer living, for example, disease, fire, and natural disasters. Many were built on flood plains as these were sites with alluvial soils good for crop production and close to waterways for trade and transport but thus were prone to flooding. They were also subject to internal political and economic problems over the creation and distribution of wealth. Rivalries occurred between urban and rural populations and between cities.

In Europe, by medieval times, city-states were not uncommon. The basis of their wealth arose from trade and the growth of the craft guilds producing the new equipment for agrarian production and the commodities for the merchant class and the wealthy elites (Pirenne 1956). The opening up of trade on a global scale through voyages for the 'explorers' paved the way for colonialism and the extraction of commodities and raw materials from around the world and the bringing of these back to Europe. The pre-capitalist world made its money largely through land-based production and trade. The cities that grew were those strategically integrated into these activities. The dominant 'global' cities of the sixteenth and seventeenth centuries were therefore those which held a key position within the mercantile world, with London, Amsterdam, Antwerp, Genoa, Lisbon and Venice being the most significant. As political fortunes changed across Europe in the eighteenth century, to this group were added Paris, Rome, and Vienna (Robertson 1992, Knox 1996).

Industrial City

The major transformation of the pre-industrial city took place with the rise of the industrial world. The new cities were the result of a combination of technological change and the creation of a new economic system, one based not on trade, but upon the creation of wealth through use of capital. The nineteenth century saw the development of a new form of urbanism, the industrial city. This brought a new set of cities to the fore, as key nodes in the system of global cities – among these were Manchester, Chicago, Detroit, Pittsburgh, cities of the Ruhr region of Germany (Essen, Dortmund,) and North East France (such as Lille). The growth of these industrial cities was rapid. In Britain, for example, in 1801 London was the only city of over 100,000 people and this contained 4.7 per cent of the United Kingdom's population. London, at this time, was also the largest city in Europe. By 1901, one hundred years later, there were thirty-five cities of over 100,000 containing 25.9 per cent of the population. The growth occurred most rapidly in the second half of the nineteenth century.

A major shift occurred with respect to time. The clock tower in the industrial village of Loefsta in Sweden, built in the early eighteenth century to accommodate Flemish ironworkers, marked the need for accurate timekeeping. The ironworks operated on a shift system; six days a week with Sunday off. The 'village' was carefully planned to reinforce the social order and create an 'ideal' environment. The central axis was the manor house, paymaster's house and the church. The workers' houses ran from this central axis to the periphery according to the worker's place within the industrial workforce. The shift from agrarian to industrial work thus brought about far-reaching changes to patterns of work and social arrangements, bringing in a new social hierarchy, based around ownership of industrial production and possession of factory-based work skills.

The rise of the industrial city thus saw the creation of both factory production and urban residential districts close to the new forms of employment creating areas often of tenement dwellings. The new physical structure was one of narrow streets and crowded dwellings. In these circumstances, dwellers suffered from diseases arising from the new environmental conditions. Pollution of the air arose from the shift to carboniferous fuels as the basis of industrial energy and residential heating creating smoggy conditions and reducing sunlight to many of the areas of residence. Water supply also became problematic, as drainage was often poor and infectious disease spread (McDermott 1973). Nutrition was often deficient due to lack of money and knowledge.

One disease, which appeared in the industrial city, was rickets, a bone disease. Research during the late nineteenth and early twentieth century centred on whether this was the result of environmental conditions or nutrition (Loomis 1973). Eventually, it was discovered this was probably the first 'pollution-induced' disease and arose largely from the lack of sunlight getting through to children living in the new urban slums. The narrow streets and tenements created alleys and courts where little sun penetrated, especially during the winter months. And this problem was exacerbated by the smog. It was particularly widespread in the poorest districts of the large urban areas – the 'narrow alleys and haunts of the poor' (Engels 1971).

One of the earliest analysts of the industrial city was Frederick Engels who wrote an account of early industrial life in Manchester in 1843. In this, he chronicled the conditions of life in the great towns. He began with life in London where he noted the poverty in the East End areas such as Bethnal Green. Another acute observer of urban life in the nineteenth century was Charles Dickens who also drew attention to the plight of the urban poor and the conditions under which they lived at this time. The Engels family had acquired a cotton mill in Manchester, the cradle of industrial capitalism, and, in his twenties, Frederick Engels moved from Bremen in Germany to train as a businessman and help manage the family mills. This brought him to one of the new industrial cities at the time when it was beginning to expand rapidly. He thus saw Manchester as a typical example of the new form of urbanism. The physical structure of the city demonstrated, for Engels, the separation of the classes that was the hallmark of industrial capitalism. The new class structure that was emerging was built into the very structure of the city.

Engels' work identified a number of urban zones. The centre of the city was where the commercial district was to be found, just under a kilometre long and a kilometre wide, containing offices and warehouses, no permanent residences and intersected by the main roads. Moving out from this area the next zone was that of a working-class district around the commercial core about two kilometres wide and beyond this lived the upper middle class in regularly laid out streets and in villa-like houses surrounded by gardens. The transport system stretched out along the main roads bisecting the working-class areas. Along these roads spread the shops and other businesses of the lower middle class. Thus the commercial, lower middle-class areas acted as a buffer between workers and the richer upper middle-class residential districts.

Engels' (1971) writing was not just a descriptive account of the new spatial patterns. It also included an argument as to why the city was spatially organised in this particular way. He argued that the riches of the upper middle class were the direct result of the level of exploitation. Here, he reflects Marx's analysis in seeing all wealth arising out of the unpaid labour of workers (surplus value). The privileges of the upper middle class could only therefore be maintained through the exploitation of the workers. The poor living conditions, which were found, were seen as part of the shift from pre-capitalist to capitalist forms of production. The result was that thousands of workers and their families were living in houses and neighbourhoods without drains or sewers. A number of writers, as the century progressed, drew attention to the statistics of life in the industrial city. Life expectancy was low, and city death rates were higher than average for the country as a whole. The increase in urban population was maintained during this period not by natural increase but through migration from the countryside.

Two factors were important in shaping the structure of the city as the nineteenth century progressed to its end. These were rising affluence created by the new capitalist industrial economy and the growth of urban reform movements. Real wages rose by the end of the century allowing at least some of the workers to escape from the poverty and overcrowding of the slums. Transport systems were improved enabling commuting to take place across greater distances. The development here was of the rail system (Kellet 1969), to be followed by electric trams and buses in the early decades of the twentieth century and finally the private car. The latter had a major impact on the spatial arrangement of the city and led to the rise of the suburb. With suburbanisation, also came tenure shifts and the increasing role of home ownership.

The rise of reform movements was the second factor of significance. Here, the public health movement and the rise of epidemiology was significant. These drew attention to the linkage between the incidence of disease and spatial factors which in turn led to the realisation that diseases were related to such things as sanitation, clean water supply, and proper drainage systems. The development of an improved physical infrastructure led to a dramatic improvement in the physical condition and overall health of the population such that mortality rates fell and fertility improved. The work of Booth on poverty, which linked this to income deprivation, occupation, residence and overcrowding, and that of the early social statisticians in the late nineteenth and early twentieth century further documented life in the cities. This, in turn, assisted in the creation of a reformist agenda pushing for greater regulation of urban development and improved physical and social conditions (Abrams 1968, Thorns and Sedgwick 1997).

Suburban Development in First-world Cities during the Twentieth Century

The reforms and expansions of the economy provided opportunities for mobility, occupationally and geographically. The public health and housing improvements led to strong population growth. Cities expanded outwards aided by new forms of relatively cheap transportation. Thus began another transformation: from the concentrated to the more dispersed urban form, which became typical of the majority of western cities. The older cores changed in their function and population composition as the century progressed as a result of slum clearance, renewal and gentrification. Major tenure shifts took place within the UK, for example, the population shifting from one largely living in private rental to one mainly in owner occupation by the mid 1960s. The move to ownership and suburbia was based on an increased level of privatisation and privatism (Saunders 1990a). The triumph of individualism was seen to have occurred.

A key factor in this transformation was the changed nature of industrial production. The early capitalist enterprises were small in scale and often family owned. As the twentieth century progressed, it became dominanted by the new corporations, initially national in scale but later transnational and, by the end of the millennium, global. The Ford Motor Company was one of the first such corporate organisations established within the auto industry. Henry Ford is credited with two important innovations. These arose from his realisation that it was not sufficient to produce cars, it was also necessary to sell them. Thus, workers needed to earn sufficient money to be able to afford a model T Ford and also they needed to have time to enjoy it. Ford increased wages and reduced the length of the working day solving both these 'consumption problems'. This strategy stimulated demand and thus increased production, sales and profits. The system, which this heralded, was that of mass commodity production. Hence, this period is often dubbed 'Fordism' (Harvey 1990, Amin 1994).

The high point of modernism is often seen as the period in the twentieth century during which both 'Fordism' and 'welfarism' predominated. This was a time when both economic and state activity was designed to increase production and output and incorporate all individuals into an increasingly standardised pattern of mass consumption. It was the period of suburban growth and the proliferation of single-family dwellings on their own plot of land. Suburbs were considered to be a perfect design to stimulate the production of household commodities such as washing machines, fridges, mowers, televisions and video recorders – the hall-marks of the mass consumer. The rough time frame for modernism (although strong vestiges remain with us) is 1800 to the 1970s. In the latter decade, the processes that ultimately became associated with the post-modern began to emerge.

As noted earlier, Fordism is the shorthand for the development of large-scale, mass production-based industries, built around the technologies of the assembly line (Cooke 1989). Such industries produced standardised commodities in hierarchically structured organisations. Originally, they were nationally organised but as they grew in size they moved to become multinational in scope but still with a firm base in the country of origin given the requirements for large plant, equipment and a local labour force. The application of scientific management techniques associated with Taylorism[1] to the labour process was part of the way work relations were organised through wage regulation and control. Workers completed single tasks on the assembly line rather than working on the total product. This required specialisation and differentiation amongst the workers leading to an extensive division of labour. Work was largely gendered with skilled workers being predominantly male. Unionisation, because of the large plants, was generally strong. Wages had to be set at a sufficient level to allow workers to purchase commodities and they also had to have suffi-cient leisure time to enjoy their use. Thus, hours of work were reduced and hourly pay rates improved both as a result of unionisation and the need of the capitalist producers to encourage the buying of commodities. The creation of demand also required the creation of a marketing and advertising industry linking consumer items to lifestyle requirements cre-ating the 'suburban way of life' which was written about in the 1950s and 1960s in both popular and academic literature (Dobriner 1958, 1963; Berger 1960; Gans 1967; Thorns 1972; Clapson 1998).

The system was designed to produce a standard product. For this system to be successful, it had to overcome the resistance of the labour movement. Consequently, there were struggles within the advanced European, American and Australian and New Zealand societies to bring about change and create the necessary conditions to enable this new form of capital accumulation. In these struggles, the state played a prominent part and assisted in the formulation of wage-setting procedures and union recognition through the use of arbitration and wage awards. In particu-lar, struggles intensified in the 1920s and 1930s during the time of the Depression. Further, the 1939 to 1945 wartime period was a crucial one as it provided greater opportunity for both employers and the state to bring about the necessary reorganisation of the labour process, under the guise of war-time necessity, to facilitate the full development of the 'Fordist' system in the 1950s and 1960s.

The other pillar of the system was welfarism. The intervention of the state to assist in the regulation and setting of economic conditions for the success of capitalist production was a characteristic of the New Deal in the USA and the Keynesian welfare state of Britain, Australia and New Zealand (Castles 1985, Thorns 1992). This was the time of collective bargaining, national wage regulations and centralised planning designed to ensure national and regional economic growth and development. The successful combination of state, capital and labour organisations into a period of 'corporatist' management created a time of sustained economic growth. At the level of urban planning, this system brought about an emphasis upon rational comprehensive planning, the development of city and regional plans and planning authorities. One major consequence was the separation of activities, through zoning and other similar regulatory devices, creating segregation between areas of residential, industrial, commercial, shopping and entertainment land use. One major separation occurred where public life took place in the inner city and where private 'domestic' activities dominated the suburbs. This separation was also strongly gendered with the 'city' being the preserve of men while the suburb, especially during the day, was the place of women and children often in under-serviced neighbourhoods (Hayden 1980, McKenzie 1980, Saegert 1980, McDowell 1989, Saville-Smith 2000). The gendered nature of city spaces is well captured by Doreen Massey where she describes her recollections of travelling into Manchester on the top deck of the bus and observing football and rugby pitches along the way stretching across the Mersey floodplain she passed – all were given over entirely to boys (Massey 1994). It was, therefore, not just residential space that was gendered but also the public spaces for urban leisure and recreation. Such divisions were incorporated into the design of urban spaces and reflect the patriarchal nature of the industrial city and its managers – the politicians and planners within local government.

Economic growth appeared assured under this system of economic, political and social organisation as the initial post-war decades were characterised by affluence and the creation of full employment with labour shortages rather than surpluses, which necessitated an increased rate of migration to satisfy demand.

Migration and natural increase stimulated housing production with strong growth in residential development and the creation of companies such as Levitt and Sons (USA), Wimpey (UK) and A.V. Jennings (Australia) as major suppliers of housing (Gans 1967, Kilmartin and Thorns 1978). There was thus a substantial increase in home-ownership rates in such suburban-based societies. For example, in Australia, a society with strong encouragements for home ownership it reached 74 per cent by the end of the 1960s and became clearly the dominant mode of tenure (Stretton 1970, Kemeny 1981). New surburban spaces were created, designed around individual family households dedicated to privatised forms of consumption and increasingly dependent on the private motor car rather than public transport systems.

The result was a strong expansion of private detached housing in peripheral suburbs based upon the ownership of a private car and an expansion of consumption, especially of household commodities (for example, fridges, washing machines, televisions, motor mowers, videos, microwave ovens, and so on) with private cars eroding public transport and adding to each individual's possible flexibility. This expansion of consumption led to a greater degree of homogenisation across class boundaries as more people enjoyed the mass consumption economy that was created (Dunleavy 1979). The 'Fordist system' began to show signs of crisis and decay in the 1970s as the underlying structural conditions changed and the ideology that had helped to underpin it came under increasing attack.

The Fordist form of urban growth and expansion is often thought of as characteristic of first-world cities. The case of Sao Paulo, in Brazil, shows that this is too limited. Sao Paulo's history of urban development in the twentieth century is one of growth and expansion based around an 'industrial-commercial metropolis' creating a city of suburban living and segregated neighbourhoods (see Box 2.1). Further spatial changes took place re-enforcing patterns of segregation in the latter part of the last century.

Box 2.1

Sao Paulo, Brazil: industrial change

- Population 2000: 17.8 million, 4th largest city in the world

- Population 2010: estimate 19.7 million – would still be the 4th largest city in the world

History of the city

- City founded in 1554 by Jesuits located at a 'critical intermediary point in the transportation routes between coast and interior plains' (Godfrey 1999).

- Initially, relatively poor colonial settlement without extensive resources.

Continued

- Significant change came with coffee, European immigrants (largely from Italy) and immigrants from other areas of Brazil from the late nineteenth century.

- By 1928, population had grown to its first one million.

- Industrial structure developed in the twentieth century, assisted by tariff barriers.

City structure

Rapid growth created three cities within the twentieth century. In 1933, the city was an 'industrial-commercial metropolis' with 'quite homogeneous districts' arranged around a 'compact core'. Its shape was not unlike the classic Chicago school model. With the Boulevard Plan (1930s) for reshaping the centre around major avenues, large scale redevelopment took place which included demolition and redevelopment, new transport systems and office and commercial development in the downtown area. Suburban housing development was encouraged by the opening up of new transport lines.

Urban segregation occurred as the city grew, with distinct districts for workers around the factories both near the centre and in the outlying districts where new industrial plant was located. The wealthier groups within the city sought the higher ground in the city's southwest creating a series of fashionable suburbs.

After the Second World War, the city was reshaped again by urban renewal, automobile transport, peripheral industrial and retail development and suburbanisation. Accompanying the growth was residential segregation by social class. In 1960, 21.6 per cent of population lived outside the central city. By 1990, this had increased to 40.7 per cent indicating the rapid growth of the wider metropolitan region.

The 1990s has seen a third stage of development with economic restructuring leading to the de-industrialisation of the core and further metropolitan decentralisation. Industry has moved out and relocated looking for cheaper locations. This has meant job losses creating increased levels of unemployment (Da Silva 2000).

The urban economy has become 'tertiarised' favouring finance, commerce, and other service sectors. Downtown has been redeveloped around high-rise office and residential accommodation for the wealthier urban service class which has emerged. These changes have created greater wealth and poverty which are spatially segregated and located in contiguous neighbourhoods leading to increased levels of 'fear' of crime and disorder leading to 'defensive architecture and heightened security measures' (Caldeira 1996).

City web site: *http://www.uoregon.edu/~sergiok/brasil/saopaulo.html*

Explanations for the Growth and Shape of the Industrial-Modern City

Introduction

The analysis of the industrial city was initially examined as part of the transformation of societies from a pre-industrial form to an industrial one.

The first generation of writers therefore emphasised the 'contrasts' between city forms and the rural world which they were replacing. Durkheim and Tonnies are two influential writers from this tradition.

Contrast Theories

The key theorists were Comte (1876), Durkheim (1960), Toennies (1956) and Weber (1921). The newly-emerging urban industrial world was seen by most of these early writers as typified by competition, conflict, contractual relations and utility, whereas community was the antithesis of these things, based around cooperation, integration, and kinship relations.

Comte, for example, grew up during the period of the French Revolution and the breakdown, as he saw it, of an ordered society. He was critical of this breakdown, which he saw as spreading anarchy and rampant individualism. The restoration of order for him was a priority. Consequently, he saw community as people's natural habitat, which was being destroyed along with other traditional forms of association by revolutionary change. The creation of 'communities' would thus be part of the process of rebuilding an ordered, industrial, modern society.

Durkheim (1960), writing towards the end of the nineteenth century, feared the disintegration of social relationships into 'anomie'. This constituted a situation where the norms and expectations surrounding behaviour were no longer known. The onset of industrialisation would create normlessness and social breakdown. He identified, as a key feature, the shift from a community based upon mechanical solidarity to one based upon organic solidarity. Mechanical solidarity was where the moral ideas and values of a society were shared by all members, collective authority was absolute and deviants were not allowed. Conformity to the rules was expected of all the population and was enforced by strong sanctions. The basis of this form of solidarity was the homogeneity of moral beliefs across the population. In contrast, organic solidarity was based upon social differentiation and a key integrating role was played by the division of labour. The new form of solidarity was thus based upon the interdependence of specialised parts. Norms, rules and laws were organised, not around repression, but through contracts between individuals and groups which were legally binding and enforceable via the judiciary and court system. Stability and integration would be rebuilt on the basis of necessity. None of us could survive in the new industrialised urban world on our own; we all depended upon the activities of each other. The new solidarity that Durkheim saw emerging came out of our diversity rather than being imposed by our homogeneity as it had been under 'mechanical solidarity'. He thus termed this new form of solidarity 'organic solidarity'.

A second analyst of the transformation from the pre-urban to the urban was Ferdinand Toennies. Toennies published an influential book, *Gemeinschaft and Gesellschaft* (Community and Society) in 1887. In this, he laid out the characteristics of two stages, the first was *Gemeinschaft*. Here, human relations are intimate, enduring and based upon a clear understanding of where each person stands in society. The worth of the individual is related to the person rather than what they have done, so status is ascribed and not achieved. The second stage, which increasingly characterised industrial society, was *Gesellschaft*. Here, the large scale and impersonal shapes human relations and the contractual ties that were apparently increasing. Status was achieved rather than ascribed, giving greater importance to individual actions and motivations. Toennies thus saw society as moving through a transition from one form of social organisation to another, and his work is an attempt to theorise about the changes that industrialisation makes at the level of social relationships, and social groups.

Of the two stages, *Gemeinschaft* is based on homogeneity, group orientation, informed and shaped by tradition, and guided by sentiment with each person feeling that they are part of the overall community (Table 2.1). Being a member of the community was more important than doing one's own thing. Thus individual desires were subordinate to those of the wider group. The collective nature of society meant that individuals were not specialised and so were 'Jacks and Jills of all trades'. Finally, primary relationships, that is face-to-face relationships between friends and close kin, were the most typical form.

In contrast, in *Gesellschaft*, heterogeneity was the normal basis for society with a greater emphasis upon individualism. Individuals are guided by rationality and by actions which enhance their own self interest rather than the collective interests of the community or wider society. Tasks are specialised so, rather than 'Jacks and Jills of all trades', people become experts or specialists in particular tasks. A consequence of this is that they have to link up with others to get tasks completed. Relationships, rather than being based around a knowledge of the whole person, are more transitory and linked to the accomplishment of defined tasks. For each task, a particular combination of people are grouped together but once the task is finished the reason for that association is lost. Thus, relationships are more fluid than under the Gemeinschaft-based society.

Table 2.1 illustrates the contrast between community and society that gradually became a major organising theme for this group of nineteenth-century social theorists. The terminology is a little different across the theorists. However, the differences are relatively minor as they all focus upon the idea of a contrasting typology based around notions of community and society.

Table 2.1 Ferdinand Toennies (1855–1936)

Gemeinschaft	*Gesellschaft*
Homogeneity	Heterogeneity
Group oriented	Individual oriented
Tradition dominates	Business and commerce dominate
Individual guided by sentiment	Individual guided by rationality
Each person part of the overall culture	Preponderance of subcultures
Each person jack-of-all trades	Job specialisation
Relationships among people valuable in and of themselves	Relationships transitory, superficial
Primary relationships predominate	Secondary relationships predominate

Twentieth-century writing within this tradition developed more complex typologies of 'contrast' and built what became known as the rural-urban continuum. Most of the contrasts developed identified the 'rural' with the small-scale, integrated social group and set this against the 'urban' which was seen as larger in scale and more individualistic in orientation (see Wirth 1938, Redfield 1960, Pahl 1975).

Critique of Contrast Theories

The rural-urban continuum and its ideal types had a number of serious weaknesses as an informing model for the analysis of cities. The first problem was that it was, in fact, only a dichotomy. The two polar types of 'rural' and 'urban' were reasonably clearly defined but the stages in between were not. What needed to change for a locality to become urban in its social characteristics, or how many of the contrasting elements had to change? Questions such as these got little attention. The result was that the model was essentially a static presentation capturing two points in time and articulating their social and cultural base. Thus, it was not able to deal with social change. This difficulty arises in part from the reliance on 'ideal types'; these are abstractions from, and often simplifications of, the real world and are used to examine actual situations to see how closely they conform to the model. Such models lack historical depth and often prevent an analysis of change.

The second major weakness was the incorporation into the analysis of an implicit bias in favour of the countryside. This was largely anti-city and saw the city as the location where 'community' had become lost and where rebuilding would require intervention and conscious 'community development' on the part of planners and others. This position favoured a particular notion of community as integrated social relations bound by common values and traditions. It denied or chose not to investigate the fact that small towns and rural villages were also the place of petty tyrannies, power imbalances and unequal relationships (Dempsey 1990). Conformity and stability were often the result not of choice and consensus, but of power and oppression.

The third deficiency was that the model was generated out of the experience of a largely European society at a particular moment in its development. There is, therefore, a question over how far such analysis is transferable to situations where the historical experience has been different. The transition from a rural, small-scale peasant society into an industrial urban one has been far from a universal experience. A number of variations have occurred. For example, in cities created as part of colonialism, in such areas of the world as West and South Africa, cities were often initially administrative and political cities with trading functions. Their structure was created to reflect the power and cultural values of the colonial elites rather than being a product of industrialisation (King 1976).

Urban Ecologists

A second generation of urban analysts can be located in the work of the Chicago School. The founder of the school was Robert Park, who was a somewhat unusual academic as he came to the university via journalism. He was very much grounded in his experience of living in Chicago, which in the 1920s, was experiencing tremendous growth. Chicago had a unique position as a trade, financial, manufacturing, and transport centre for the opening up of the Midwest. What intrigued Park (1952) were the patterns of urban growth and the development of distinctive subcultures located in different parts of the city. What then were the linkages between the social and the spatial structure of the city that contributed to a residential form that exhibited a considerable degree of residential segregation on the basis of ethnicity, household type, income and activities?

For an explanation, Park turned to a combination of Darwin and Ricardo. From Darwin, he drew upon the idea of competitive evolution – the harsh striving for dominance amongst species which led to the survival of the fittest (Bulmer 1984, Smith and Feagin 1987). This led to the idea of 'natural areas' produced by the sequence of invasion, succession and domination; a process taken from plant ecology to describe how a particular plant species became the dominant one in a landscape. Park saw migration as a key aspect of this process. New migrants from Europe, from the southern states and from south of the border came to Chicago in search of work and the American dream of a better life. On arrival, they lived in one of the transitional areas, close to the central business district, which constituted the urban core. Once established, they moved into other areas where they tended to join other migrants from the same ethnic and regional group. As these clusters grew, they had a tendency to drive out other residents, so creating the dominance of a particular ethic group, creating the Little Sicily, black belts, and Chinatown found in Chicago at this time. From Ricardo came the importance of the land market and the level of ground rent. This clearly had an important impact on both the activity within any particular area and the likely occupants. The market worked according to the 'hidden hand' described by Adam Smith. This, rather like Darwinian competition, was conceived largely as an asocial process rather than one based around sets of human social actors such as landowners, real estate agents, financiers, and developers. The resulting view of the city was rather mechanistic and left little room for considerations of culture or social values in the formation of behaviour.

Alongside the competitive processes of evolution and the land market, Park also recognised the importance of communication. People were social beings and, as such, had the capacity to organise themselves socially into groups through interpersonal interaction. This level Park called the socio-cultural and saw it as contributing to the creation of 'sub cultural areas' where different ways of life became crafted by the occupants. These were the subjects of his students' ethnographies of everyday life within the city such as Zorbaugh's *The Gold Coast and the Slum* (1929).

Parks' students, Burgess (1967) and McKenzie (1933), translated these ideas of social ecology into the famous 'bulls eye' model of urban structure showing a series of concentric rings flowing outwards from a central core. In this model, the engine room of the city is the central business district, which is the destination for the majority of commuting traffic, and is where transport nodes are centred. It is the place where there was a high daytime population but a low residential population once the working day is finished. Moving out from this zone the immediately surrounding area was seen as a 'zone in transition' and was where both population and land uses were fluid and changing. Commercial activities encroached and led to land price changes, forcing out existing uses, and bringing in new ones. Further, the area had the lodging houses which provided the entry point for the migrants into the housing and labour market of the city. Beyond this zone, there was that of working-class housing, where the more established workers bought themselves property and became more firmly anchored into the American way of life. Further out still was the zone of middle-class housing with the more substantial properties of the more affluent. Finally, there was the commuting zone which stretched out for an ever-increasing distance as the means and speed of commuting improved.

Later theorists, working within this tradition, modified this concentric zone model based on further empirical analysis of other North-American and European cities. Hawley (1950) redefined the zones as sectors and showed how cities tended to grow along transport lines with both road and rail creating wedges or sectors of development rather than concentric rings. The patterns within the sectors were similar, however, to the rings and the model was still based around the central business district as the point of origin and growth. Later still, the idea arose of 'multiple nuclei' (Hoyt 1939) where there was still a central business area but with a more dispersed and increasingly large urban area. Regional centres emerged around the edges which then formed either sectors or rings of differing size and composition around these new regional nodes.

The work of the early ecologists was thus largely concerned with the internal characteristics of the city and with the process of residential segregation of the population. The writing of Park in some ways paved the way for the discussions during the 1950s and 1960s of the role of mass society upon individuals. The move to the city and modern industrial society were intimately connected and both were seen to have had differentiating effects upon the individual, leading to a loss in personal freedom and autonomy. This theme is taken up in the writings of, for example, Riesman (1961) who in the *Lonely Crowd* wrote about how individuals feel isolated within the mass society of the city as they are surrounded by people who are strangers and with whom they find it difficult to establish meaningful social relations. The city was seen as a large and varied place where individuals became less important and therefore needed social support from public and voluntary agencies to restore them to a more wholesome path and more integrated set of social relationships. Community development was thus encouraged in many countries in the late 1960s and 1970s.

Critique of Urban Ecology

The ecologist's explanation for change derived from deterministic views about social change, and contained a mixture of biology and market forces. Both tended to rely on hidden mechanisms appearing to be independent of human agency and driven by their own logic. They privilege the level and nature of technology in their explanation for urban and suburban growth and thus the shape of the city. Transport is considered a crucial variable here. The city was shaped first by the distance we could comfortably walk, then by travel using a variety of means of public transport beginning with the horse-drawn omnibus, followed in the twentieth century by the electric tram, suburban and subway rail lines and the private motor car (Dyos 1954). Alongside these factors were also those of infrastructure and services: the patterns of water reticulation, electricity and gas supply, waste removal and so forth. Here, the questions arise as to whether it was the technology and provisions that drove development or the conscious actions of class actors and other social- and political-interest groups.

Ecologists were also influenced by the idea that society needed to maintain stability and order. This again reflected their evolutionary thinking and the stability that followed the rise of a new form of local domination. This then secured stability until the next wave of change, either in land use or population, took place creating in its turn some short-term instability. Once the process creating this instability had worked through, a new period of stability would occur (Timms 1971, Johnson 1973, Bassett and Short 1980). This emphasis upon stability ensured that order rather than change was the more dominant motif in their theorising about the city. The major weakness this exposed in their thinking was an absence of consideration of powerful social actors consciously shaping the city in pursuit of their interests. Thus, there is little discussion of the role of political parties, mayors and city planners, of captains of industry and developers, all of whom were part of Chicago in the 1920s and 1930s. Fortunes were made, and no doubt lost, on land transactions because speculation was rife as the city grew. Just as the political actors are absent, so too is any consideration of collective social actors, There is no consideration of class action or struggles over the use and changes in land values and occupancy, or of associations formed among and between the new migrants to the city (Castells 1976). The ecologists' legacy is that of a detailed description of the distribution of people and activities across the urban area rather than a strong analytical scheme which answers the questions as to why these distributions occurred or how they reflect underlying and surface differences in power and privilege amongst the urban dwellers. For answers to these questions, we have to turn to the urban managerialists and political economists.

In the 1950s and 1960s, the original ecological work was strengthened through the addition of more sophisticated statistical, analytical procedures working with census tract data. These were social-area analysis and factorial ecology (Berry and Kasarda 1977). Neither added substantially to the theory of city growth articulated earlier. What they did was to provide a greater range of analyses of cities in various parts of the world, showing how the urban areas and subareas were characterised by forms of residential segregation, household structure, and ethnic concentrations. In some ways, this led to urban studies becoming something of a theoretical backwater. This position changed with first a Weberian-inspired critique leading to the focus upon the 'urban managers' and then a

Marxian-inspired critique focusing upon the production and reproduction of urban space and the formation of urban social movements.

Urban Managerialism

In the late 1960s, an English urban analyst, Ray Pahl, wrote a book entitled *Whose City?* (1975) and introduced the idea of the urban manager and gatekeeper into the debate about city soci-spatial structure. Pahl drew upon Max Weber and his work on power and bureaucracy and the significance of administrative systems within modern societies.

Weber's approach suggests a political theory about domination and power (Kilmartin, Thorns, and Burke 1985). Power in these terms is the ability of one person to enforce their will even against the wishes of another. How this is done varies according to the nature of society. Weber distinguished three types of domination: traditional, charismatic and rational-legal. Traditional authority was more characteristic of pre-industrial societies where power lay in the hands of temporal and spiritual rulers by virtue of their position, usually inherited, within the social structure. Legitimacy was maintained through appeal to the authority of the past, of the inherited mantle of spiritual recognition. In contrast, charismatic authority was related to the person and their ability to command a following through their personality, skills, ideas and accomplishments. Charismatic power was useful, if not necessary in periods of transition and change from one form of domination to another. Rational-legal domination was the final form and was characteristic of modern society. Here, legitimacy was based on administrative and/or bureaucratic skills and rules, which are underpinned by rationality and science. Authority lay in the position rather than the individual and gave significance to credentials and achievements over ascriptive criteria and inheritance. The important shift here is towards the recognition of the existence of key social actors who could manipulate the citizens. Their life chances were affected by the decisions of the powerful, a dimension notably absent in the work of the urban ecologists.

Alongside the work of Pahl was that of Rex and Moore who analysed the changing patterns of housing allocation within inner areas of Birmingham, UK (1967). Their study was focused on the nature of the zone in transition, around the central area where the middle class were vacating properties and areas which new migrants were then moving into and changing the ethnic and class composition. However, the analysis carried through showed that the allocation of housing in this area was crucially affected by the workings of the housing market and the rules of allocation practised by public housing authorities. This further added to a growing critique of the Chicago School and their insufficient attention to the political framework of resource allocation.

The city, therefore, within this mangerialist framework became understood as a set of resources to be allocated and distributed by political and bureaucratic processes. The question thus became what were the resources being allocated? The key resources were seen as land, capital in its various forms (human, social, cultural), the built environment (housing, and industrial and commercial buildings) and social resources (transport, education, health and recreational). The next step was to discover how these urban resources were spatially distributed and managed by various urban gatekeepers. Research sought to describe and examine the allocative practices, rules and procedures, of central and local states, especially in the area of housing, which in the UK, particularly, was considered a key urban resource. Access to housing also determined the household's or individual's location in the city and thus the facilities and other services available within a particular urban neighbourhood. Research quickly showed that the distribution of such urban resources as libraries, playing fields, community centres, shops, and bus services were not evenly spread across the urban area but were unequally distributed. The source of this inequality displayed itself in the processes and interplay of power within local political systems. This involved both public officials such as planners and policy-makers and private-sector actors such as bankers, real estate interests, property owners, landlords and local business owners. Analysing the outcomes in terms of the spatial distributions of resources provided a means to understand the nature of urban social inequality, and peoples' differential access to structures of power.

Critique of Urban Managerialism

One of the key issues which has arisen in critiques of the managerialist position is that of who manages the managers? What is the structure of power within the urban system, of which managers are the 'front line'? Here, the argument arose that managerialism appeals to those with power as it directs attention away from the power-holders and towards those who are, in effect, intermediaries between those with power and the city residents. Further, it was seen to appeal to those at the bottom of the social scale as it identified, for them, a group who were the cause of their oppression (Williams 1978).

The initial examination of urban managers by urban researchers was shaped by a desire to improve their efficiency and performance by identifying weaknesses in both their training and in their delivery of services. This approach attracted criticism from two sources. The urban political

economists who emerged at more or less the same time as the urban managerialists delivered the first counter-attack. They argued that urban
managerialism inflated the autonomy and power of the urban managers
and ignored the broader socio-economic processes, which constrained
the decision-making of urban managers. To use the analogy used by
Gouldner (1979), the urban managerialist ignored the top dogs in society
and targeted the middle dogs. The urban residents in this analogy would
be the underdogs. The critique of the urban political economists is perti-
nent – they point to the role that is played by flows of both local and international capital and the creation of a new international hierarchy of urban
centres into which cities are linked.

The debate on who controls the managers within the city parallels the
debate taking place in industrial sociology in the 1960s. In both contexts,
the analysis focused upon the nature of modern complex organisations
and how these have routinised the making of decisions and created new
categories of specialist administrators with their own values, training
and allegiances. In both urban and industrial sociology, by the mid to
late 1960s and into the 1970s, there was a growing critique of this managerialist position which argued that a fundamental question was who
manages the managers and what was the nature of the ownership and
control of urban resources, especially those of land development capital?
Thus, for example, where urban manangerialism might look at the problems of public housing and call for more efficient allocation policies or
better trained workers, the political economists would ask why is there
not enough low income housing? This approach would suggest that the
urban managers were not key actors but middle-level functionaries constrained by processes such as technological change, industrialisation and,
of most importance to the political economists, capitalism. Many political
economists saw the urban managers as tools of capitalism as they
exercised their rules and procedures to essentially control residents and
facilitate the profit-making of business interests.

As if proving that public sector actors are damned if they do and
damned if they don't, in more recent times, the notion of urban managers
has become increasingly under attack from the right. In these arguments,
urban managers, particularly planners, are obstacles to, rather than the
facilitators of, change because they prevent the effective working of
market allocation thereby inhibiting economic growth. The growth of
'market rationalists' as a dominant group within policy-making has meant
an increasing shift towards the use of the market as a more effective means
of meeting individual requirements (Pusey 1991). The new orthodoxy sees
the bureaucrats of the state agencies as 'regulators' controlling social
behaviour and inhibiting market initiatives. Consequently, it is preferable

to reduce their role and allow greater individual choice by the downsizing of the public sector and deregulation of many programme policy areas. The remaining public servants, however, are to adopt a new managerialism, which is much more commercially oriented and purportedly client focused. The managerialist attacks of the right, in some respects, can be seen as no more than a group of ideologues who simply want to replace the old urban managerialist philosophy with a new philosophy and structure whereby the new urban managers are more compliant to their political masters and are not guided by objectives of equity or fairness but efficiency and acceptability.

Urban Political Economy

The final set of analysts, are those who drew on the Marxian tradition. There are two streams here, which have been influential. The first is the work of Castells (1977b) and Harvey (1973, 1989, 1990) in the late 1960s and 1970s which renewed the Marxian analysis of the city through strong attacks on existing work by the ecologists and managerialists which they saw as at best descriptive and, at worst, ideological obscuring rather than illuminating the economic and social forces which shape the city and urban social life. Returning to Marx, both saw the way forward as identifying the circuit of capital as it was expressed through the urban form. The four main spheres within capitalist social formation identified by Marx, therefore, were the starting point for analysis, namely the production, circulation, consumption and exchange processes within capitalist society and how these were worked through in the urban context. To these initial four, later neo-Marxist writers added those of legitimation and contradictions (Kilmartin, Thorns and Burke 1985). The second are those neo-Marxist writers who were influenced by the French Regulation School and developed analyses based around a model of regimes of accumulation and modes of social regulation. This view saw the 1970s as a period of crisis in global capitalism leading to a 'restructuring' around a new set of activities taking the world economy to a new level of global activity and new forms of spatial distributions leading to the emergence of 'global cities' based around financial services and information (Sassen 1991, 1994, 1996, 1999; Knox and Taylor 1995).

In respect to the first form of analysis – the circuit of capital and the city – in order to understand the working of production and the city it was necessary to see the city as the site of both the production of material goods and the reproduction of labour power. From the earliest days of the industrial city, workers were drawn to the city to supply labour power for the expanding manufacturing plants. Workers also became the consumers of the new commodities. As the capitalist system has changed over time, new spatial arrangements, both globally and locally, have occurred leading to the decline of some cities and the growth of others in various regions of the world. Capital has been relatively footloose and production has shifted to new and cheaper labour markets creating the de-industrialisation of the cities of the earlier periods of capitalist industrial expansion (Massey 1984). Marxists would suggest that the structure of the city and its dispersed shape in the twentieth century arose from the 'needs' of capitalist commodity production. It was necessary to create the individual consumer and create demand for such things as private cars, whiteware, housing, and roads. These analysts saw suburbia as the ideal form for the expansion and stimulation of consumer demand and the creation of landscapes of consumption (Zukin 1991).

Marketing, advertising, taste making and levels of real income shape the consumption of goods and services. Initially, the consuming of goods and services could be achieved through the single-earner family wage. As the twentieth century progressed, however, this became increasingly difficult so that by the late 1950s the need for additional household earning capacity had become apparent and by the 1970s two full-time incomes were increasingly considered essential to lift the household into the upper income level and thus enable continued participation in contemporary consumer culture. Dolores Hayden writing about the American dream of home ownership and Mrs Consumer noted that:

> Mrs Consumer moved the economy to new heights in the fifties. Women who stayed at home experienced what Betty Friedan called the 'feminine mystique' and Peter Filene renamed the 'domestic mystique' . . . With the increase in spatial privacy came pressure for conformity in consumption. More and more women joined the paid labour force, as the suggestible housewife needed to be both a frantic consumer and a paid worker to keep up with the family bills (Hayden 1980:174).

There are two aspects to urban consumption, namely an individual one and a collective one. The dispersed spatial structure of the city owes a lot to the individual consumption emphasis which flows from owner-occupied separate housing on its own plot of land. Urban form is created here which is most conducive to commodity consumption, the low-density, private transport-oriented, owner-occupied city. The second aspect is collective consumption. The collective consumption of goods and services such as health care, education, transport, parks and recreation spaces expanded with the growth of welfare state social democratic policies from the 1930s and 1940s to the 1960s (Dunleavy 1979, 1980; Saunders

1990b). The global crisis of capitalism in the 1970s created a reappraisal of the state's role and, with the rise of the neo-liberal agenda in the late 1970s and 1980s, the reduction in the level of collective provision began and the reassertion of individualised and market solutions to the supply of goods and services was embraced. State restructuring occurred and greater targeting and 'user-pay' schemes were introduced into the supply of collective commodities such as health, education, transport, and pensions. A reaction was expected to this restructuring, by those affected, and Castells (1977b, 1983) predicted the rise of urban social movements and suggested that urban based struggles would occur surrounding this shift from state to market provisions and this would provide a focus for the development of new forms of collective consciousness and thus an impetus for change (Lowe 1986).

A further aspect of the realisation of profits from the consumption process is that the time between when a commodity is produced and when it is finally consumed is an important contributing factor to its price. Pressure therefore exists to shorten this period of time and simplify the stages which sit between the manufacture of a commodity and its ultimate sale. The costs to be addressed include those of getting the workforce and other inputs to the workplace, moving the commodities produced from the workplace to the retail outlets, and getting the consumers to the developing retail outlets. The new super malls and out-of-town shopping centres, such as those at West Edmonton and Gateshead's Metro Centre, have been crucially important in encouraging more consumer spending (Shields 1992, 1996).

A key area of change in urban consumption has been in the transport infrastructure. Road developments, the privatisation of the railways, the introduction of containerisation and reform of the ports, and the development of larger airliners (747 jumbo jets and the proposed new airbus to carry over 500 passengers) have all been centrally important in reducing time and cost in this area. Also important is credit and the possibility this creates of spending before you have saved. Good examples include consumer spending through hire-purchase and finance-company loans, the use of credit cards and electronic banking for the purchase of goods. These changes have been a further factor in restructuring the spatial form of the capitalist city where freeways link workers' 'homes' in the suburbs with workplaces and encourage the push for rapid transit systems from suburbs to downtown city centres. In these debates and decisions, the relative political influence of the road-transport, private-transport and rail lobbies upon the decision-makers has crucially shaped the outcomes.

Profit is not realised within this circuit of capital until sales have taken place, thus exchange is a further crucial component. Market transactions enable commodities, labour, materials, and finished goods to be exchanged for money so it is the precondition for both consumption and for 'realisation of surplus value'. The purchase of property, not for its use value, but its exchange value has also been a major factor in the urban land market. Speculative pressures have led to a pattern of boom and bust through the 1960s to the 1990s meaning that there have been winners and losers rather than an even rate of accumulation (Hamnett 1999).

Finally, two additional factors have been suggested: those of legitimation and contradiction. This raises the role of the state, both national and local, in urban development. Marxists see the state's role as very much facilitating capitalist development through maintaining conditions favourable to accumulation and market-based activity. The state needs to ensure that the majority considers such activity 'legitimate' and thus the ideological activities of the state are an important aspect contributing to urban development. The nature of planning laws and government incentives and support for development is significant. In many countries, special zones have been created giving favourable conditions to businesses to establish new ventures such as in the recently created Chinese Special Economic Areas such as Pudong in Shanghai. Another way of assisting capital to develop activity is through the use of incentive grants and tax write-offs, and finally there have been 'brown site' redevelopments as at Homebush, the Sydney 2000 Olympic site, with the aid of government grants (Searle and Bounds 1999). The final issue of contradiction arises from the necessity to manage the inherent contradictions within the capitalist mode of production and serves to temper the extremes. Wages cannot be depressed too far as this will result in workers not being able to afford commodities and in turn will lead to surpluses and falling sales creating a crisis of over-production. Another contradictory force operates around the need to manage conflict and ensure legitimacy for the policies being pursued. This is where we see recourse to the rhetoric of the public interest to legitimate action at both local and national government level.

A very influential set of neo-Marxist writings, particularly within Britain in the 1970s and 1980s, analysed the relationship between economic restructuring, urban and regional change and political conflict. The work here of Massey (1984) has been the most extensive and drew attention to the spatial consequences of the de-industrialisation of this period. British industrial areas in the North East, North West and the Midlands lost skilled work with the restructuring of such industries as shipbuilding, steel-making, and car manufacturing. Much of this was relocated either to other parts of the world, for example steel making to South Korea, or to areas where there had not previously been a history of this type of industrial activity such as the 'sunbelt states' in the southern part of the

USA. Part of the reason for these locational choices arose from the class and political cultures of the various regions with industry shifting to places where labour could be obtained at lower cost and without strong unionisation, thus enabling increased rates of capital accumulation and a restoration of profits.

In the 1980s and 1990s the growth of 'regulation theory', a development with its roots in French Marxist scholarship, especially the work of Aglietta (Jessop 1990), was taken up by urban analysts, particularly those analysing Los Angeles, as a way of explaining 'urban restructuring' (Soja 1989; Storper and Scott 1989; Davis 1991). Regulation theory seeks to analyse the crises of capitalist accumulation and the need for new sets of social mechanism to help 'regulate' the form of capitalism, which is appearing. This new form is seen as flexible, unstable and chaotic. Aglietta separated out the 'mode of accumulation' from the 'mode of regulation' and argued that capitalism required the generation of social mechanisms to ensure social stability during periods of accumulation. Once the regime of accumulation breaks down, crises ensue in both the economic, social and political structures requiring a new form of both economic and social regulation. Most regulationists argue, that over the 1970s and 1980s, there was a period of crisis brought on by over-production leading to a decline in profits, a rise in unemployment and the need for restructuring to restore profitability to capitalist accumulation. The focus on 'restructuring' required both an analysis of economic activities, for example, the shift to financial and consumer services and the knowledge economy and a spatial analysis where the de-industrialisation of urban regions and the displacement of activity from one area of the globe to another have had major implications for urban growth and decline (Bluestone and Harrison 1986, Cooke 1989, Zukin 1991). There is continuing debate as to whether a new regime of accumulation and social regulation has yet been formed or indeed will be formed. Most regulationists would agree that 'Fordism' is in decline and we are entering a 'post-Fordist' world. There is, however, disagreement as to whether a new regime can or will eventuate. Harvey (1990) is the theorist who has been most certain about the formation of a new regime, which he sees as one of 'flexible accumulation'. This regime is based on a more global set of interconnections and is held together through individual contractual relations. This is seen as in sharp contrast to the previous 'Fordist regime' which was

> underpinned by the development of large corporations with high profits based on near monopoly conditions, collective bargaining and the development of a unionized working class with middle-class powers of consumption, fine tuned

with Keynesian macro economic management technique and government redistribution (Smart 2001:2).

However, others in this perspective are not as certain that a new regime has yet emerged and are unsure as to whether or not this is now a possibility. This reflects a concern with the way that nation-states are ceasing to be the nodes of the new economy. Rather, the new sets of economic relations that are emerging are based on global flows of information and financial transactions and thus are not constrained by national borders or governments. In this emerging world it could well be that cities also become key nodes, rather than nation-states. It is further suggested that cities are increasingly being drawn into competition with other cities, both in their own 'nation' and transnationally. The result of this pattern may well be a less coherent and more fluid set of economic, political and social relations and these may not cohere into a single 'regime of social regulation' (Kennett 1994).

Critique of Urban Political Economy

The analysis of the city developed by the urban political economists has been criticised for its over determination, emphasis upon material structures and its limited view of human agency. The theory was not particularly sensitive to difference in experience across the cities of the world. Not all followed an identical path. The regulationists attempted to meet some of these objections through the widening of the Marxist argument to look at how social and political relations intersected with economic forces to shape the particular national patterns of accumulation. However, in the end, the fundamental driving force of the theory is the wage relation and the imbalance of power between those who own and control the means of production and those who must work for wages. The theory thus emphasizes structural relations rather than the agency of the various actors and it effectively excludes those who are not in the regular paid workforce. This has increasingly generated criticism as the strength of class relations, as a basis of social organization, has been challenged in the latter part of the twentieth century by the rise of other forms of social movement. The very breakdown in the coherent set of social and political relations that regulationists have drawn attention to as part of the 'crisis' also released a whole set of other social forces of change, for example, ethnicity, gender, peace, environmentalism, that have also provided alternative sources of social mobilisation contributing to the more fragmentary nature of social and political relations towards the end of the twentieth century.

The increasing emphasis on diversity has encouraged the rise of post-structural and postmodern theory embracing a more contextual and contingent set of explanations and rejecting the universal style of explanation favoured within the political economy tradition. These newer currents of theory will be further examined in Chapter 4.

Summary

The chapter has examined the growth and development of the industrial city, which is the key representation of the modern city. Urban analysis grew up alongside this development and provides a number of lenses through which to view the changes of urban living that took place. The four reviewed here are those of the contrast school, the Chicago School of urban ecology, the urban managerialists and the political economists. In the last decades of the twentieth century, a key question became: have we reached a new point of transformation? Are we leaving behind the 'modern world' produced out of the set of interrelated political, economic and spatial changes of the late eighteenth and nineteenth centuries and entering a 'postmodern' world? One of the key aspects of this debate relates to the structure and distribution of population, both urban and rural and the pattern of migration. It is to these that we now turn prior to examining the arguments for, and evidence of, a transition to a postmodern globalising urban world.

Note

1. Taylorism is often used as synonym for scientific management. Taylor pioneered the reorganisation of work tasks (time and motion study), payment methods (incentive payments for rationalising tasks) and industrial discipline in nineteenth century to improve efficiency and output (Mann 1990).

Further Reading

Elliott, B. and McCrone, D. 1982, *The City Patterns of Domination and Conflict*, London: Macmillan – now Palgrave Macmillan. Chapter 3 'The Emergence of the Modern City', pp. 51–77. This chapter from their book on the modern city gives a good account of how cities developed from independent centres in the medieval period to the 'corporate' cities of the late twentieth century.

Hayden, D. 1980, 'What Would a Non-sexist City be Like?' *Signs: Journal of Women in Culture and Society*. 5(3) pp. 169–87. This is an important article which has had considerable impact on challenging the gender-blind nature of much urban analysis. Hayden also sets out a model for change.

Saunders, P. 1986, *Social Theory and the Urban Question* (2nd edn) London: Hutchinson. This is still an excellent analysis of the work of the 'modern' theories of the city. Clearly written, it provides both an analysis of the various theories and a critique. Chapters 2, 3 and 4 would be particularly useful to extend this chapter's discussion of the theories.

Savage, M. and Warde, A. 1993, *Urban Sociology, Capitalism and Modernity*, London: Macmillan Press – now Palgrave Macmillan. Chapter 3, 'Cities and Uneven Economic Development', pp. 34–62, gives a good account of the way capitalist economic systems structure cities. It draws particularly upon the work done by economic geographers.

Web site

http://www.uoregon.edu/~sergiok/brasil/saopaulo.html

3

Demographic Change and the City

Introduction

The global demographic transition is one of the key features of the twenty-first century and one which is critical for the global shape and pace of urban development and change. Since the publication in the 1960s of Ehrlich's *Population Bomb* (1968), the focus in debate has been upon the consequences of rapid population growth and the need to moderate fertility rates to ensure that the population does not exceed the carrying capacity of the planet and that Malthus' dismal prophecy does not become a reality. Thus, population policy has principally been about birth control and the reduction in growth rates, particularly in the developing parts of the world, for example, the development of the one-child family in China. Within the population mix, however, there are other significant changes. The regional distribution of population across the globe is changing, countries are ageing at varying rates, and the rural-urban balances are still moving in the direction of the cities. Thus, even if, overall, the population may be going to peak at some stage during the present millennium, there will be profound distributional and profile changes which will impact upon the social structure, economic capacity and socio-political relations between nation-states and ethnic groupings arising out of the relative changes in the size and shape of the various populations within the cities around the world.

Demography of Global Cities

The first question to explore is what is likely to be the total population of the world which needs to be accommodated within settlements, be they urban or rural? Where will this population be concentrated (Andrieu 1999)? The size of the world population is a function of natural increase and changing longevity. As economic, social and health conditions are

41

improved, life expectancy increases. The distribution of the population both within and between cities, regions and nations is further influenced by patterns of migration. Thus, with respect to migration, it is necessary to consider not just rural to urban movement but also urban to rural, international and urban to urban and rural to rural movement.

The world's population is still growing at a fast rate although the growth is quite uneven across the various countries within the world. Although growth is now predicted to slow down and eventually peak around the middle of the present century, we are still experiencing a growing total (Figure 3.1). The six billionth child was symbolically welcomed into the world by Kofi Annan, the UN Secretary-General, at Sarajevo in October 1999. The world having added this last billion in the short time of 17 years, the rate of growth is slowing down. In 1998 the population of the world was 5.9 billion. From 1975 to 1995 it showed a steady growth of 1.7 per cent per annum. Over the last five years, this rate of growth fell to only 1.3 per cent per annum (UNCHS 2001b). Of this population growth, 80 per cent occurred in the less developed regions of the world. Estimates for future growth are always somewhat problematic as they depend on a range of assumptions about the fertility behaviour of the population. Thus, the UN predictions cover a range from high to low fertility options. The middle prediction would see the population rising to around 8.04 billion by the year 2025 and peaking around 9.37 by the year 2050, whereas the high option assumes a slower rate of decline in

Figure 3.1   World population size: past estimates and medium, high and low fertility variants, 1950–2050

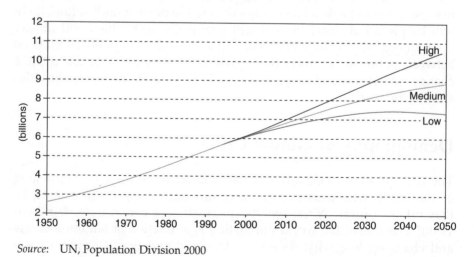

Source: UN, Population Division 2000

population growth and thus yields a total of 10.7 billion by 2050. Finally, in the low variant, a more rapid decline in population is assumed to produce an estimate of 7.3 billion by the same date. The middle- and high-growth projections assume that after 2050 the world population would stabilise and then begin to decline.

What the figures show is that despite the decline in fertility in many countries as a result of both explicit population policies, for example, that of the Peoples Republic of China, and social changes in western countries such as later childbearing, the changing position and role of women in society and the workforce, and decline in marriage rates, the overall population number is still increasing. The present global fertility rate at an average of 3.0 children per woman still needs to decline to 2.1 (replacement) by 2035 to make the 9.4 billion target used in the middle-level prediction. The pattern of fertility is quite uneven across the globe with high and low fertility countries. The developed world, on the whole, has the lowest levels of fertility. The high fertility countries – Pakistan, China, India, Indonesia – still have rates well above the 2.1 children per woman, which is seen as the replacement level. From 1995 to 2000, 21 per cent of world population growth was accounted for by India and a further 15 per cent by China. The ten countries expected to make the greatest contribution to the increase expected over the next decades to world population, in addition to the four above, are Nigeria, Brazil, Bangladesh, Mexico, the Philippines and the USA. The US position is interesting as this growth is within a developed country and thus seems to be against the overall trend. The growth here is, however, amongst the Hispanic and Black American population rather than amongst people of European origin.

The link between fertility and affluence has been long established through demographic and social research. Such classics as Bank's *Prosperity and Parenthood* (1954) pointed to the reduction in family size amongst the British middle classes to ensure that their children had the best opportunities in education and social advancement. The increased survivorship which came about through health and social improvement to the physical environment within the developed cities of the world decreased the need for large numbers of children leading to a fall in the birth rate. Thus, as countries increase their level of affluence and development, birth rates tend to fall. This is shown in data for all countries in the 1990s except Africa. In Africa, there are signs of the beginning of decline in some countries in east and southern Africa. The situation here, and the data, is complicated by the political instability leading to large-scale migrations and ethnic 'cleansing' associated with inter-ethnic conflicts (for example, Rwanda, Uganda, Zaire, and so on). There has also been the impact of diseases, especially AIDS (acquired immune deficiency syndrome) upon the population. In the twenty-nine African countries where the impact of

AIDS has been studied, life expectancy at birth will remain low. It is predicted that by 2015 life expectancy will reach 47 years instead of an estimated 64 years without the AIDS epidemic. Thus AIDS has shortened life
by an average of 17 years. This clearly has a significant effect on the rate
of population growth (UNCHS 1996, 2001b; Rakodi 1997).

In the next decades, all the growth in the overall population of the
world is expected to be contributed by the developing countries with
around 3.68 billion people (between 1995 and 2050). Over the same period,
the developed world will shrink by about ten million. This will lead to
considerable regional changes, which are likely to affect the global, political and economic agendas.

Asia and Africa are the regions of the world where the population
growth is most likely to be concentrated reflecting the current demographic profile of most of these societies. Overall, Asia is likely to have an
extra two billion people by the middle of this century. This growth is at a
declining rate with the average dropping from just over three children per
woman to 2.54 by 2001. It is also uneven across the countries of Asia with,
for example, Japan having one of the most rapidly ageing populations
within the world and will be faced with a substantial fall if current demographic conditions within the society continue as its fertility rate has fallen
substantially below replacement rate. It also has over 25 per cent of its
population in the over 65 category (International Longevity Centre 1996).
Long-term predictions for Japan, released by the Ministry of Health and
Welfare, indicate that the population could fall to 'about 500 in the year
3000'. This is a result of Japanese women having only 1.4 children each on
average, well below the replacement level (Browne and Reeves 1999).

Africa is the other area where there is still high fertility and this region
is expected to contribute a further 1.3 billion to the total. Here, the high
fertility rate has been moderated by the rising mortality rate caused
by the series of wars, disease episodes and natural disasters that have
occurred in the final decades of the twentieth century. If these are moderated then population growth could accelerate.

In Latin America, population growth appears to have slowed down and
a low fertility pattern is becoming established with, for example, women
in Brazil now having on average 2.3 children down from 6.3 in the 1960s.
This will not prevent some further growth and thus an increase in fertility potential, due to the relatively youthful nature of much of the population. It is expected that the growth here will be around 334 million. In
contrast to this pattern of growth, the European population is set to
decline by 27 million by 2025 and a further 64 million between 2025 and
2050. These changes will affect the global balance in the world population
quite significantly. In the 1990s, Europe's share of the world population
was 12.8 per cent, similar to that of Africa. By 2050, on the assumption of

decline of 74 million and growth of 1.3 billion for Africa, Europe will contain only 6.8 per cent of the global population whereas Africa will have 21.8 per cent.

The two main demographic factors, which shape the growth in population, are the number of live births and the life expectancy within the population. The survival rates of both infants and adults have improved in the developing countries but are still below those in the developed countries. The gap is closing. In India, survival of infants has improved giving a total fertility rate of still over 4, well above replacement level. Further, the life expectancy of the population has increased dramatically from an average of 45 years in the 1960s to 62.5 years by the 1990s. These two factors together account for the strong growth in the Indian population. Male children are seen as a significant asset thus their survivorship is considered crucial for the long-term well-being of their families in many developing countries. Often, there is little in the way of a welfare system and land succession still provides limited opportunities for women making it important to have male children. In the 1996 UN Conference on Human Settlement (Habitat 2), one of the key areas of debate was around the issue of women's rights to land and thus to a choice in life. Many marriage contracts operate around access to, and control of, land distribution. One of the consequences of a large surviving population and limited access to land is to create a surplus rural population which is then forced to migrate to the cities in search of work and income.

Household Structure Changes

Total population growth is not, however, the only factor which creates demand for accommodation and thus shapes the pace and nature of urban growth. The other significant variable is the structure of households and their long-term stability. Household size and composition has become one of the most significant growth stimuli within the developed societies maintaining the pressure for more housing construction, even in those societies where overall fertility has fallen below replacement level.

The middle years of the twentieth century witnessed a marriage and baby boom within the developed countries of Europe, America, and Australasia. This was the product of both the delay in marriage and childbirth brought on by the global depression of the 1930s and the disruption of peoples' lives by the Second World War (1939–45). The relative affluence and stability of the 1950s and 1960s also helped encourage population expansion. This was a euphoric time characterised by widespread confidence in the technical capacity of the age to solve the problems of economic and urban growth. This optimism was punctured towards the end of the 1960s as the limits to growth started to become apparent and the destruction of the environment that a high energy consuming society was causing began to filter into the consciousness of the affluent societies. *The 'Silent Spring'* by Rachel Carson (1962), Ehlich's (1968) challenge regarding the population expansion, and the emergence of the environmental, peace, anti-nuclear energy, and feminist movements raised questions about the 'sustainability' of the social and environmental aspects of the suburban boom.

The suburban boom of the 1950s and 1960s stimulated the growth of a consumer economy and increased aggregate demand for housing. This was the period of the Levittowns within the USA and the growth of a debate about a suburban culture and way of life replacing the urban (Thorns 1972). The flight to the suburbs was seen as a reflection of the demography and household-forming practices of the more affluent post-1940s cohorts. They embraced home ownership and separate dwellings with space to raise the family. The analysis pointed to the strength of 'familism' amongst this group. Work was a means to an end – family life in the burgeoning suburbs. Life was child centred and focused around the communal institutions associated with childrearing and family life – the school, taxes in the locality, keeping the area and its tax base secure, and seeking newer forms of leisure and consumer durables (Seeley, Sim and Loosely 1956). This led to arguments about the growth of privatisation and privatism (Pawley 1978).

The baby boom turned into a baby 'bust' in the late 1960s and latter decades of the last century. Fertility rates fell, marriages became less stable and thus a greater variety of both size and form of household have emerged. What some demographers have described as the echo marriage boom, when the initial cohorts of baby boomers reached marriage and childbearing age, created not an increase in fertility, which might have been expected, but a fall. This generation has married later, if at all and many have delayed childrearing or chosen to stay childless (Cameron 1997). For women, a greater variety of opportunities for career options and the ability to control fertility and thus make choices now exist. Further, there have been major changes in social values regarding the role of women and men in society. Here, the growth of second-wave feminism and its challenge to patriarchal structure and attitudes has been particularly significant. Feminist writers were a key group in developing the critique of suburbia and the way it limited and disadvantaged women (Hayden 1980; McDowell 1989, 1997; Massey 1994).

The net effect of these social and demographic changes has been the creation of many smaller households and also greater household instability. The one-child family is now the fastest growing household in many countries. In America, they have grown from 9.65 per cent of all families in 1976 to over 17 per cent in 1998. In Germany, more than 50 per cent of 12.9 million families with children in 1999 had only one child and in mainland China, the birth rate has shrunk to such an extent that the Government is beginning to rethink its one-child policy.

Youth versus Age

One of the far reaching changes taking place is that of the shifting balance between younger and older people. This arises from changes in both the behaviour of younger cohorts and increased longevity. Amongst the young, there has been a growth of the one- or no-child household. At the other end of life, there has been increasing longevity and relatively large ageing cohorts reflecting the periods of higher fertility, especially the 'baby-boom' generation. The net result is that the population of the world will age much faster over the next fifty years. In 1998, the median age in the world was 26.1. By 2050 this will have risen to 37.8. Part of this change is accounted for by the declining percentage of children within the total population (Figure 3.2). In 1998, 30 per cent of the world's population comprised children under the age of fifteen, whereas those over 60 made up ten per cent. By 2050, projections indicate that the proportion of children will have fallen to 20 per cent and that for the over-60s will have more than doubled to 22 per cent. In actual numbers, this will mean an increase from 580 million to two billion over 60s. Europe will be the region of the world most affected by these changes where the percentage of children will fall from 18 per cent (1998) to 14 per cent (2050) and southern Europe, especially Italy, Greece and Spain, will have the oldest populations. Spain and Italy, with current fertility rates of 1.15 and 1.18, are amongst the lowest in the world and these, if unchanged, will lead to a substantial decline in both the Spanish and Italian populations by 2050. To preserve total population in these countries without a significant change in fertility behaviour would require massive migration. This would create greater cultural and social diversity but also, for some, the sentiment that 'Italy would be no longer Italian'. At their summit in 2000, the European Union (EU) leaders, recognising the policy implications of population decline, sent out a message to the 380 million citizens to 'make more babies'. The declining population is already creating labour shortages across Europe and these are set to intensify. However, solving them through more migration exacerbates the inter-ethnic tensions that have appeared in many European cities which are not politically popular. Thus, the current emphasis is on more children through exhortation and a raft of new financial incentives to encourage more babies to European parents. Recent EU surveys show that most European couples in fact want more children but

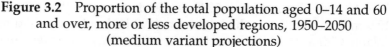

Figure 3.2   Proportion of the total population aged 0–14 and 60
and over, more or less developed regions, 1950–2050
(medium variant projections)

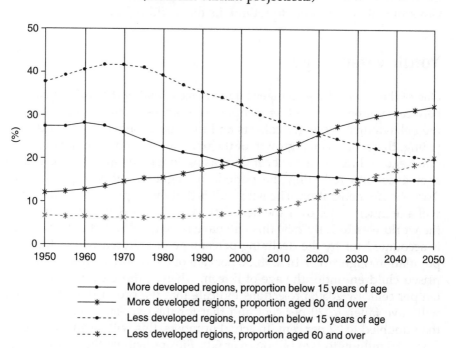

Source: UN, Population Division 2000

are deterred by the challenge of balancing jobs and family life. In contrast, a recent Australian study found that the most common explanation was not job and career oriented but purely a lack of interest. The study quotes one 32-year old as saying 'I have no maternal urges and I'm just too busy with other things'. The study indicates that personal and social goals were becoming more diverse and that being childless was more socially acceptable. Therefore, to have children or not was a choice (Australian Institute of Family Studies 1996).

As Figures 3.3 and 3.4 show, a further change will be the growth in the numbers of the over 80s. This group comprised 1.1 per cent in 1998 and is expected to grow to become 3.9 per cent in 2050. Within this increase, there will be more women than men as is shown in Figure 3.4.

The ageing of the population coupled with the rapid decline in fertility poses the problem of an increasing proportion of elderly retired compared to the continuing working-age population. This in turn leads to an increase in the dependency ratio. Since the 1970s, especially in developed

Figure 3.3 Age composition of world population, 1998

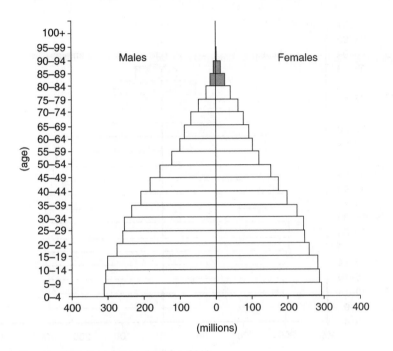

Source: UN, Population Division 2000

countries, this has made a significant change to demographic profiles. In 1950, 131 million of the world's population were aged over 65. By 1995, this number had tripled to 371 million. By 2025, the expectation is that the number will have risen further to 742 million and, by 2050, to 1.4 billion, ten per cent of world population (6.4 per cent in 2000). One of the consequences of the growing proportion of elderly citizens is the emergence of a debate about the capacity of the various societies, in which they are a substantial and growing component, to finance this sector of the population. The debate has focused upon the degree of dependency and the estimated cost of ageing usually in terms of superannuation and health care. The problem is greatest in the developed countries within the OECD (Organisation for Economic Cooperation and Development). A recent IMF (International Monetary Fund) study concluded, for example, that:

> under existing public pension arrangements, which rely heavily on PAYG [Pay As You Go] schemes, aging of the population has started to contribute to serious fiscal stresses in most major industrial countries, and that these are likely to get worse over the next few decades (Chand and Jaeger 1996:32).

The Transformation of Cities

Figure 3.4   Age composition of world population, 2050

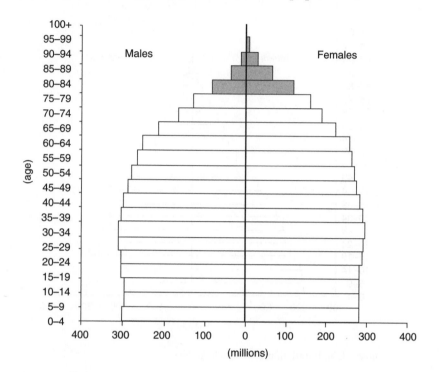

Source: UN, Population Division 2000

The construction of the 'problem' has been one where the elderly, those drawing pensions, have been seen universally as a burden upon the rising generation and this rhetoric has then been used to create a political momentum for the adoption of more restrictive welfare and pension provisions.

Countries where such a debate has emerged in the 1990s are the USA, UK, Canada, Japan[1] and Aotearoa/New Zealand. In the first four cases, strong growth is seen in the proportion of those over 65 during the next 50 or so years (see Table 3.1) dramatically increasing the dependency ratio. Further data show a strong growth in the very elderly, those over 75, which means a longer period of high dependency is likely with its attendant higher costs for health care in addition to pensions.

The emergence of an intergenerational debate about the elderly appears to be linked to the adoption of fiscal and social policies inspired by the new right economic and social agenda. Greater individual responsibility, and a desire to reduce the level and cost of publicly provided welfare ser-

Table 3.1 Demographic trends and dependency ratios, 1995–2050

Demographic trends	1995	2000	2010	2020	2030	2050
US						
Population	100.00	104.80	113.00	119.80	124.70	127.20
Elderly dependency ratio	19.20	19.00	20.40	27.60	36.80	38.40
Very elderly ratio	42.70	46.30	45.80	40.50	45.80	55.60
Total dependency ratio	52.70	52.00	50.50	57.40	68.00	68.80
Canada						
Population	100.00	105.00	113.20	119.70	123.10	122.70
Elderly dependency ratio	17.50	18.20	20.40	28.40	39.10	41.80
Very elderly ratio	39.90	43.30	44.60	40.20	44.40	55.80
Total dependency ratio	48.60	48.30	47.50	56.30	69.00	71.90
Japan						
Population	100.00	101.30	102.20	100.60	97.60	91.60
Elderly dependency ratio	20.30	24.30	33.00	43.00	44.50	54.00
Very elderly ratio	37.80	38.30	44.50	47.20	56.30	58.10
Total dependency ratio	43.90	47.20	56.70	67.80	70.50	84.00
UK						
Population	100.00	102.20	102.20	103.50	103.90	102.00
Elderly dependency ratio	24.30	24.40	25.80	31.20	38.70	41.20
Very elderly ratio	42.90	45.30	46.30	44.50	45.80	57.20
Total dependency ratio	54.30	54.00	52.30	58.30	68.00	71.20

Source: Chand and Jaeger 1996:4

vices such as pensions, health and housing and replace these by a greater degree of 'user pays', lies at the heart of this agenda. The focus on intergenerational issues suggests that dependency is a 'natural' phenomenon associated with chronological ageing rather a social problem related to how the social position of the elderly within society is constructed (Walker 1982, 1990; Calasanti and Bonanno 1989).

The 1996 IMF report, for example, states: 'in principle, individuals should be responsible for making adequate provisions for their own retirement' (Chand and Jaeger 1996:1). Changes to pension schemes and social security provisions have encouraged increased targeting and limiting eligibility. In order to create a new political culture in which such change is more acceptable, it is argued that a debate regarding the position of the elderly within society has been engendered which allows questions to be raised about the equity of current arrangements and intergenerational financing of pensions and other welfare provisions.

The debate tends to focus on a limited number of facts and repeats these to create a sense of fear amongst the population often with simplistic associations between the numbers in the workforce and those who are 'dependants'. Such discussions do not distinguish between those who are dependent on the state in retirement and those who are covered by their own private provisions. This conflates the elderly into one undifferentiated category which is patently absurd. Among the elderly there are those who are income and asset rich as well as those who have neither and are solely dependent upon state pensions. Crude dependency ratios are simplistic forms of demographic analysis (Bedford and Pool 1997, Thorns 1998).

Ageing is not the only factor leading to smaller and less stable households. A major change to the pattern of household formation is the dramatic increase in households headed by women. Over the last 20 years of the previous century, this was particularly dramatic and resulted in around one fifth of all households globally now being headed by women. This change reflects the changing nature of family relations (Stacey 1990, 1996). There has also been an increase in the number of blended households arising from second and subsequent relationships amongst couples. This impacts again on both the size of the household and the accumulative possibilities that are linked to family formation, ownership of land and property and inheritance (Hamnett, Harmer and Williams 1991, Hamnett 1999). All these factors have historically been important for the maintenance of social status and position amongst the middle class within a variety of societies. One of the features of many cities is thus the more fluid nature of family relationships and fragmented nature of relationships amongst and between kin members.

The low birth rate and ageing are likely to have significant urban impacts in those countries where these conditions are present (for example, Spain, Italy, Japan). The building industry, for example, is likely to suffer a decline, as there will be fewer new households coming onto the housing market. The long-term decline in the size of the population across Europe and in Japan are likely to create vacancies within the housing market at a greater rate than they are required to meet the demands of new households. Migration here could be factor preventing or at least moderating the rate of decline. This would require the rethinking of policies by a number of European societies. Population decline and vacant properties are likely also to have consequences for the value of houses and land and may well rework the relationship between housing and the accumulation of wealth, which in turn impacts upon the financial status of the older citizens and exacerbates the problems of financing the ageing population in their later years when they are no longer members of the paid workforce. These effects are likely to be regional and local in nature and will reflect decisions made by older cohorts with respect to retirement – for example, whether they continue to 'age in place' or whether retirement villages and centres are constructed. Clearly, more attention within the planning and building industry, will be focused on the requirements of older citizens than has been the norm in the past, when much of the focus, especially from the 1950s to the 1970s was upon young nuclear families in suburban houses.

Having now identified the global population parameters, the likely increases and their regional locations, we now need to turn to examining how the population is likely to be distributed within the regions of the world. Particularly important for our project will be the likely impact upon the urban population and thus on the growth and decline of cities.

Regional Changes – Urbanising World

At the beginning of the new millennium the urban population exceeded the rural. For the first time, over 50 per cent of the world's population are living in urban areas. One of the problems of analysis here, however, lies in the way 'urban' gets defined in the various countries around the world. Despite these ambiguities it does seem clear that the trend is still towards urban living and thus the twenty-first century will be the first in which we are living in a predominantly urban world.

The transition to the urban industrial world has already been discussed in Chapter 2 where we traced the growth of the modern city. It is important to recognise that, despite the shift to an urban population in the developed world during the nineteenth and early twentieth century, within the developing world there are still considerable numbers of rural dwellers. In fact, as late as 1950, most of the world's workforce was still employed in agriculture. By the 1990s, the transition to new forms of employment meant that the engine of growth within the various economies had shifted from agricultural commodities to services, many of which were urban based. The twentieth century was thus one in which there was a steady decline in rural population and rural-based employment. This contributed to the growth, during the same period, in both the number and size of cities.

In 1950, for example, the average size of the 100 largest cities in the world was 2.1 million. By 1990, this had more than doubled to five million. The last decade has seen the further rise of the mega city – cities of over ten million inhabitants (see Table 3.2). The majority of these are now in the developing world. Between 1980 and 2000, Lagos, Nigeria; Dhaka, Bangladesh; Cairo, Egypt; Tiajin, China; Hyderabad India, Pakistan and Lahore, were added to the list and, by 2010, Lagos is projected to become the world's largest city (UNCHS 2001b).

The European cities, which were at one time dominant in the global league, have declined in their percentage of total urban population and as

Table 3.2 Trading places on the Top 30 list of the world's largest cities (*population in millions*)

	1980		1990		2000		2010	
1	Tokyo	21.9	Tokyo	25.1	Tokyo	26.4	Tokyo	26.4
2	New York	15.5	New York	16.4	Mexico City	18.1	Bombay	23.6
3	Mexico City	13.9	Mexico City	18.1	Bombay	18.1	Lagos	20.2
4	Sao Paulo	12.5	Sao Paulo	17.8	Sao Paulo	17.8	Sao Paulo	19.7
5	Shanghai	11.7	Shanghai	13.3	New York	16.6	Mexico City	18.7
6	Osaka	10.0	Bombay	12.2	Lagos	13.4	Dhaka	18.4
7	Buenos Aires	9.9	Los Angeles	11.5	Los Angeles	13.1	New York	17.4
8	Los Angeles	9.5	Buenos Aires	11.2	Calcutta	12.9	Karachi	16.5
9	Calcutta	9.0	Osaka	11.0	Shanghai	12.9	Calcutta	15.6
10	Beijing	9.0	Calcutta	10.9	Buenos Aires	12.6	Jakarta	15.3
11	Paris	8.9	Beijing	10.8	Dhaka	12.3	Delhi	15.1
12	Rio de Janeiro	8.7	Seoul	10.5	Karachi	11.8	Los Angeles	13.9
13	Seoul	8.3	Rio de Janeiro	9.7	Delhi	11.2	Metro Manila	13.9
14	Moscow	8.1	Paris	9.3	Jakarta	11.0	Buenos Aires	13.7
15	Bombay	8.1	Moscow	9.0	Osaka	11.0	Shanghai	13.7
16	London	7.7	Tianjin	8.8	Metro Manila	10.9	Cairo	12.7
17	Tianjin	7.3	Cairo	8.6	Beijing	10.8	Istanbul	11.8
18	Cairo	6.9	Delhi	8.2	Rio de Janeiro	10.6	Beijing	11.5
19	Chicago	6.8	Metro Manila	8.0	Cairo	10.6	Rio de Janeiro	11.5
20	Essen	6.3	Karachi	7.9	Seoul	9.9	Osaka	11.0
21	Jakarta	6.0	Lagos	7.7	Paris	9.6	Tianjin	10.0
22	Metro Manila	6.0	London	7.7	Istanbul	9.5	Seoul	9.9
23	Delhi	5.6	Jakarta	7.7	Moscow	9.3	Paris	9.7
24	Milan	5.3	Chicago	6.9	Tianjin	9.2	Hyderabad	9.4
25	Tehran	5.1	Dhaka	6.6	London	7.6	Moscow	9.4
26	Karachi	5.0	Istanbul	6.5	Lima	7.4	Bangkok	9.0
27	Bangkok	4.7	Tehran	6.4	Bangkok	7.3	Lima	8.8
28	St Petersberg	4.6	Essen	6.4	Tehran	7.2	Lahore	8.6
29	Hong Kong	4.6	Bangkok	5.9	Chicago	7	Madras	8.2
30	Lima	4.4	Lima	5.8	Hong Kong	6.9	Tehran	8.1

Source: UNCHS 2001b

significant 'mega cities'. For example, by 2000, London had fallen from 16th in the world by size to 25th and does not make the top 30 in 2010 estimates. Other European cities to fall out of the top 30 by 2010 are Milan in Italy and Essen in Germany.

Some of the cities within the 'mega cities' list exert extreme dominance within their own nations states. Tokyo, for example, accounted for 27 per cent of Japan's retail and wholesale sales, 60 per cent of invested capital and 50 per cent of university students (Yeung 1997). Figure 3.5 shows how the mega cities are distributed across the regions with 50 per cent of them

Figure 3.5 Percentage of world's mega-city population by region, 2000

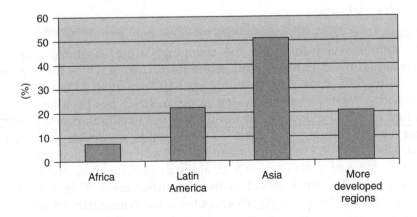

Source: UNCHS 2001b

Table 3.3 City population by regions of the world, 2020 estimates

Region	2020 Population living in cities (millions)	Estimates of total population living in cities (per cent)
Africa, sub-Sahara	440	46
Arab	260	66
Asia-Pacific	1970	46
Highly industrialised countries	547	84
Latin American/Caribbean	391	75
Economies in transition	420	78

Source: UNCHS 2001b

now in the Asian region compared to 20 per cent in Latin America and under 10 per cent for Africa.

Table 3.3 moves our attention to the size of the city populations within the various regions of the world and is an indicator of the degree of urbanisation. The data shows that the highly industrialised (Western European and North American) countries have the highest proportion of urban dwellers followed by the economies in transition (Eastern European countries such as Poland, Hungary and Russia, formerly part of the socialist bloc) and Latin America and the Caribbean. The least urban is sub-Saharan Africa and the Asia Pacific region with 46 per cent of their populations living in cities.

Changes to Regional Spatial Distributions

Deindustrialisation

The figures reviewed reflect the changing nature of global economic activity and the deindustrialisation and restructuring which has occurred within the old 'core' nations in the post-1970s period (O'Loughlin and Friedrichs 1996). The restructuring of urban space has been an ongoing feature of urban development throughout the twentieth century. Again, over the last decades, a more varied set of trends has developed. There is increasing attention on the centre of the city as a place to live, giving rise to new waves of gentrification and, at the same time, there are those still committed to the outer suburban and peri-urban areas. This is shown by the growth of the 'life-style' block outside the boundaries of the urban areas in what were rural farming zones. Some of this change has led to the focus upon the growth of so-called edge cities at the intersection of freeways and feeder roads on the periphery of the urban area stimulated by the car and the need for parking and the growth of hypermarkets and commercial centres (Garreau 1991).

The patterns of urban growth and decline from the mid-twentieth century were a reflection of the 1950s and 1960s metropolitan growth, which concentrated much of the post-war expansion of population and industrial manufacturing within the USA and Western Europe into these areas. During the 1970s and 1980s, the impact of a series of economic crises led to a re-structuring of economic life (Massey 1984, 1995). Massey, for example, identifies the process of deindustrialisation in Britain and shows how decline in manufacturing and traditional male-based skilled and semi-skilled work had major impacts on the industrial cities of the Fordist regime of accumulation in the North of England and the Midlands creating long-term problems within the local labour market which affected house and land prices (Hamnett 1989, 1999). Bluestone and Harrison (1986) in their study of the deindustrialisation of America document a similar set of changes showing how cities in the USA, such as Detroit, Columbus Ohio, Buffalo, and New England industrial towns based around manufacturing suffered substantial decline and the loss of major forms of wealth generation as urban growth and new employment shifted south and west to the 'sunbelt states' and California.

The flip side of the change was the growth of new hi-tech industries. Good examples include the USA along Route 66, and in the San Fernando Valley in southern California where the electronics and computer-based industries flourished. By the 1980s, these too were being affected by the shift in micro-process manufacturing and assembly to South East Asia, for example, to Hong Kong, and Taiwan (Henderson 1989). A further set of growth links was to defence establishments and the related research and development sites (Cooke 1989). New economic activity tended to favour green-field sites where non-union labour was attractive and the presence of subsidies and assistance from local and national governments in the form of tax breaks and low infrastructure costs could be obtained. In Europe, similar growth occurred where there was access to European Union regional development funds, for example, in Spain and Ireland. What this period of economic and urban development demonstrated overall was an increasingly 'footloose' capital moving spatially to find the most attractive sites for the type of activity desired (Hill and Feagin 1987, Soja 1989).

Ageing and Retirement Zones

The other spatial shift leading to new patterns of urbanisation has arisen from the ageing of the population as the baby boomers move towards retirement. This generation has been one whose working lifetimes were mostly constructed during relatively affluent times where they were able to maintain their working lives without breaks and an increasing number reach retirement with substantial investments – mostly based around their own house. At retirement, there has been a growing trend for the more affluent to relocate to a 'retirement zone'. In the USA, the growth of Florida, southern California and Arizona as retirement locations has been a significant factor in the development of these regions. In such areas, the new residential form has been the purpose-built retirement village offering older citizens security and safety within an age-limited 'community'. In Britain, the popularity of the south coast for retirement has been important in shaping the housing market of such places as Hastings, Eastbourne, and Hove.

Migration and City Change

Up to this point in the chapter, we have been concentrating upon the contribution of natural increase to the growth and change in cities. Equally significant to urban population growth and composition has been migration. Migration is diverse in form. Each form has an impact in its own right. It is, however, the combined effects of rural to urban to rural and urban to urban and international migration, which help to shape and reshape the city.

There have been progressive waves of migration around the world linking it into one global system since at least the seventeenth century. As Held et al. (1999:283) have observed:

> People have always been on the move and they have moved great distances. There are many impulses behind these movements: victorious armies and empires have swept across and implanted themselves into new territories; the defeated and dispossessed have fled to defensible land and safer havens; the enslaved have been torn from their homes and relocated in the lands of the enslaver; the underemployed and unemployed have searched for work; the persecuted have sought asylum; the curious and adventurous have always been traveling, drifting and exploring.

Migration is thus not a new phenomenon but has been a significant part of human experience. There have been times when there was more and less movement and movement has been structured according to different prevailing forces. Amongst these, as noted above, have been a mix of push factors such as the consequences of war displacing people, economic depressions and unemployment and pull factors related to people's aspirations for a better life and their desire for change and adventure.

The first phase of global migration to consider is that from the seventeenth to the nineteenth century. The direction of flow was principally from Europe, which was at this stage seen as the centre of the world politically and economically. The flow was to the Americas, both South and North and involved the movement of Spanish, Portuguese, Dutch, British, Irish and French peoples. Initially the migrants established colonies of the 'mother country' relocating many of the institutions and practices of those countries in the new location. Over time the colonies grew and eventually asserted their desire to be independent of the motherland. Canada, the USA, Australia, South Africa, and Aotearoa/New Zealand were all settler societies strongly shaped by out migration from Britain, Ireland and Holland (especially to South Africa). A further source of movement, although not this time voluntary, was the slave trade. This trade lasted from the sixteenth century through to the nineteenth and was responsible for the enforced movement of an estimated 9–12 million people (Curtin 1997). The 'trade' transported Africans from the sub-Saharan coast of West Africa to the plantation economies of the Americas, North and South, and the Caribbean, as plantation workers, – slaves with no political or social rights. This movement created the basis for the multi-ethnic societies which have evolved to the present in those regions and lay at the centre of the segregation of both rural and urban areas. The final group were the Indian and Chinese indentured workers who migrated to South Asia and North America.

The second phase that can be identified is that from 1850 through to
1920 and is the migration associated not with plantation settlement, and
the need for labour to operate this form of commodity production, but
with industrialisation. Transport had by now improved and the cost of
migrating had fallen and surplus population had been created through
agricultural changes creating rural poverty and unemployment. This led
to a drift to the cities and to the attraction of the move to a new land for
a new life. In these new lands, industrial expansion created a need for
wage labour, rather than slave labour. The pull of markets and possibility
of an increased standard of living became at least part of the incentive to
migration. The rapid growth of European cities had resulted in overcrowding, housing problems and poverty which created one of the stimulants to continuing emigration from Europe to the new world where
opportunities for advancement were offered by promoters of settlement.
The pull of the assisted passage and the promise of opportunity were
powerful incentives and deliberate recruitment took place by some of the
promoters of development in Australia and Aotearoa/New Zealand to
create the 'perfect' mix of population for the new societies. Edward
Gibbon Wakefield, for example, promoted settlement in both Australia
and Aotearoa/New Zealand along lines which would reproduce the
English class structure (Pearson and Thorns 1983).

The pattern of migration was continued outward movement from
Europe to America, South Africa, West Central Australia and Aotearoa/
New Zealand. Some of this flow was facilitated through the provision of assisted passages for immigrants to Aotearoa/New Zealand and
Australia. Also of note was the movement of Chinese and Californians
to Australia and Aotearoa/New Zealand stimulated by gold in the
1860s. After the gold ran out, some of these migrants stayed on and turned
to other activities such as market gardening and retail business activity.
In the mid-nineteenth century, the slave trade ended and this left a
problem for the colonial economies as it deprived them of cheap labour.
This was solved through the system of indentured labour, mostly from
Asia. Workers were drawn from India, China, Japan, and Java to work in
American, British, French, German, and Dutch colonies in Asia, Africa,
the Pacific and the Caribbean (Potts 1990; Clarke et al. 1990). This form
of labour was based on short-term contracts often linked to discharging
debts incurred on transit to the new country. The largest proportion were
Indian and estimates suggest a movement outwards of around 30.2
million between 1834 and 1937 giving a net migration figure of around six
million. The legacy of this movement can be seen in the substantial Indian
communities across the Pacific (for example, to Fiji where they comprise
just under half the present population), Africa (East and South) and the
Caribbean.

The final phase began after the Second World War in 1945 and was the time when a contra flow becomes established. Instead of the movement being predominantly from the centre to the periphery the flow is now towards the centre. War and the subsequent consumer boom created labour shortages throughout Europe and the USA and to solve these problems they turned to migration, both internal and international (Castles and Kosack 1973). The empires of the colonial powers were now to be seen as places where labour could be recruited. Britain brought labour from the Caribbean, India and West Africa. Originally, these migrants were given the right to settle rather than guest-worker status. A similar pattern existed in Belgium, and the Netherlands, drawing upon their colonial territories. The recruitment was to fill mostly semi- and unskilled work in industrial and service jobs such as transport, with many ending up working on the bus and rail system. For France, the migrants were drawn from their territory in North Africa, Algeria, and West Africa. For the USA, the workers came from south of the border and from the islands of the Caribbean, Cuba, Puerto Rico and Jamaica.

The first waves were composed mostly of single males and it was assumed they were temporary residents rather than settlers. Over time, this pattern shifted to family reunion and a more settled population creating growing numbers of ethnic sub-areas within the major cities across Europe. Migrants had become permanent residents and were demanding better access to citizenship rights in their new countries. This in turn fed into political opposition and the growth of racist sentiment.

West Germany, Luxemburg, Sweden, and Switzerland developed a different system of migration; that of the 'guest worker' who was only allowed into the country on a temporary permit and had no rights to settle. Over time, this pattern created settlers who then wanted to bring their families. Thus, a wider range of migrants arrived leading to the establishment of a permanent 'sub-community' within many European cities. This phase was dominant by the mid-1970s with second-generation migrants engaging in struggles for political rights and improved conditions and status. Issues arose for European countries of the social cost of migrant labour, especially when they became long-term residents and lost some of their mobility. Under these circumstances it became more attractive to capital to look at taking work to where cheap labour was to be found increasing the attractiveness of the newly developing countries of Asia such as the Philippines, Thailand, Malaysia, Indonesia and China, places where labour was cheap and incentives were provided by the state, often in the form of special economic zones, offering tax breaks and relatively weak labour laws.

The changing national, regional and global function of European cities has been a major factor contributing to their patterns of migration. For example, Brussels became a significant regional centre as both NATO (North Atlantic Treaty Organisation) and the European Commission established their headquarters in the city in the 1950s (see Box 3.1). This generated new labour demands that in turn encouraged a number of streams of migrants to the city who had to be housed within the city and its hinterland impacting on the social structure and the spatial distribution within the urban region.

Box 3.1

Brussels: impact of migration

- Brussels-Capital Region's territory consists of 19 communes and stretches out over 161 km^2.

- On 1 January 1995, there were 951,580 inhabitants (average density per km^2: 5896).

The history of Brussels over the second half of the twentieth century is a good example of the way in which the socio-spatial structure of the city has been reshaped by both the position of the city within the global world and through the entry to the city of migrants.

Brussels, in the period from 1945–73, developed as 'dual city' with an east–west split related to its physical environment and historical patterns of settlement. The more favourable land was to the east of the centre and this became home to the city's wealthier classes. In the 1960s, economic development was characterised by internationalisation. This created both low skilled jobs – filled mostly by 'guest workers' from the Mediterranean area – and the growth of tertiary level occupations arising from the city's increasingly important function as a site of international organizations (for example, NATO headquarters established in 1958, followed by the European Commission). Thus, by the 1990s, the proportion of foreign nationals in the population had risen from 8 per cent in 1960 to 30 per cent in 1995 (Kesteloot 2000).

The changing nature of the economy provided upward social mobility opportunities for the Belgian population and created suburban expansion as planning controls were weak at the periphery and home ownership was encouraged. The gaps in the labour market for semi- and un-skilled work were solved through the migration of temporary workers.

In the 1970s, a downturn occurred leading to slow growth and restructuring. One consequence was the halting of migration in 1974. However, the numbers of migrants continued to grow through family reunion and marriage. The migrants entered the housing market in the older working-class areas vacated by the upwardly mobile local population, thus creating inner-city areas in the east dominated by immigrant groups. This growth is further strengthened by their younger demographic profile and higher fertility rates. The lower levels of upward mobility open to the working class, as a consequence

Continued

of economic restructuring, has led to a further consolidation of ethnic neighbourhoods in the inner city.

In the 1990s, renewed growth has occurred based around 'flexible production and consumption processes' leading to further decline in industrial-based employment and a 'deepening of the opposition between ethnic neighbourhoods' (Kesteloot 2000:198). In the eastern half of the city, new investment, associated with the growth of the city's new economy, such as the high speed train stations, luxury hotels, office spaces and shopping centres together with upper-market residential innovation and gentrification projects, has resulted in further increases in property values and thus desirability. A consequence has been increased separation between the wealthier and poorer areas. The migrant neighbourhoods of the inner city have also been encroached upon by the growth of offices, new transport systems and roads to bring into the centre the middle-class professional and administrative workers now working in the TNCs (transnational companies) and international organizations centred in the city.

At the beginning of the twenty-first century, Brussels continues to be a socially and spatially divided city and clearly shows the impact upon its composition of the migration of guest workers in the 1950s and 1960s – many of whom subsequently settled and created their own sub-cultural areas within the city.

City web site: *http://www.bruxelles.irisnet.be/*

In the 1980s across Europe, there was a general tightening of immigration and citizenship rights in response to changes in political, economic and employment conditions. The most significant political change was the demolition of the Berlin wall and the subsequent upheavals in Eastern European countries including the breakup of the USSR and the reunification of Germany. These changes in their turn created a different set of migratory processes across Europe, especially movement from east to west and to destinations that were previously restricted. In the 1990s, for example, with the change in policy towards Jewish emigration from the former Soviet Union, there was a movement of two million Soviet Jews to the state of Israel.

The last decades of the twentieth century also witnessed major changes in migration patterns within the Asian region associated with uneven economic development and the growth of significant global cities in Singapore, Hong Kong, South Korea (Seoul), and Taiwan (Taipei) (Laquian 1996; Castles 1997; Wang 1997; Findlay, Jones and Davidson 1998). In all these cases there has been a switch from net emigration to immigration. The Asian crisis of 1997–99 has only had a temporary effect on these flows and, with recovery over the past two years, the speed of flow has increased again. The patterns are quite different from those we have described for Western Europe as they are much more strongly influenced by both intraregional movements and the present phase of globalisation which has created a transnational group of migrants who are mobile and relatively footloose and move from global city to global city and are employed in high-value financial and information services. This group is mostly drawn from Japan, the USA, and Canada. To service this high-earning group, there is also a need for a 'service class'. This creates demand for domestic workers, predominantly female, who have been recruited overwhelmingly from the Phillipines and Indonesia.

Hong Kong, for example, has had a pattern where immigration has consistently exceeded emigration and, in 2001, was still receiving 151 new migrants a day. With the shift in the economic base of Hong Kong away from manufacturing and towards information and financial services, a need for different types of migrants has been generated. There has been a substantial increase in the flow of domestic, mostly female, workers as maids drawn from the Philippines and Indonesia, professional and highly-skilled workers from Japan, the USA, Canada and Australia, and finally construction workers from Thailand, to assist in the increased building programme of both commercial and residential real estate.

Singapore is another Asian city-state where there has been a history of significant immigration, raising the current population to over four million. The pattern has been shaped by a public policy seeking to control immigration through a system of temporary permits, for example, for Malayan and Thai construction workers and domestic maids from the Philippines, Sri Lanka and India. In terms of permanent migrants, the policy has preferred those ethnic groups such as Malays, Indian and Chinese, which reflect the pluralistic nature of the Singapore population.

In both Japan and Taiwan, there has been an increasing use of migrant labour to solve the labour shortages that have emerged due to the ageing of the population. For example, in Japan, in 1998, there were 1.5 million foreign nationals drawn predominantly from Korea and China. However, there were also an increasing number of female workers who entered the labour force from the late 1980s to provide workers in the 'entertainment' and domestic employment market as maids and as age care workers – reflecting the ageing of the Japanese population and the shortage of medically trained staff (Yeung 1996; Hirano 2000; Hirano, Castles and Brownlee 2000).

The Asia region has thus developed a pattern of interregional migration that is well organized with workers from different countries serving specialised functions within the economies of the region. The system is organised as can be illustrated by looking at the Philippines, a net exporter of labour, and the ways this has been developed by a mixture of public and private agencies indicating the significance of networks for the recruitment of workers through the region (Schmidt 1998). In the

Philippines, Manila is the place where the exchange of labour is connected to the global economy and the organisations involved are centred. As part of its economic strategy, the Government from the 1970s adopted a policy of overseas employment as one way of both generating 'export' income and assisting in reducing internal unemployment. It first attempted to do this through government-created agencies. However, these were not very successful and by the 1980s had given way to a mix of public and private agencies (Tyner 2000). The recent history of Manila shows that cities can have a global function not solely as 'destinations' of migrant labour, but also as a supplier. Just as migrant workers arriving in a global city can cause dislocation, disruption and cultural transformation, so too the loss of particular age and gender groups can disrupt traditional family and marriage practices and cause transformation in the sending cities.

Substantially greater urban heterogeneity has been the result of these patterns of migration so that by the end of the millennium in the cities of Europe, the USA, Canada, and Australasia there were substantial urban sub-populations of many nationalities. For example, in Toronto at the beginning of the twenty-first century, there were over 100 different nationalities present within the urban area bringing an increasingly diversified and multicultural, multi-ethnic culture to the city with the downtown markets along Spadina Avenue displaying a rich array of Chinese and Caribbean foods, clothing and other items for sale. Further, the increased range of ethnicities has also provided a large number of festivals and cultural events, including parades by the various ethnic groups. For example, the largest dragon in North America, is annually paraded through central Toronto by the Chinese community.

This increased diversity of nationalities, through migration, gave rise to a far greater cultural diversity in many cities which has led to an extensive remaking of the neighbourhoods and communities within those cities. Melbourne in Australia, for example, has large Italian and Greek populations from migration in the 1960s and more recently a substantial Turkish and Asian population – the latter both from migration and from refugees from Cambodia, Laos and Vietnam (Collins 1988). This has resulted in an increased variety of restaurants and markets and community organisations reflecting these migrant communites. In Aotearoa/New Zealand, Auckland is now where the world's largest Pacific island community lives and in total there are 54 different ethnic groups now resident, influencing the housing types, recreation needs, education and cultural diversity. Further evidence of increasing ethnic diversity comes from data on the current school population. This shows that 52.7 per cent is European New Zealand, 17.5 per cent Pacific Island, 14.5 per cent Maori and 12.7 per cent Asian. In the inner cities of the UK in the late 1990s, as a result of the migration patterns of the 1950s to the 1970s, up to 33 per cent of the population did not have English as their first language. In the restructuring of the 1980s and 1990s, many of the descendents of the post-war migration streams, now second generation migrants, have found themselves the victims of rising unemployment and have become scapegoats for unemployment and falling urban living standards leading to a rise in racial tensions (Sivanandan 1990).

A final aspect of late twentieth-century migration has been the continuing flow of refugees, created by war and famine in different parts of the world. One of the most affected has been Africa. Here the refugee population has grown from an estimated 300,000 in 1960 to about 7 million in the late 1990s. The major areas affected are the Sudan, where the civil war has displaced an estimated 3 million people, and in Rwanda and Burundi. United Nations Centre for Human Settlement (Habitat) has estimated that of the total of 25 to 30 million refugees, some 14 to 15 million have been displaced within the borders of their own state. In Europe, the most recent source of refugees are as a result of conflict in Bosnia and Kosovo. In South East Asia, East Timor has been the site of a struggle for independence from Indonesia that has created new streams of refugees.

In the twenty-first century, the patterns of migration could well shift from the migration of essentially low-paid workers to take up relatively unskilled jobs in industry and services, which formed the bulk of the migration to Europe and America in the 1950s and 1960s towards more elite migration featuring both professional and technical workers and business migrants who are global migrants and travel and locate within a network of increasingly global cities. The preoccupation of the developed societies tends now to be much more with the 'brain drain'. The loss of highly skilled, educated and professional people who are increasingly seen as a global commodity in the drive to create new forms of wealth generation around the 'knowledge economy' is now acknowledged as a problem in many countries. The migration of ' brains' comes not just from the developed world but also from the developing, taking away from these countries potentially their most able people. The lure of high returns is hard for the smaller, both developed and less developed countries to combat. In Australia, for example, a debate has recently emerged around its immigration policy and whether it will be able to attract the 80,000 immigrants a year set in its new policy. The fertility rate has declined to below replacement at 1.78 and thus to maintain and expand the population will require immigration. However, there is increasing recognition that the people wanted – with the skills to promote the development of the knowledge economy – are those in high demand around the world. Clearly the falling birth rates, we identified earlier, and the subsequent pressures within societies with falling birth rates – mostly European, but also including a number of Asian and Pacific countries including Japan and Australia – to maintain their standard of living and level of economic activity, are likely to generate a new round of migration from the less developed to the developed world, once again changing the face of these societies and their cities.

Summary

The analysis of the patterns of demography and migration allow us to more clearly understand the context of urbanisation in the next fifty years. Projections are not always accurate as they cannot always foresee people's fertility intentions, thus there will be a range of scenarios produced. Nonetheless, many of the people who will age are already on the planet. They are going to age and they will live longer and this will have a major impact upon urban life over the next decades. Already we can see the impact of the baby boomers upon the urban property market and upon urban lifestyles. Fewer children, fewer years out of the workforce and longer life expectancy for a substantial proportion of the developed world's urban population have enhanced their consumption capacity.

Having now identified some of the parameters of change, the next questions to consider are whether the 1980s and 1990s were marked by sufficient change to suggest that a major period of transformation is occurring, creating a new 'postmodern' set of urban spaces and whether these spaces are best understood within the frame of globalisation.

Note

1. For an extensive discussion of changes in East Asia, see International Longevity Centre (Japan) (1996).

Further Reading

Held et al. 1999, *Global Transformations: Politics, Economics and Culture*, Cambridge: Polity Press. Chapter 6 'People on the Move' pp. 283–326.
    This is a very comprehensive analysis of patterns of migration. The material includes both historical and contemporary analysis.
UNCHS. 1996a, *An Urbanizing World: Global Report on Human Settlements*. Part 1, pp. 3–24. Oxford: Oxford University Press.
UNCHS. 2001a, *Cities in a Globalizing World: Global Report on Human Settlements 2001*. London: Earthscan Publications Ltd.
UNCHS. 2001b, *The State of The World's Cities Report 2001*. Nairobi: UNCHS.
Web site for report: *http://www.unchs.org/istanbul+5/statereport.htm*
These three reports produced for Habitat 2 and Habitat plus 5 are the most comprehensive data sources available on trends in urban growth and change. They contain both commentary and extensive tables, graphs and charts of changes taking place. The most recent one can be accessed via the web site given above.

Web sites

UN data and discussion

http://www.unchs.org/
http://www.global-city.org/
http://www.uni-duisburg.de/duisburg/yearbook.htm
http://cities.canberra.edu.au/

Most national statistics offices have their own web sites which will be a great source of data for your own country. Below is the New Zealand national site.

http://www.stats.govt.nz/

United States Census Bureau

http://www.census.gov/

Migration research, Asia-Pacific region

http://www.uow.edu.au/research/centres/capstrans/apmrn/apmrn.html

4

Global Cities

Introduction

The last two decades of the last millennium have seen the rise of the 'post-modernist critique' and a vigorous debate as to whether the modern industrial world has now transformed itself into the post-industrial world. At the heart of this debate is one about the nature of the economic and social forces shaping both collective and individual life. Giddens, in his recent analysis of the *Third Way* (1998), identifies three major revolutions taking place during this period. They are globalisation, the transformation in personal life affecting relations between individuals and communities, and in our relationship to nature. Here, the growth of the debate about genetic engineering and the environment has refocused our attention on the links between nature and science and nature and society. The central question is whether the dominant paradigm through which we view this relationship is still to be one around the notion of universal progress and scientific advancement in order to reshape the natural world, or is there to be a shift towards a more reciprocal relationship as is incorporated in the debate about 'sustainability'? All these transformations have influenced urban life. The city looks very different at the beginning of the new millennium.

In 1973, I travelled to Aotearoa/New Zealand to take up a position at the University of Auckland. On the first Saturday, I took a trip to the centre of the city. The first thing that struck me as odd, coming from Britain, was that on a Saturday morning there was a very infrequent bus service. Where were all the people living in Auckland I wondered? What did they do with their weekends? Arriving in the centre of the city, I discovered it was not like the European city centres with which I was familiar. It was almost deserted, a bit like a ghost town. Life was suburban in focus at this time and domestic in orientation. Shops were closed and the range and nature of other recreation and leisure activities in the city centre were sparse. Twenty-seven years later, at the beginning of the new millennium, the urban world in Aotearoa/New Zealand is very different. The city centres at a weekend are now alive with activity, shops are open, cafes have emerged onto the pavements, recreational and leisure opportunities have increased incorporating such seemingly now universal urban redevelopment features as harbour front redesign, casinos, tramways, museums, leisure districts, convention centres, restaurant and cafe cultures. The result is a remarkable transformation of empty spaces to ones thronging with people and activity.

The structure and form of the city has become much more highly differentiated. The growth of new forms of wealth generation, have led to the restructuring of the spatial structures, within the former industrial and administrative cities. Manufacturing has declined as the key engine of growth to be replaced by a new set of activities more centred around information (Castells 1996, 1997, 1998; Sassen 1991) and leisure, recreation and tourism (Lash and Urry 1987, 1994; Zukin, 1991). Consumption landscapes have become the new focus of much of western scholarship. Consumerism is seen as one of the driving forces of economic, political and social life. The global nature of the world requires us to see urban change as an interrelated process. Industrial activity has been relocated to new regions and cities, growth and decline has occurred, the demographic and social structures have changed. In this chapter, the objective is to examine the key aspects of this change and to look at how this has led to a rethinking of urban analysis and the emergence of a different set of agendas to those we have observed in the analysis of the modern industrial city as we confront the increasingly global interconnectedness of the present urban world. The chapter begins with the debates and analysis around the questions of postmodernity and postmodernism and from there moves to the issue of globalisation and finally to the nature of the global city.

Modern to Postmodern Cities

The analysis of the city has been strongly affected by the growth of the postmodernist critique of social analysis. For some, this represents a major epistemological break with the past and the development of a whole new set of ways of thinking about culture and society. Soja for example has observed that the postmodernist position contains:

> a deep critique of all modernist thought . . . a critique of totalising discourses, master narratives of essentialism, exposure of silences within the literature, a rethinking of the concept of difference and otherness . . . a critique of historicism . . . a new interest in hyperreality, hyperspace, simulation and simulcra (Soja 1993:484).

Soja is drawing attention to the fact that the postmodernist challenge is related not only to how the city has changed but also to how we are to conceptualise that change. Can we still generalise about sets of cities or is what is now occurring much more place specific and therefore contingent? The shift to simulation and simulcra reflects the growing attention to the signs as well as the actual structures and behaviour contained within the city and also links to the fact that much of our knowledge about place and urban life comes through the media, the television and films we watch and the increasing access that some have to the Internet and WWW as the source of information (Lash and Urry 1994; Lyon 1994). Through this, it is argued, we come to believe we know places we have not physically visited creating a new sense of hyper-reality (Baudrillard 1988, 1998).

For other writers, the postmodern condition is seen more as an extension of the 'modern' world into a new phase, largely as a result of the restructuring of capitalism around a new mode of production. Such writers identify the shift as a move from 'Fordism' to 'flexibility' and draw substantially upon regulation theory (Harvey 1990; Jessop and Sum 1999). In short, the term postmodernism is ambiguous; sometimes it is being used to describe a stage in history, whereas on other occasions it is used to describe an analytical method and a cultural expression.

It is thus necessary in any analysis of postmodernism to appreciate that the argument has both a socio-economic analysis (the stage in history – postmodernity) and a debate about the nature of knowledge (the analytical method – postmodernism). It is thus necessary to identify the main aspects of each of these two themes.

Socio-economic Analysis – Postmodernity

The next section will examine the themes of production, the labour process, the role of the state, ideology and spatial relations and draws from a range of both theoretical and empirical work seeking to analyse the transformation from modern to postmodern economic, political, social and spatial relationships and practices (see Table 4.1).

Production

The significant changes have been the move to a greater level of global activity with the pre-eminence of the transnational corporation as a 'footloose' institution, which no longer has strong ties to particular nations, regions or localities. Such corporations make their location decisions on the basis of what is most suitable to enhance overall profitability regard-

Table 4.1 Key aspects of modern and postmodern cities

Modern (Fordism)	Postmodern (flexibility)
Industrial-manufacturing-based economy	Information-based economy

Production

National/international	Global transnational
Mass production (Fordist)	Small-scale production runs. Just-in-time procedures
Uniformity (assembly line)	
Standardisation and hierarchically organised	Flexible processes
	Demand-driven, market-based consumption
Mass consumption	Total quality management (worker participation)
Wage control and regulation via unions and employers collective agreements (national awards)	Individual and workplace contracts

Labour Process

Single tasks performed by workers (assembly line model)	Multiple tasks
	Horizontal labour organisation
Specialisation (job) tasks broken down into small components extended division of labour	Flexible working hours and pay contracts
	Enterprise and site agreements and individual contracts rather than
Vertical labour organisation	National awards
Differentiation based on skill levels and gender	Core-peripheral workers as new divide

State

Regulatory and interventionist	De-regulative shift from a provision model to a rights model of state actions
Collective agreements (for example, wage bargaining – income policies)	Neo-liberal – privatisation
Centralised planning (national, regional and local levels)	Competition

Ideology

Welfarist (state should provide for citizens)	Individualism
	Entrepreneurship
Rational planning based on scientific research/evidence	Competition
	Individual 'life style' consumption and display
Mass consumption	

Space

City versus suburb (dualistic view of the city)	Blurring of dualism – urbanisation of the suburbs, gentrification of the inner city (infill housing)
Planning and segregation (zoning) separation of residential and employment activity	Development of edge/regional centres/hypermarkets

less of whether this means operating in Australia, South East Asia, Europe or North America. We are now living within a global economy in which transnational corporations and their associated elites are the key actors. There is a greater contrast between the mobility of capital which is high, and that of labour which is restricted and often unable to follow work, creating localities and regions which have experienced 'deindustrialisation'; and production technologies have altered to reflect new ways of producing commodities through computerised inventory and control systems (bar coding at supermarket check outs) and the development of 'just-in-time' systems of production. These require smaller plants and more flexible production runs which are linked to the requirements of particular customers. This means that the new production systems are more demand driven and individual-consumer focused with a more varied pattern of output. Gone is the large-scale, and standardised commodity plant. Instead we have the introduction of multiple products, and with this a multi-task rather than single-task workforce. Such changes necessitate the construction of a more flexible workforce. Thus radical changes have taken place in the labour contract with a move from national awards to site bargaining and agreements over hours and days worked, pay scales and rates. It is important to recognise the variety of experiences that have emerged indicating there is not one single pathway being followed (Thorns 1992).

Labour Process

The labour process under Fordism was characterised by the assembly line and single tasks performed by workers in factory-based production. The jobs they did were broken down into smaller and smaller components in the interests of efficiency. This system was designed to produce large numbers of standardised products for a mass-consumer economy. The changes to production allowed by new technologies and the shift to a service-based economy in many advanced capitalist societies has resulted in substantial changes to the way work gets done and thus to the size and structure of the labour force. More flexible working practices have been initiated and the assembly-line system has given way to more varied arrangements designed to produce a more diversified range of products for much more diversified and fragmented markets. Workers in turn have moved from secure systems of employment in many countries to more 'flexible' contracting forms of employment rather than permanent systems. And jobs and skills requirements are now seen to be subject to constant change.

State

The key change here has been the retreat by the state, in many of the advanced capitalist societies, from the support of publicly-funded welfare. Policies have been adopted over the 1970s and 1980s, which progressively reduced the role of the state within welfare provision and instead moved to promote user charges and privatisation, the sale of state assets and contracting out (Pusey 1991). Welfare assistance, for those who have been marginalised, made unemployed or redundant by economic and social changes, has increasingly fallen upon the voluntary sector (for example, religious and other community groups) which has established food banks and emergency housing. This again illustrates that the new forms of economic activity have created winners and losers. Homelessness and poverty have also increased, as has the wealth of those in the upper sectors of the employment structure (Daly 1996a, b). The increasingly global nature of economic and political relationships has posed a challenge to the continuing centrality of the nation state in this new, more global social order. For some, the new arrangement could well be between large trading and political blocks, such as the European Union and a network of global cities each with an increased level of economic and political autonomy.

Ideology

The shift in ideology is away from a welfare-based society to one centred around individualism where social responsibility becomes much more the concern of the individual who is free to exercise choice over how they meet their needs and desires. The state sees its responsibility confined to targeting those unable to help themselves adequately through unforeseen circumstances. This tends to introduce a strong moral component to decisions regarding social expenditure reminiscent of previous debates about the 'deserving' to be assisted and the 'underserving' who are to be excluded from state benefits. The state is recast as an 'enabling state' moving back from actually providing services to encouraging the formation of new partnerships with the third sector and the private sector.

Space

The key change here has been within the nature of the culture and way of life which has developed amongst contemporary city dwellers. The postmodern world is one where social life is much more framed around individual taste and experience. Gone is the homogeneity of the 'mass consumption' surburban landscape. Housing styles have become more varied and a new wave of urban gentrification has taken place (Smith and Williams 1986; Smith 1987; Rose 1990). The rise of new middle classes, separating themselves from the mass, and pursuing a more distinctive lifestyle creating a new urban ideology, is a crucial component of change. Greater social differentiation is the result with two distinct lifestyles appearing. The first is that of the 'yuppie', a person who is dedicated to an individualistic lifestyle built around conspicuous consumption and whose wealth has been created in the new service economy and in the financial boom of the early to mid-1980s. According to one recent writer:

> apart from age, upward mobility and an urban domicile (yuppies) are sup-
> posed to be distinguished by a life style devoted to personal careers and indi-
> vidualistic consumption (Smith 1987:151).

The second is an 'underclass' of the excluded, a growing group of welfare beneficiaries, unemployed and homeless people who are often also divided from the majority by their ethnicity and gender (Dear and Wolch 1987). One of the consequences here has been the growth in tensions, crime and urban violence leading in turn to a greater use of surveillance and security systems to protect property and people, the most extreme form of which would be the guarded and gated residential area.

Patterns of Transformation

Global shifts are not always worked out everywhere the same way. For example, in Australia, the shift towards more flexible work practices was resisted longer than in some other capitalist nations due to the strength of the labour movement and the fashioning in 1981 of an Accord between the labour movement and the incoming Labour Government. Despite such policy there has been a gradual erosion of the terms and conditions of employment and a retreat from centralised wage fixing towards more localised arrangements as part of the transition to a more 'flexible' regime of accumulation; a process greatly accelerated since the election of the State and Commonwealth liberal governments in the 1990s. There has thus been a shift from an industrial- to an information-based economy that has led to the growth of a new managerial professional and business class and the increased significance of real estate.

Hazeldine (1998) in an analysis of these changes within Aotearoa/New

Zealand draws attention to the increased number of managers to workers now required. In the 1950s, the ratio was one manager to every twenty workers. By 1981, this ratio had changed to one manager for every nine workers and, by 1996, had further reduced to one to four workers. This increase in managers changes the structure of the wages bill and helps create a more affluent segment of the workforce. Hazeldine, for example, calculated that for Fletcher Challenge Ltd, Aotearoa/New Zealand's largest corporation, there are now 2301 in the plus NZ$100,000 league netting a total of around NZ$292 million per year (Hazeldine 1998:125).

It is largely in the metropolitan centres that this transformation to the class structure has happened reflecting the new nodes within the world economic system. Alongside the new 'service' class, there is also a new 'servant' class providing the labour for the leisure, recreation and pleasure industries that have also grown alongside the class with an increased disposable income. Much of this work is part-time and casual. This leads to a divide between the 'core' workers who are assured of secure full-time jobs within the new growth sectors and the peripheral workers in less secure, often part-time and casual work. This often extends into the formation of an extensive informal economy where non-monetary exchanges become a significant aspect of everyday life. A transformation has also occurred alongside these changes in the position of women in the labour market and through the rise of a new wave of feminism. Women have markedly increased their presence in the labour market. The information economy has expanded the tertiary areas of the economy which have been occupied disproportionately by women workers whereas the decline in the manufacturing base has affected men more than women (Massey 1984, 1995). These shifts have assisted in changing household dynamics with a breakdown of the old stereotypes and gender divisions within domestic labour (Massey 1994). The whole urban pattern had previously been based upon the idea that someone, usually the wife (female partner) would bring together the disconnected processes (separate social services and provisions across such areas as education, transport, health and recreation). The increasing absence of women from suburbs and local community activities as a consequence of higher rates of employment results in a need for a reorganisation of local activities.

Two Faces of the Postmodern City

The result of the set of transformations examined is that the postmodern city has two faces. The first is the face of the successful which displays a glitzier and entertainment-centred culture of restaurants and wine bars, shopping malls and casinos. It is thus not surprising that the 1990s have seen casinos open in many cities around the world, for example, in Melbourne and Sydney in Australia, and Auckland, Christchurch and Queenstown within Aotearoa/New Zealand. In both cases they generate employment and other economic activity in the central areas of the cities where they are located although at the cost to other areas is unknown. The second face is that of the excluded who create new urban ghettos composed of the homeless, the asset-poor households, those displaced through the new wave of gentrification, the elderly renters on state pensions, and those on public housing assistance. The city has thus become more, rather than less, polarised. These two faces of the city are seen in the growth of the city as a centre of festival and display, gentrification and the increased level of homelessness, urban crime and fear (Davis 1995; Dear 2000).

This separation is somewhat masked by the illusion, created through the print and celluloid media, of the whole globe increasingly being drawn into a common cultural experience through access to the same sources of information (Internet) and entertainment (television via satellites, cable television and common programmes). So, increasingly, we are told that we all share the same sets of visual and aural images, restructuring our images of the social world. For Baudrillard (1988), there has been a disappearance of the difference between what is real and what is imagined and he sees the whole of the city as a 'gigantic theme park'.

Postmodernism – Epistemological Challenges

The second aspect of the postmodern position is that of the epistemological debate about the basis of knowledge. The argument here is that the economic and social structure has gone through a major change, equivalent to that of the 'great transformation' of the eighteenth and nineteenth centuries that ushered in the modern world of industrial society. The modern world was also the world of science and of rational thought and analysis. It was the one where social theory was developed to help explain the transition and the nature and shape of the society that was produced. The second major theme of the transition from modern to postmodern, therefore, is that of the forms of analysis that should be used and a rejection of the enlightenment project's commitment to scientific discovery and the quest for truth. The two epistemologies that have characterised this form of endeavour were those of positivism and realism. They have increasingly been constructed as being rooted in western culture and understanding rather than a universal set of interpretations. They are thus ethnocentric and increasingly inappropriate in attempts to make sense of the global world.

Positivism

Urban analysis in the 1950s and 1960s was strongly shaped by the positivist belief that empirical facts could be collected by rigorous, usually quantitative, procedures and by objective researchers who could distinguish between 'facts' and 'values'. The process required the generation of information and, on this basis, plans and programmes would be developed by experts, rather than by politicians and community members. Patrick Geddes (1949) dictum of 'survey before plan' was seen as a touchstone of such rational comprehensive urban planning. The positivist approach, it was argued, would reveal how the urban system operated and would thus allow generalisations and interventions by planners and others to improve the urban environment. It was committed to an idea of social progress, via social engineering and the intervention by planners to achieve specified ends. Usually such plans involved ideas of social balance, greater social equity and increased access to resources and facilities. These social planners would be impartial and dedicated to the truth and wider 'public interest' unlike the politicians, 'social activists' and other groups who acted out of more restricted information and on a 'partial understanding' (Gans 1972; Simmie 1974, 1981; Angotti 1993).

Realist Critique

The positivist view was subjected to considerable criticism with the development of a more 'radical' or critical urban social analysis in the 1970s shaped particularly by Marxist and neo-Marxist writers (Pickvance 1976; Harloe 1977; Kilmartin and Thorns 1978). This position, typified by Castells' essay in the early 1970s, 'Is there an Urban Sociology?', (1976), dismissed previous urban analysis as ideological and characterised positivist empirical science as simply reinforcing the status quo as it assisted in the legitimation of the powerful who could claim they possessed objective scientific knowledge of social activities and relationships. Neo-Marxist and Marxist urbanists mostly subscribed to a realist epistemology that still sought to establish a scientific basis for urban study, thus they were still committed to the enlightenment project (Keat and Urry 1975; Duncan and Goodwin 1988). Realists claim that there are structures that

The Transformation of Cities

shape actions and these are to be sought through theoretical endeavour as they are often concealed beneath the surface. It's a bit like peeling the layers off an onion to get to the core of the explanation having rejected the surface and superficial explanations which confuse or get in the way of the truth. The objective was, as with the positivists, to develop explanations for events which were universal and generalisable to provide theories which could be used to shape action and change.

Postmodernist Critique

The postmodernist critique of both positivist and realist urbanists is that there are no overall scientific explanations for events. There is in fact no order to be discovered or structures to be revealed (Table 4.2). The layers of the onion here are all of equal value and interest rather than representing a progressive move to understanding and explanation. The objective of study is thus not understanding and universal explanation but to identify and celebrate the distinctiveness of urban cultures and ways of life.

In *The Postmodern Condition* (1984), Lyotard identifies a series of historical changes in the type of knowledge produced within societies. In pre-

Table 4.2 Modern and postmodern epistemologies

Modern	Postmodern
Scientific explanation Generalisation Foundation narratives	Rejection of overall explanation Individual narratives
Objectivity (facts-values separation)	Rejection of objectivity in favour of individual positioning
Prediction	Understanding
Distinctions Dichotomies	Differences Collapse of distinctions and boundaries between 'disciplines'
Classifications	Rejection of classification and taxonomies
Politics: Rational/informed decision-making Survey before you plan (Geddes) Planning/overall schemes	Politics: Identity politics Women, ethnic groups, gay, lesbian, aged, disabled, and so on Differences celebrated

modern society, a narrative style of knowledge prevailed which was bound up in stories, legends and myths about society, and its origins, shape and place in the world. Modernity challenged these narratives dismissing them as superstitions, as ignorant and false accounts of nature, as the creation and structuring of social relationships and sought to replace these 'narratives' with the 'meta-narrative' of scientific explanation based on empirical knowledge. The final shift Lyotard identifies is to the postmodern condition. Here the meta-narratives that have been created by social scientists are in decline and are fragmenting in the face of change and the emergence of multiple narratives and more individualised accounts of experience. Thus, as modernists sought classification and generalization, postmodernists seek to collapse these distinctions and see urban society in terms of differentiation, fragmentation and an emphasis upon the individual and her/his identity.

The work within urban studies has been strongly influenced by the French post-structuralist writer, Baudrillard (1988) and his notions of hyper-reality. Baudrillard argues that increasingly signs and symbols shape society, what he terms simulcra, to such an extent that there is a breakdown between the real and the imagined. The rise of the theme park and the extension of recreation and leisure activities has also changed the shape of the city with a re-emphasis upon the playful and the entertaining. This is seen in the growth of festivals and street theatre and the turning of sources of information and cultural transmission, such as museums, into accessible and interactive experiences rather than repositories of classified information for the educated. It sees popular culture as being as significant as the so-called 'high cultures' more dominant in modernist analysis and thus seeks to democratise knowledge.

The postmodernist critique has led to a new agenda for urban studies that privilege the individual 'narrative' or account as the key source of information. This is seen as putting back the people and their voices and social positions into the analysis. The city is seen as the 'text' so buildings, signs, symbols, spaces (squares and parks) as well as the people need to be analysed and 'read'. All these facets, therefore, need to be analysed and recorded. There is a shift from economic analysis of the city, strongly present in the 1970s' Marxist and neo-Marxist work, to the cultural and the aesthetic. The diversification of the urban population through, for example, migration, noted earlier, has created a greater social differentiation within the city population and helped form ethnic sub-groups who have, in the late 1980s and 1990s, begun to celebrate rather than hide their cultural differences. Thus, it has become common to identify people as Greek-Australian, Italian-Australian or Irish-Australian rather than just Australian, to demonstrate cultural attachments and origins. Consequently, studies have re-emerged which analyse these cultural variations and provide histories of development that are presented through the eyes and voices of the local residents.

Urban political debate tends to shift from questions about how to redesign the city to increase equality and social justice more generally, to ones more focused around the politics of identity. Here, the rise of gender, sexual and environmental politics has been of crucial importance. The concerns within these new social movements are more likely to be expressed around individual lifestyles and desires to reclaim autonomy over personal spaces than around issues of class politics. These changes also tend to lead to a move from the institutional arena of formal political activity within the state or federal system of government to more local actions and movements (Seidman 1994).

Postmodernity represents, therefore, a set of arguments about the changing nature of the economic system. Here, it captures the transition from a mode of production based around large-scale mass activity carried out in large plants linked to an interventionist state which produced a seemingly standardised urban form (the post-war suburb). In addition it also entails a set of arguments about the epistemological basis of knowledge. Here, it represents a rejection of the enlightenment view of scientific knowledge and explanation in favour of one which is based around differences and more individual accounts. It dismisses claims to objectivity and universal truth in favour of 'positioned' accounts and the actual voices of the subject group. It seeks individual freedom rather than collective change and sees the future as one of ambiguity and uncertainty rather than in terms of predictions from known facts. It attacks the cultural imperialism of western knowledge and draws attention to the significance of indigenous knowledge, and the importance of culture in the construction of knowledge.

From World Systems to Globalisation

One of the key questions that emerged in the latter years of the last millennium was that of the creation of globalisation. How is this different from the previous understanding of the world system? What set of forces has shifted us to this new conceptual agenda? Or is it in fact just the old agenda dressed in new clothes? Is it a worthwhile idea at all, or just a catalogue of everything that has changed since the 1970s (Marcuse 2000; Marcuse and Van Kempen 2000)? For example, Wallerstein has suggested that:

> Globalisation is a misleading concept since what is described as globalisation has been happening for 500 years. Rather what is new is that we are entering an 'age of transition' (2000:249).

He does thus concede we are entering a period of profound change which does challenge our thinking and previous sets of explanations. In our discussion, we will first examine the debate about the formation of world systems and then move to the debate about 'globalisation'.

World Systems

The idea of the world system arises out of neo-Marxist scholarship, particularly the work of Wallerstein (1974, 1979, 2000). For Wallerstein, the present world system emerged in the sixteenth century with the discovery by Europeans of the new world. This allowed the population of the European world to expand beyond its carrying capacity through importing resources to supplement those within the existing nations. This set in train a system of dependency and exploitation that led to the colonial expansion and the system of markets and dependencies shaping the world into 'core', semi-peripheral and peripheral nations. The core nations initially dominant were the maritime and later industrial powers of Europe; Britain, the Netherlands, Spain and France. The system was initially built around trade, within which the European powers explored and obtained commodities for sale in Europe. These included spices, silks, and new foods. The dominance of the core was secured through their wealth and their military and naval capacities. With the discovery of new worlds, migration then settlement occurred, firstly, of the Americas and later of Southern Africa and Australia and Aotearoa/New Zealand. One of the consequences of this migration was to create what some have called dominion capitalist societies (Armstrong 1980). What characterised this group of countries was their dependency on land-based production. The beef ranches of Argentina and the sheep farms of Australia and Aotearoa/New Zealand played a significant role in the chain of food production for the industrialising populations of Europe. A consequence of this particular pattern of production and its orientation to exporting has been a different pattern of urbanisation with cities being built on the coast and serving as entrepôt, transportation and service centres rather than bases for industrial production and attractors of rural domestic populations (Mullins 1981a, b; Berry 1983, 1984; Denoon 1983). In Aotearoa/New Zealand, for example, it was not until the post-second-world-war period that the indigenous population shifted from being rural to urban based. In 1945, the distribution was 74 per cent rural and 26 per cent urban. By 1971, this had reversed to 71 per cent urban and 29 per cent rural (Thorns and Sedgwick 1997).

The second group was that of the semi-peripheral nations of southern Europe around the Mediterranean and linked to the core through trading relations and a dependency limiting their internal development, leading to a relatively slow rate of economic and social development. The reasons for the existence of the semi-periphery are both economic and political. Like the middle class in class systems of capitalist societies they are a buffer between capitalist and worker, and thus they confuse the directness of the relation of exploitation and appropriation. Semi-peripheral countries, such as Aotearoa/New Zealand, have some opportunities to use their role as a go-between to develop trade and other strategic alliances. These are limited. The world system model also allows for the shifting of nations within these categories giving the system a dynamic quality. The third part of the system was the periphery, the outer edge of the system, originally Eastern Europe, which sold cash crops to the core extending outwards to incorporate parts of Africa and Asia with the expansion of nineteenth-century colonialism.

In this scheme the world constituted a single division of labour organised around production for sale in a market (Hill and Feagin 1987). It was hierarchically organised and based around unequal exchange – thus exploitation. The unequal exchange is reinforced by political interference on the part of strong states in the weaker (less powerful) states using their power in global economic and political institutions. The system is seen to operate in a similar way to capitalist labour relations where the employer appropriates 'labour power' from the worker to make a profit (surplus value). In a world context, the powerful countries at the core appropriate wealth from the peripheral countries and so engage in an exploitative act. The relative level of this will vary both over time and between countries depending on the nature of the resistance and the degree of dependency (Frank 1981; Walton 1987).

The analysis of the world system in terms of a core–periphery model is a holistic one which assumes a relatively high degree of integration and control of markets by multinational companies and arrangements between nation-states. The unequal nature of the exchanges that take place sets up the major social stratification within the world system between countries which exploit, for example, the USA and Europe and the rest of the world (the exploited) which is then designated as the periphery or semi-periphery with various degrees of differentiation having been identified over time by world system theorists.

The majority of adjustments within the system occur at times of depression and/or recession within the world system as these allow the rise and fall of a particular nation's position within the international stratification system. In the latter decades of the twentieth century, the newly industrialising countries had particularly dynamic growth rates. In the late 1990s, the 'Asian Crisis' saw this period of growth sharply reversed and falling currencies and rising unemployment created problems for the Asian societies and cities which had grown rapidly on the backs of the expanding economies. Some of the former core nations, for example Britain and Spain have declined. This has led to the rise of new sets of alliances as counterweights within the system. Here, the rise of the European Union as a rival to the USA, and the 1989 breakdown of the Berlin Wall and collapse of Eastern Europe and USSR, have been of major significance.

A further development on Wallerstein's work came through the emergence of the New International Division of Labour work of Froebel, Heinrichs and Kreye (1980). They saw a combination of changes to the role and structure of labour with an increasingly large reserve army, a new set of technologies, which facilitates changes to the organisation of production, and a set of reorganised financial systems, which allows the more rapid flow of international capital. One of the main consequences they saw of these shifts was a relocation of production towards the periphery (Froebel et al. 1980). This analysis gave rise to the concept of the sunrise and sunset industries and the spatial shifts both within and between nations as capital sought competitive advantage as it restructured following the world depression of the 1970s and its series of fiscal crises (O'Connor 1973).

Globalisation

The emergence of globalisation as the key focus for debate occurred in the 1980s. The reason for its appearance at this time connected with a series of events giving currency to the view, in both academic and more popular discussions, that we were now living in a new kind of world. Schaffer argues that:

> Two dates – 1494 and 1969 – stand out as important moments in the history of the world as a global place. . . . Since the fifteenth century, people have slowly come to think of the world as a global place. This process was aided by the widespread use of maps and globes in schoolrooms. . . . (In 1969) the astronauts's photographs of earth gave currency to the idea of the world as a global place. (Quoted in Khondker 2000:17).

The impact on peoples' consciousness of images of the globe is quite significant. Many of us were brought up on maps that were created using a Mercator projection, which flattens the globe and therefore exaggerates the size of countries at both the top and bottom of the globe. As most maps were produced in Europe, not surpisringly Europe is the centre of the map, and the maps were coloured to reflect the colonial empires of the European powers. The de-colonisation of these countries from the 1950s and the unravelling of former Soviet Union and Eastern Europe and the

Balkans have provided a radically altered map of the world. The transformation in communications systems – providing instant and lower-cost
possibilities of connecting with people around the globe – has also transformed our knowledge and capacity to link up with others. It creates new
global flows of information and provides new ways of networking,
for example, school children 'chatting' via the Internet across ethnic and
spatial boundaries, senior's surfing the net and maintaining links with
their children and grandchildren who are part of the mobile service class.
The compression of time and space is thus real and is significantly restructuring our thinking about the world. We are undoubtedly at a period of
transition in our history and moving through a stage of disintegration and
rebuilding (Wallerstein 1998). The outcome of this may well not yet be
clear, nor what are the best conceptual tools to analyse these shifts. One
conceptual tool that has been suggested, and which has gained considerable currency, is that of globalisation.

Globalisation is a troublesome term that is currently fashionable. Its
use is diffuse and vague and there is no consistent definition as to what
it constitutes (Waters 1995, Larner 1998, Marcuse 2000). Robertson and
Khondker, for example, argue that:

> In spite of a number of attempts on the part of social scientists to conceptualise
> globalization in a careful analytical fashion, there is now so much loose and
> negative talk of 'globalization' that serious scholars of the compression of the
> world as a whole, in long historical perspective, face the increasingly difficult
> task of maintaining their intellectual seriousness in the face of slipshod and
> often heavily ideological employment of the word (1998:26).

Their critique reminds us forceably of the need to see globalisation – the
compression of the world and the reduction of time-space 'distanciation'
that has occurred – within its historical context (Giddens 1998). Each new
invention to increase the speed of travel and communication brings with
it the suggestion that social relations will be fundamentally changed. The
latest set of technological innovations has created a new era in global-
based communication and the speed of reaction is now frighteningly fast.
This was clearly shown by the collapse of the stock markets in the October
1987 crash, when computers triggered sales and the effects rapidly flowed
around the world quickly leading the downturn into a major collapse.
The ideological overtones within globalisation can have negative conno-
tations, for example, the obliteration of difference, the homogenisation of
different aspects of life and the resulting loss of national identities,
cultures and traditions (Ritzer 1998). Many see this as an extension of
'colonialisation and westernisation' leading to the domination of non-
western societies through a new form of imperialism (Jacobs 1996).

It is important to recognise that there is not just one discourse sur-rounding globalisation. The first is the economic, which has been fairly dominant, and suggests that we now live in a world of intensifying global economic competition. The world is a single marketplace controlled by relatively few large players. Nation-states are weakened and the embrac-ing of a free trade and open borders policy is critical to economic pros-perity and growth. According to Friedman, globalisation:

> may include a loose combination of free trade agreements, the internet and the integration of finance markets that is erasing borders and uniting the world into a single lucrative, but brutally competitive market place (1995 A15).

There is a strong and weak version of the economic argument. The strong version sees a shift over time from national- to international-based economies, though here companies are still based within a nation-state, and to the present 'global economy' dominated increasingly by trans-national companies (TNCs). The TNCs are less tied to territory and in their most extreme form can operate as 'virtual' companies, not requiring any spatial reference point (Waters 1995). The growth of franchising arrangements means that control can be exercised at a distance from the actual location of the operation, whether this is producing Hamburgers (McDonalds and Burger King) or selling real estate (Century 21). In this new world, national-level processes are of secondary importance and the new global markets are seen as uncontrollable by single national govern-ments. Thus, the significance of the nation-state is eroded. Companies need to become as 'competitive as possible' to survive, thus open borders and free trade are advocated (Therborn 2000). The strong reading of eco-nomic globalisation, however, stresses the impotence of nation-states and social movements to resist the forces of globalisation and therefore under-plays the strength of transnational bodies and institutions such as the IMF, World Bank, OECD, G8 (USA, Canada, UK, France, Germany, Japan, Italy and Russia) WTO (World Trade Organisation) and the UN and its various constituent bodies. These organisations are based around sets of relations between nation-states rather than TNCs and thus have some capacity to exert control over the operations of such companies (Hirst and Thompson 1996). They are, however, a continuation largely of western-based power and are part of a north-south view of the world that does not fully recog-nise the 'post-colonial' nature of many societies (Jacobs 1996). The analy-sis also tends to disregard the role of resistance by groups within the local and international population. Social movements do exert influence both through the international bodies (for example, the peace, feminist, envi-ronmental (Green) movements and coalitions of indigenous peoples) and at the local level through a variety of forms of mobilisation and resistance (including both labour and community-based movements, NGOs (Non-governmental organisations) and community-based organisations). The rise of the anti-free trade movement, and the series of violent protests in Seattle, Melbourne, Prague and Quebec between 1999 and 2001, is an indication of the continuing significance of social movements and social protest.

Weaker forms of the economic argument would still privilege the economic processes connected with globalisation, such as the spread of TNCs, increasing competitiveness, the relatively footloose nature of capital, and the significance of new forms of electronic communication and thus global economic organisation. Proponents of this argument would, however, be less certain that this was inevitable and they would preserve the possibility of human agency and would advocate the formation of counterweights to TNCs via international organisations and agreements and the formation of global social movements (Waters, 1995, Hirst and Thompson 1996).

The second reading of globalization has focused upon culture rather than economics and revolves again around arguments about homogenisation or diversity as the outcome. Here, the compression of the world and the dominance of the new information and entertainment media, and its owners and controllers, which feed all of us a common diet of TV, films, music and advertising has been at the centre of debate:

'Man buys the world'
This headline appeared in Business Week magazine on the occasion of the acquisition by the international entrepreneur Rupert Murdoch of the full assets of the Hong Kong-based Star TV (*Guardian*, July 1995). Murdoch, whose business career started when he inherited the Murdoch family newspaper empire in Australia, is, at the time of writing, head of News Corporation, a media-centred global conglomerate spanning TV, cable vision, and print media as well as satellite broadcasting and information technology industries across four continents. Familiar names such as *The Times* newspaper of London, Twentieth Century Fox Films and TV, Harper Collins, the world's largest English-language publisher, as well as Star TV, broadcasting to 54 Asian countries, are all part of this empire. Deals have recently been signed or are pending with the Globo organisation, the largest TV network in Brazil, for a Latin-American satellite service, and with the *Chinese Peoples Daily*, to bring the Communist Party newspaper into the world of global technology. Meanwhile, Murdoch renounced Australian nationality for American citizenship in order to pursue media acquisitions in the USA, thereby surmounting legal restrictions on foreign media ownership (Holton 1998:50).

Holton is here drawing our attention to the global nature of control over the media, what counts as both news and entertainment, and also the root-lessness of the corporate citizen who apparently changes citizenship to facilitate the expansion of their global empire. Commitment to national identity became subservient to the pursuit of entrepreneurial activity. The power of the media over sport has recently been illustrated in the 'Super League' battles in Australia where News Corporation, Murdoch's company, attempted to set up a new league alongside, and competing with, the existing Australian Rugby League to ensure the sport was fea-tured on the Murdoch-owned Sky TV. Similarly, the same company fought a takeover battle for Manchester United football club. It was rumoured that as part of this plan they wanted to import into the side a Japanese player to improve the ratings in Japan, rather than add significantly to the playing capacity of the team. Media controllers, as the new sources of power and corruption in a global world in which the old enemies of cap-italism and socialism have now been removed, also featured in the 1997 James Bond film *Tomorrow Never Dies*.

In this construction of the globalisation debate, there is also a dispute regarding the extent of human agency. Can we resist this global flow of information and entertainment, this process of what has been described as 'mcdonaldisation' or 'coke-isation', drawing attention to the standard-isation of tastes and eating and drinking habits and entertainment expe-riences resulting in a loss of the local cultural differences and increased similarity. The alternative line of argument has pointed to the emergence of greater local variation with the rise of ethnic and other identities as part of the decay and transformation of the previously dominant 'global' empires of colonialism and communism.

Central to the debate has been the crucial significance of new forms of communications including the electronic fax, internet, email and WWW. Here, however, access to such technology is far from even and research and policy has increasingly identified a growing digital divide between those people and countries integrated into the new information technol-ogy and those excluded, creating the possibility of network ghettos being formed (Thrift 1996). The digital divide is about access and has two dimen-sions, one is about age and the other about the provision of connections. According to the computer experts, 25 is the 'digital' divide. People over 25 have not grown up with the 'digital age' and therefore are not com-pletely absorbed into this culture and way of exploring and knowing the world. The other form of divide comes through who is linked into the information system. Is this the privileged world of the rich countries and populations? Or has the spread been such that it has led to greater access to information and knowledge and thus served to break down barriers.

The research is still unclear. There has been a tremendously rapid spread of computers and internet use but there are still significant clusterings and also quite varied levels of technology and access.

Will these shifts to new technology free up time by dissolving distances? Graham, commenting on this possibility, raises some interesting questions.

> Those social groups with access to sophisticated telematics can often now begin to transcend the physical limits and rhythms associated with traditional urban life. Services, amenities and jobs can increasingly be accessed in electronics space without (necessarily) moving into physical space (through teleworking, teleshopping, telebanking, and so on). For many (usually those with high physical mobility) it also encompasses the use of a multitude of electronic networks and spaces as phones, faxes and electronic mail are used to keep in touch, distant computers support the petty transactions of everyday life (Graham 1997:25).

One question this raises is whether or not there is a continuing need for interpersonal, face-to-face relations within the global city or in the future will all these be done via cyberspace? For new networks to be created and old ones maintained and refashioned for contemporary circumstances, the establishment of trust and understanding is required. For this, it is usually necessary to have some interpersonal communication and engagement. As Fitzpatrick (1997:6) has observed:

> Global cities reflect the economic realities of the twenty-first century. Remote working from self sufficient farmsteads via the Internet cannot replace the powerhouses of personal interaction which drives teamwork and creativity. These are the cornerstones of how professional people add value to their work. Besides, you cannot look into someone's eyes and see they are trustworthy over the Internet.

The visual connection is not, however, far away so will this reduce the necessity for face-to-face relations or are these a deep-rooted part of human experience, such that we will never want to remove them from our lives?

Research has also shown that, far from eliminating spatial factors in access to information, there is a new spatial concentration being formed. Work, by Graham (1998, 1999), for example, indicates over 50 per cent of all long-distance calls in the USA are taken by only five per cent of customers and that dominant within this group are the TNCs. Further support comes from work that shows 55 per cent of all private telecommunications circuits that terminate in the UK do so in London, and

Manhattan also has a high concentration of telephone and internet connections. In the case of telephones, Manhattan has more connections than all of the nations of sub-Saharan Africa. Further, it has the highest rate of internet activity anywhere in the world and is also a major location for internet-provider and multi-media companies (Rothstein 1998).

In respect to information technology the dominance of TNCs such as Microsoft is marked and this has a profound effect upon both how we communicate with each other and what we do. In Hong Kong, in 1999, as part of the repositioning of the city after its return to Chinese rule, two scenarios were suggested, both by overseas groups of experts, one from MIT and the other from Harvard; the 'Hong Kong Advantage' and 'Made in Hong Kong'. The first recognised the decline in manufacturing and promoted trade, finance, and high technology. Hong Kong was to be the hub around a knowledge- and information-based economy with access to mainland China, Asia, and the Asia-Pacific region. The second proposal focused on high-technology manufacturing of brand name production and original design, and the idea of moving from low-cost manufacturing to higher-value added goods. The adoption of the service, information, and knowledge strategy showed the connections desired with the global 'cyber gods'. The power of the 'cyber gods' was seen in the desire to have them present at the launching of Hong Kong's new development strategy:

> After the official announcement, this new object of urban governance seems to have resonated within a global-regional-local community comprising local capital (for example, Richard Li and Pacific Century), the Government . . . and other regional capitals (for example, Microsoft's Bill Gates, Yahoo's Jerry Yeung and IBM's Craig Barrett). The latter group of 'cyber gods' flew to Hong Kong to publicly endorse the idea (Jessop and Sum 1999:25).

Our knowledge of events around the world is now both greater and more instant, so we all can share in the action without leaving the comfort of our armchairs. This homogenisation is seen as an aspect of western, or more often American, domination of the world, changing habits, taste and culture into a globalised sameness (Rojeck and Urry 1997, Ritzer 1998). Travel and tourism fit into this as resorts, cities, and even countries develop a similar range of attractions for mass tourists to visit and experience. Stopping this tide of change is seen as well nigh impossible (Ritzer 1998).

The last dimension of the globalisation debate is about what has been termed globality (Therborn 2000). This is about planetary survival and the way humans and the wider eco-system have interacted in the past and are doing so in the present and thus what the future may hold for the globe as a complex eco-system. Environmentalist and a series of global conferences and reports have shaped the growth in this global discourse. The key contributions to this debate were from the Club of Rome in the early 1970s, followed by the first UN Habitat meeting in Vancouver in the late 1970s. Then, in the 1980s, the Brundtland Report (1987) that placed sustainable development on the international agenda was particularly influential. In the 1990s, there was the Rio Earth Summit in 1992 and the second Habitat conference in 1996 at Istanbul. These, among other events, social movement activity (for example, Greenpeace) and public discussion have led to a greater global awareness of our interconnectedness and the need to move beyond national-based solutions to address such complex issues as climate change, pollution of the oceans, the spread of diseases, and forms of development that reflect the limitations of the earth's resources. These questions will be explored more extensively in Chapter 9 where we will also consider the extent of linkages between these various strands and the analysis and debates about the future shape and size of the city.

Global Dynamics

The city is an increasingly central locale for the world's population with the fastest-growing urban regions now lying outside of Europe and North America. It is to Africa, South America and Asia that we must look for the most dynamic, in terms of growth, of the world's cities. The growth of the large metropolis is one of the most significant facets of urbanisation. In 1990, 270 cities had in excess of one million inhabitants and housed 33 per cent of the world's population. Of these, 22 cities had between five and eight million, and 20 mega cities contained ten per cent of the world's population. How will this pattern change, as the twenty-first century unfolds? Will the trend continue to mega cities or will a reverse flow be a feature of the century? Demographers are, for example, now predicting that, by the middle of the present century, the population of the world will have passed its peak and we will be facing questions in many regions and cities not of population growth but of decline. Clearly the future shape of the population of the world is a crucial aspect of the global context.

The largest cities at the present time are, Tokyo with 26.4 million, Mexico City with 18.1 million, Sao Paulo with 17.7 million and New York with 16.6 million. Within this discussion, however, it would also be necessary to take into account the nature of the regions within which these cities were set and the existence of the urbanised eastern seaboard of the USA and the greater Tokyo region which contain a population of over 30 million. The global cities may form the core of these urbanised regions but the various urban nodes have quite distinctive global functions. New

York, London, and Tokyo are widely considered to be the global cities of greatest strategic importance (Sassen 1991, 1994, 1999, Friedman 1995). This relates to their key role in the global network of telematics and their place as financial and information centres not only for their respective countries but also for the world as a whole. Global cities are now the key sites for the control, coordination, processing and distribution of knowledge that makes them the engines of growth within the present stage of capitalist development. The requirements of information technology make new demands on the built environment and in New York these have resulted in shifts of financial services activities from buildings in the Wall street area to new mid-town locations.

Box 4.1

....

New York: global city

- Population 2000: 16.6 million, 5th largest city in the world

- Population 2010 (estimate): 17.2 million, 7th largest city in the world

Global city

In contemporary analyses of the global city, three cities are always identified as leading exemplars – New York, Tokyo and London – as these three cities are at the centre of the financial and information economies (Sassen, 1991). However, one interesting aspect of the debate has been about the degree to which continued spatial concentration is necessary in an increasingly 'global' world based around electronic means of communication. Recent research on New York City is informative as it shows that there are continuing spatial constraints arising from the fact that modern communications technology is still dependant on 'hard' wiring (fibre optic cable).

New York's financial district still retains the headquarters of more 'fortune 500 companies' (leading global companies) than any other American state and its economy is increasingly dominated by the information sector (Graham 1999).

Information technology requires 'smart buildings' and this has privileged new buildings over redesigned existing buildings. This produces a shift in where the new activities are located. A study by Longcore and Rees (1996) shows that New York's financial district has undergone significant geographic change as its world-city function has grown.

In 1960, the downtown financial district was a compact area centred on Wall Street and Broadway. By the mid-1990s, with the greater reliance on advanced information and communications technology, the demand for space and for buildings able to accommodate the demands of these new services led to the centre of gravity shifting from the

Continued

traditional areas around Wall street to 'mid town' and a new generation of buildings leading to a loosening of the historic locational ties with the downtown area of Wall Street. Thus, Wall Street by the mid 1990s has become a sub-centre rather than the financial centre and buildings increasingly have vacancies. For example, 40 Wall Street (had 80 per cent vacancy in 1996), 44 Wall Street, 50 per cent and 45, 90 per cent (Longcore and Rees 1996:366).

Longcore and Rees (368) conclude:

> As highly competitive major financial firms retreat to secretive, security conscious structures and a building technology that stresses large horizontal over vertical spaces, the traditional, tightly focused, financial district land market may finally demonstrate geographical flexibility.

Global processes thus are complex in their effects on urban structure and do not necessarily remove the effects of physical location or reduce the need for contiguous location. The need for particular buildings and technologies is an additional factor, along with the continuing need for networking and social interaction which contributes to the resilience of the global city to dispersal of its functions (Thrift 1996).

The work of Friedman has been significant in shaping the analysis of the global city over the past few decades. Friedman developed an agenda for research into global cities and marked out the parameters of the debate which has been conducted through the late 1980s and 1990s. For Friedman, cities are spatially organised socio-economic systems (Friedman 1995). The key aspect highlighted by Friedman is the fact that cities serve as centres through which flow money, workers, information, commodities and other economically relevant variables. They thus become spaces of global accumulation. As such, they possess economic and political power and this provides a magnet to attract population so increasing their spatial variety and complexity. The population increasingly takes on a cosmopolitan character as the driving force comes not from locals but from the increasingly powerful, relatively footloose, transnational capitalist class. Membership of the global city league is not fixed but is the subject of fierce competition amongst and between 'world cities' for activities facilitating economic growth in the contemporary world. The access to cyber ports, information flows, financial markets and institutions are seen as the prize goals. Biotechnology, bio-engineering, and genetic engineering are some of the key growth enterprises. Around 2000, such companies exist globally, but mostly located in the northern hemisphere and concentrated in the USA. Such companies are at the centre of the growth of the so-called knowledge industries.

Global and the Local

Cities now compete in a global system where there are new hierarchies of power and opportunity with New York, London and Tokyo as the core cities where the world's information and financial super-highway is centred. Regional and local centres intersect with this global system in a variety of ways, creating the differences and local variations which are visible across the cities of the world. Although all cities are increasingly drawn into a system of global relations, local identities have survived and are part of what, in the end, creates their competitive advantage as increasingly the quality of life becomes a significant factor as well as the economic returns. It is important to also appreciate that cities are not homogeneous entities but are made up of sets of social actors, divided around such things as class, gender, sexuality, and ethnicity. Thus, what is good for one group may not be for another. In the global repositioning of cities, these internal divisions may be exacerbated or diminished.

Clearly, the positioning of nation-states within the global system influences the cities within those nations, leading to the rise or fall of their significance globally. The impact of these changes can be considerable on the level of economic activity and wealth generation and thus on the lives of the urban dwellers. Being out of the global circuit can lead to an increased level of urban poverty and exclusion, changes in the job market and in the extent to which the city is included within the international division of labour.

Summary

This chapter has explored the changing global context within which the city, in the twenty-first century, needs to be understood. It has tracked the epistemological shifts in focus from national to world, and most recently, to global urban systems. Each of these shifts is a reflection of changes in economic, political, cultural and spatial relationships that through restructuring have created sets of winners and losers amongst the largest cities of the world. The emergence, in the last decades of the twentieth century, of a set of global cities, providing the hub of the new information and knowledge economy has reinforced the dominance of the 'north' in global terms, yet where both population and cities are likely to grow over the next decades is in the south (especially Africa) and in Asia. Having set out the broader context of globalisation and identified some of the key components, the next two chapters explore the way urban life is being reshaped at both the everyday level and within the wider sphere of urban consumption and the remaking of the images and places within the city.

Further Reading

Postmodernity and the City

Dear M. 2000, _The Postmodern Urban Condition_, Oxford: Blackwells. Chapters 1 and 2. This is a good discussion about the rise of the postmodern critique and postmodern school of urban analysis based in and on Los Angeles.

Soja, E. 2000, _Postmetropolis_, Oxford: Blackwells. 'Part 2, Six Discourses on the Postmetropolis'. Soja has been a leading writer working within this framework since 1989 when his book on Los Angeles challenged much of the contemporary thinking about the city and how it was to be analysed.

Globalisation

There is a huge literature now emerging. Some publications that are particularly useful are:

Friedman, J. 1995, 'Where Do We Stand: A Decade of World City Research'. In Knox, P. and Taylor, P., eds, _World Cities in a World System_. Cambridge: Cambridge University Press, Chapter 2, pp. 21–47. One of the most informative papers of the last decade which has helped to shape the agenda of research on world/global cities.

Hirst, P. and Thompson, G. 1996, _Globalization in Question_, Cambridge: Polity Press. Chapter 1, pp. 1–17. This is a valuable critique of the more determinist economic positions on globalisation.

Marcuse, P. 2000, 'The Language of Globalization', _Monthly Review_, July–August. This is a short but stimulating paper which questions the degree to which globalisation is in fact anything new.

Robertson, R. and Khondker, H.H., 1998, 'Discourses of Globalization'. _International Sociology_, March, 13(1) 25–40. Robertson has been a significant writer in this area and one who draws attention to the long historical view necessary in understanding contemporary globalisation.

Sassen, S. 1991, _The Global City: New York, London and Tokyo_, Princeton, NJ: Princeton University Press. A significant analysis of three key global cities.

Scholte, J.A. 2000, _Globalization: A Critical Introduction_, London: Macmillan – now Palgrave Macmillan. Chapter 1, pp. 13–40. A very comprehensive account of contemporary globalisation which is clearly written and accessible to the reader.

Waters, M. 1995, _Globalisation_, London: Routledge, Chapter 1, pp. 1–10. This again is a clear and balanced introduction which allows the reader a good understanding of the main lines of debate and issues.

Web sites

Global cities

http://www.global-city.org/
http://www.council.nyc.ny.us/
_http://home.nyc.gov/portal/index.jsp?pageID=nyc_home_
_http://www.ias.unu.edu/research_prog/megacities/cities_telematics.html_

Global economic debates

http://www.wto.org/
http://www.oecd.org/
http://www.tuac.org/

http://europa.eu.int/comm/eurostat/
http://www.undp.org/

Critics of free trade agenda

http://www.greenparty.org.uk/reports/2000/meps/enlargementreport.htm
http://www.emperors-clothes.com/articles/choss/quebec.htm

5

Everyday Life in the City

Introduction

In many of the analyses of city life that were current towards the end of the twentieth century, from 'restructuring' analyses which favour the economic and suggest that urban life gets shaped largely by labour-market relations through to the recent debates about a 'globalising world', much of the focus is at the macro level. The nature of the economic, political and social relations created around that particular stage of capitalist development has been at the centre of these analyses. This, as we have discussed in earlier chapters, tends to underplay or ignore social agency. It emphasizes structural relations at the expense of meanings. The post-structuralist and postmodernist critique of the latter part of the twentieth century has re-emphasized these aspects of city life. At the level of everyday life, the city is a complex web of associations and meanings. There has always been a tradition of micro-level analysis. However, it has somewhat different roots.

The strand in the Chicago School alongside the 'social ecology tradition' that contained a strong emphasis on ethnographic fieldwork and involvement in the social life of the city in order to understand its social and cultural activities and sub-communities has one of its roots in the writings of George Simmel. Simmel (1969), unlike his contemporaries, Marx, Durkheim and Weber was most interested in the micro level of social life. The nature of social relationships, and the conflicts and contradictions emerging around them, were the central axes of this analysis. One of the variables Simmel considered to be crucial to the shaping of relationships was size of the city as this brought about greater complexity and a greater range of possible relationships. Thus, the modern metropolis attracted his attention. As Saunders notes:

Simmel's work on the social effects of size thus leads to the conclusion that, in a large group (such as a modern city), commitments become extended across a number of different social circles, the scope of individual freedom is

96

increased, the character of social relations is highly impersonal, and the individual's consciousness of self is heightened (1986:91).

Greater size enabled a greater range and complexity of relationships to be encountered thus requiring the replacement of more informal ways of relating with more formal ones. This in turn increases the possibility of individual freedom and choice but at the same time could reduce the quality of the relationship. Building from this work in the 1930s, Louis Wirth, a member of the Chicago school, developed his analysis of how increases in size, density and heterogeneity led to the transformation of social relations creating more diversity and a shift from what he called primary relations, of family and kin, to secondary more segmented relations formed through formal associations. Wirth, however, analysed the city from the top down; his hypotheses were deduced from his claims about the increased size and complexity of the city rather than from a detailed grounded analysis of daily life and, like Simmel, his analysis tended to be formalistic rather than based around first-hand accounts of peoples' actual lived experiences. In the 1950s and 1960s, there were a number of critiques of mass society that argued that individuals had become alienated and detached from fulfilling social relations. This was also taken up by those writers who saw the emergence of suburbia as a landscape of conformity, monotony and limited variety in respect to social relations.

Moving to more recent thinking about city life in the late twentieth and twenty-first century, the most significant influences derive from work which draws attention to the shift to identity as one of the keys to understanding how social life is shaped and the emergence of diversity and difference rather than uniformity and conformity. Alongside this, we can place the work of Latour (1993) who points out that social life is not, as many of the social analysts in the past have claimed, about order but about ordering. It is about social processes and thus it is an ongoing and contingent activity that is time and place bound. This provides a critique of the more extreme versions of globalisation, which assume that all places and people will be shaped by a common set of processes. Sennett (2000) is another contemporary analyst who has also recently drawn attention to the messy nature of everyday life and the dangers of trying to assume too much structure and regulation.

Identity is now seen as one of the key ways in which people situate themselves and provides a basis for social relations, mobilisation and activities (Eade 1997). Recently, in New York, I was introduced to someone who immediately told me he was 'Irish and a Poet'. This established his identity. He was born in New York but wanted to claim his identity not as a New Yorker, at least in this context, but as other. Recent Australian research has also shown that increasingly people there also want to assert their 'ethnic identity' so, rather than claiming they are 'Australian', they claim they are 'Greek Australians', Italian Australians, Irish Australians, and so on. The tendency to assert ethnic identity is not just confined to first-world cities but is increasing found globally with a strong reassertion of nationality rather than identification with a particular 'nation-state'. Such entities were, in many cases, the result of a process of colonialisation which collected together previously unrelated peoples and attempted to forge them into a single entity, often through compulsion and restrictions on individual and group freedoms. The unravelling of the former Soviet Union after 1989 and the Yugoslavian Republic and a number of central African states in the 1990s show that the lack of an underlying cohesive sense of identity makes these arrangements unstable and results in sites of conflict over ethnic identity politics.

New York, like all the major global cities, is a multicultural city containing many ethnic groups and distinctive sub-communities. The population and social life is very different in the penthouses of Manhattan from the upper West side areas of the Bronx and Harlem, or in the Russian émigré areas of Brooklyn or the middle-class apartment areas of Queens. London also has many distinctive localities. It has its east and west ends, its working-class districts such as Bethnal Green and its royal boroughs and exclusive neighbourhoods including many sub-communities. Some notable ones are the 'colonial ghetto' of Earls Court where many Australian and New Zealanders have lived during their 'great OE' (overseas experience) and the West Indian district of Brixton – now celebrated through an annual carnival rather than being seen as a deprived ghetto. Paris has its left bank areas of artists and students centred on the 5th and 6th arrondisements, or its entertainment district of Pigalle, or the artists who ply the tourist and who occupy the Place du Terre or the hippies and buskers on the steps of Sacré Coeur in Montmartre. Through these local activities the areas acquire their own identity. In the case of cities like Paris, this is both a product of the activities of the locals and the tourists attracted by the local colour and reputation as well as by the tourist promoters' 'place-making' activities.

The greater differentiation that has emerged with a loosening of the moral and social values associated with modernity and the increased emphasis upon individualism and neo-liberalism in the last decades of the previous century has created, in many of our cities, a social world based around multiple identities. For city dwellers, identities can now be constructed around such aspects as age – with the growth of both a teenage culture and age-specific activities and associations – or alternatively around ethnicity, gender, or sexuality. Sexuality is a major area of transformation with the rise of gay areas within cities and the recognition of a variety of sexual orientations and lifestyles. Dis/ability is a further aspect of identity that has become more prominent in urban planning and decision-making with greater attention to the need for 'total' mobility programmes and opportunities to ensure that the city is accessible and available to all its citizens.

These many facets of identity are all aspects of the individual and affect how we interrelate with family, friends, partners, neighbours and workmates. They also provide a basis for new forms of urban politics – those of identity. Thus the 'modernist' preoccupation with class politics, trade unions, political parties and liberal democracy through institutional politics has increasingly given way to more fluid social movements and forms of resistance. These emerge out of and around the struggles over personal and collective identities and thus provide a more varied and fragmented political and social landscape. For some, this leads to disempowerment as they see these social movements lacking cohesion and common purpose – they are for some an aspect of contemporary 'false consciousness' and thus conservative rather than emancipatory (Harvey 1990). Others see the changes as enabling a release from the stultifying politics of class and formal politics through established parties and parliamentary systems and thus potentially liberating, holding the promise of new forms of social organisation and practice (Lash 1999).

Space continues to be a significant part of how people organise and give meaning to their lives and create a sense of identity, of who they are and want to become. We all live somewhere – we have a place that we call 'home'. This may be temporary or permanent, rented or owned, large or small. It may even be just a cardboard box on the street, but it has a special quality and it is a crucial aspect of creating our sense of who we are – giving meaning to our lives and relationships. The exploration of 'everyday' life in the city in this chapter will thus start with the question of the importance of how we construct our home – both as a physical shelter and as a place of meaning. From there, we will expand the frame to think about the nature of neighbourhood and community both of which have been seen as central components of the city and urban life.

Meaning of House and Home

The home is a special kind of place and its meaning for those within in it is constructed through social processes of negotiation, resistance and resignation (Perkins and Thorns 2001b). It is a process which is never completed as the requirements and needs of the various members of the 'home' change over time. As in Latour's work, we can see that people do not so much create an order to their lives but are engaging in 'ordering'.

Thus again, it is about shifts and changes reflecting such things as gender, life stage, work, leisure and recreation, family dynamics, ethnicity and relationships. The need to analyse the differences as well as the similarities in homemaking is reinforced when the nature of this process and the meanings attached are considered across cultures rather than solely within the Anglo-American experience which has tended to dominate the literature (Perkins et al. 2001). Thus home is often constituted around single-family dwellings, on their own territory and with gardens or outside space connected to the house. This does not adequately reflect the experience of people who live in apartments unconnected with outside space, such as Hong Kong's public-housing dwellers in 40-storey tower blocks or of those who live in the squatter residences of Rio de Janeiro's favellas. Nor does it represent the world of many indigenous people who live a migratory existence and for whom land is more important than permanent dwellings and who construct temporary rather than permanent shelters (Read 2000). Yet, in each case, the people occupying the spaces are likely to be engaged in 'homemaking', the creation of their own identifiable spaces which represents their identity as both individuals and household members.

The study of the actual house we occupy has become more prominent in the late 1980s through the 1990s and into the new millennium (Perkins, Thorns and Winstanley 1999, Perkins et al. 2001). Change has taken place in family and household composition across most countries but particularly significant is that in the developed world where some of key changes have been demographic and in the status of women within the economy and society more generally. The reduction in the birth rate in the developed world and the later ages of marriage that have created longer periods of both single-family households and couples without children result in quite different 'home-making' practices and activities from those of previous generations. The greater economic opportunities for women, as a result of the activities of the feminist movement and the restructuring of work opportunities with the gradual removal of barriers to women's participation in the labour market, have been profoundly significant. Across Europe, for example, the proportion of women of working age in employment has risen in the 1990s to range from 35 per cent in Spain to 70 per cent in Scandinavian countries (Gilroy 2000). Thus, it is no longer the case that men are the breadwinners and women stay at home. How has this changed the way that the home is viewed and the activities within it are determined? The rise of the 'dual-career' family and the reversal of the caring role with male partners taking time out of the full-time workforce or being the carer rather than the principal wage earner, whilst by no means universal, are part of a broader reworking of gender and domestic relations.

A prominent strand in the analysis of the house–home relationship has centred upon the material value of the house and the role of tenure. Here, the differences between owners and renters have been drawn out. For owners, the house has accumulation potential whereas for the renter the house is simply a cost, 'it's money down the drain' being a popular sentiment in predominantly home-owning societies. Renters are also often seen as 'flawed consumers' in these societies as they have a more restricted access to credit and possibilities of contemporary consumption opportunities (Bauman 1998). What this debate starts with is the position that houses, unlike other commodities, have two separate values. These are to provide shelter (use value) and to provide a source of stored wealth as property (exchange value), and unlike many commodities, does not get consumed by its use but can in fact increase in its real value (Pratt 1982; Badcock 1989, 2000; Saunders 1990a; Dupuis 1992; Thorns 1992; Hamnett 1999). As Table 5.1 shows, housing constitutes, for many people – particularly middle-wealth holders, their most significant source of wealth and capital accumulation. This asset allows choices which are not available to those who rent and for whom housing is simply a cost. Much has been made of this distinction and there were suggestions that housing wealth accumulation could provide greater returns to individuals during times of high inflation than labour market-based activity. However, the late twentieth century has been a time of both booms and slumps in the domestic property market with gains and losses creating increased uncertainty around the rate and security of income from housing.

Property markets in cities as diverse as London and Hong Kong, for example, experienced downturns in the late 1990s giving rise to 'negative' equity for a number of households (Hamnett 1999; Lee, Forrest and Tam 2001). There is thus less confidence in the opening decades of the twenty-first century that owner-occupation will continue to deliver positive finan-

Table 5.1 Housing as a percentage of total household assets

	1980	1990	1995	1998	*Owner Occupation Rate 1995 (%)*
United States	27	27	23	21	67
Japan	14	8	10	10	61
Germany		34	34	32	41
France	44	43	42	40	54
Italy	40	37	35	31	67
United Kingdom	40	44	33	34	67
Canada	22	23	22	21	61

Source: OECD 2000

cial returns to homeowners. Further, as many people now live longer, and under conditions of decreasing public pension support, it may well be that they will consume any assets that they have accumulated within their own lifetime so decreasing the significance of property-based inheritance (Hamnett, Harmer, and Williams 1991; Forrest and Murie 1995, Thorns, 1995).

The favouring of owner-occupation as the preferred tenure form by a number of countries (Table 5.2) has also been linked to strong ideological beliefs that this form of tenure is one that confers other benefits. It is seen to create more moral and reliable citizens, more likely to support stability and gradual change, strong families and communities and a thrifty and responsible attitude towards homes and finances. Robert Menzies, the former Australian Prime Minister, catches the flavour of this view where he suggested that:

> The material home represents the concrete expression of habits of frugality and saving 'for a home of one's own'. Your advanced socialist may rage against private property even whilst they acquire it; but one of the best instincts in us is that which induces us to have one little piece of earth with a house and a garden which is ours, to which we can withdraw, in which we can be among friends, into which no stranger may come against our will. . . . My home is where my wife and children are; the instinct to be with them is the greatest instinct of civilised man; the instinct to give them a chance in life is a noble instinct, not to make then leaners but lifters (quoted in Mitchell 2000:78).

These comments show also how strongly gendered the discussion of 'home ownership' has often been. Home and family are seen as closely connected and, at least in the 1940s through to the 1960s, the 'family' was seen very much as a male-headed nuclear one.

Table 5.2   Comparative rates of home ownership (%)

Rates (selected countries)	1961	1995
United States	62	65
Australia	73	69
Canada	66	64
New Zealand	61	71
England	44	68

Source: Williams 2001

The focus on home ownership and its asset generation has been a major concern of analysts from first-world capitalist societies. With increasing marketisation in former socialist societies, home ownership has spread to the transition societies of Eastern Europe. The case of Riga, capital city of Latvia is not atypical. Here, the housing system for 50 years had been controlled, home ownership was discouraged and land was not a tradeable commodity. Housing was allocated by bureaucratic methods and was extensively subsidised. The reforms changed this pattern by shifting to greater private market allocation. Housing costs increased considerably with the reduction of subsidies and the deregulation of prices as individuals and households were now required to pay the 'market' price for their housing. The process was started in 1995 when the law on the privatisation of State and Municipal Apartment Buildings was adopted. By 2001, it is anticipated that 80 per cent of the housing stock will be transferred into private ownership (Tsenkova 2001). Hong Kong is another case where there has been a 'transition'. Here the move has been from British to Chinese control. The move does not seem to have meant a reinforcement of public rental but has allowed and encouraged state tenants to look at moving into ownership (Davis 2001; Lee, Forrest and Tam 2001). The strength of this tenure thus seems to be gaining rather than losing ground as we enter the new century. This reflects the material and non-material advantages of ownership, and reinforces the idea that where we live is a central site with opportunities to craft our sense of self and develop our personal and familial relations.

Non-material Dimensions of House and Home

In much of this work, the concentration on the house as a material object has been at the expense of the other dimensions of life which housing satisfies (Saunders and Williams 1989; Dupuis and Thorns 1996, 1998). The most significant thing here is to think about the relationship between the house, the material object and shelter, and home as a symbolic entity, which is about the creation of relationships and meaning. People consistently talk about turning houses into homes. This is an active, conscious process with deep significance for people – the first thing to be done when people move. They have to put their mark on the house and make it their own. Turning houses into 'homes' is about creating our own sense of place and identity. The putting up of pictures, the choosing of the colours, the landscaping of the garden all allow the differentiation of the house from those around and signify that this is 'our' or 'my' place. A home is a place of refuge and of memories which change through our lives from childhood to old age (Marcus Cooper, 1995). Houses also provide the space where the most intimate social relationships are developed. It is the site where people craft their sense of identity as mothers, fathers, parents, lovers, friends and companions.

Feminist critiques of research and writing on home show how homes are gendered. They are not always a place of peace and security but can also be a place of violence and oppression where women are exploited rather than liberated (Valentine 1991, 1999). They see much of the writing about home as romantic and nostalgic rather than reflecting the reality of the everyday experiences of women (Young 1997). The models often utilised are ones based around the 'nuclear family' and the 'male' bread-winner. This is the model that we saw as typical of 1950s' and 1960s' sub-urbia with its separation of public life, which took place largely in the city, and was the world of men, and private life that was domestic and subur-ban and largely the preserve of women. With the changed economy of the new millennium and women's greater participation in the workforce, this dichotomy is clearly no longer an appropriate way to view the city. The creation of new forms of work around services, rather than industrial pro-duction, has tended to change the balance of employment in favour of women. There is thus a remaking of the relations between women and men and the shifting of the basis of identity (Gilroy and Woods 1994). Men can no longer assume that they will be the dominant wage earners in a partnership; work may not be able to provide a man with his identity. These changes are likely to lead to new patterns of relationships between women and men and thus in the way that home gets constructed and re-constructed through the ongoing negotiation and renegotiation of roles and relationships within households.

Research has begun to examine the meaning of home from the point of view of the various household members. This shows significant differ-ences. Studies in Scandinavia have explored both children's and young peoples' views. Children see the home in terms of a place for their friends to come and, rather than seeing it as a 'private space', they see it as a 'semi public space open to friends' (Nilsen 2000). Work by Valentine, in the UK, has also supported this idea of the home as a semi-public space for young adults (Valentine 1999). For young people, the need for their own space comes through strongly with the 'teenage room' being one of the neces-sary components of the contemporary home (Haggstrom 2000, Ruud 2000). The Scandinavian work also did not support the findings of Ameri-can research where children saw the home as a

'field of rules' . . . Where from the moment he(*sic*) rouses into consiousness each morning, it is a consciousness of what he (*sic*) must and must not do. Without rules, home is not a home, it is a house' (Wood and Beck 1990:2).

The access of young people to the labour market and tertiary training has been restructured through both the economic changes of the latter part of the twentieth century and the increasing costs associated with tertiary education as the popularity of fees and loans has grown to reduce the cost to the state. The loans get repaid once the students are in work and this creates additional problems with respect to entry to the housing market, increasing the time that is now spent in the parents' house. What these changes point to is that the meaning, activities and the spaces within the home are likely to be reworked. How will this be done? Will it be by a process of negotiation or through the imposition by one or more members of the household upon the others (Perkins and Thorns, 1999, 2000b).

The analysis of the members of the household in addition to thinking about the household as a whole allows a further 'deconstruction' to take place and a consideration of how households come to make decisions across a range of activities. Housing mobility has often been conceived in terms of a housing career implying a high degree of intentionality and clear long-term goals to be sought. For example Abramsson, Borgegard and Fransson (2000) suggest that 'the concept of the housing career implies a progress in standards and quality of housing which is often a normative public goal'. This view was predicated on a 'life cycle' model arising out of the work of Rossi (1956) that saw households moving through a series of stages – marriage, children, empty nest old age – with corresponding changes in housing requirements. The model found favour with the planners and policy-makers who were trying to estimate the future demand for housing resources. It did, however, also serve as a constraining model and conditioned thinking and the supply of housing resources and assisted in the 'normalising' the desire for home ownership (Gurney 1999). When the model is compared to the actual experiences of those within the city, mobility is seen as a more complex affair. It is influenced by family changes, economic opportunities and labour market positions as well as by taste, desire and aspirations. Also, the unforseen and unexpected events of life create the need for housing adjustment such as the loss of partners, health problems, unemployment, and so on. Further, as noted earlier, the profile of household formation is changing with fewer children, less stability in marriage and other forms of partnering and longer periods of increasing dependency at the end of life. The less predictable nature of the job and housing markets in many countries over the latter part of the previous century also shapes the life course, aspirations and achievements of individuals and households within the city. Under such circumstances, the concept of a housing journey – containing many different possible pathways, some chosen and some forced by external circumstances, may be a more accurate reflection on social practices.

Home as a Site of Work

The home has long been a site for 'domestic' work. Such 'work' has often been discounted as it was not paid work. However, feminist scholarship has shown that this work associated with childcare and household management is still disproportionately done by women even when they have full-time paid jobs outside the home (McDowell 1999). However, a profound change is taking place in how and where paid work is done as a result of information technology (Kumar, 1995). A key question has become, will this produce more home-based work and will this mean that our homes become much more complex sites of activity and negotiation? The discussion of home-based work is often conducted in very positive language and is seen as an opportunity for greater flexibility and autonomy for workers. Advertising material in the popular media often glosses over the employment difficulties facing people as a result of work changes and suggests that they have more control over their lives than is in fact the case. A good example of this is would be where it is suggested that 'small offices in homes become more popular as more people opt for self-employment and turn their backs on air-conditioned office buildings, the popularity of the home office is on the rise' (Perkins and Thorns 2000a). The popular image of home-based work further often emphasizes the top end of the market and features professionals engaged in such activities as graphics design, software production and consulting. Whereas the full range of home-based activity would also include routine work such as on-line data entry and part-time and casual work and would involve those who, rather than having their own 'domestic workspace', often compete for this with other household members and other activities (Armstrong 1992).

Townsend (2000), in a study exploring women's views of future housing and neighbourhood, compared the views of women and those of architectural, design and planning experts on the future use of the home. All her participants saw this as likely to include a greater range of functions. For the experts, the future home would be:

- an office for home-based work
- a substitute for short-term hospital stay
- a centre for learning and substitute school room
- a virtual shopping centre
- a virtual community centre and
- a venue for technology and home-based entertainment

One function not mentioned in this study, but which is becoming a reality in a number of societies, is the use of 'home' detention through electronic tagging as a way of reducing the prison population. Shifting such people back into the 'home' environment is likely to impact upon household dynamics and on-going social relationships. For the experts, the emphasis upon technology and the idea of the 'smart house' was strong. The house of the future had its own web page and computer-controlled space – it would be possible to 'turn on the lights, move the surveillance cameras around, set the appliances to come on and off and change the air conditioning and heating levels all from a remote site through computer-based systems. Further, refrigerator manufacturers are now developing the 'smart fridge' that will provide the owner with menu suggestions from what's in the fridge and reorder goods on line as they run out. The technology is being sold as giving the individual greater control over their lives and activities. However, it could lead to an even greater dependence on technology and create a further division between those with access to technology and those without as well as encouraging less interaction between neighbours and even household members.

When a focus group of women, in contrast to experts, was asked to reflect on the question of the future of housing, they defined the future in a way that connected the home to the wider neighbourhood and were less focused upon the technology within the house. They emphasized neighbourhood cohesion, a good physical infrastructure, social inclusion, equity and safety and security with respect to the house. They also saw that the house would be multi-functional and would be more hi-tech. The choices of forms of home ownership were important alongside design and moves to make houses more 'sustainable'. The results of this research point to the need to link the understanding of individual and household practices and relations to those of the wider community and neighbourhood. How these links are being made and what changes are taking place still remain important questions for further exploration with respect to changes in everyday life within the contemporary city.

Neighbourhood and Community

The consideration of home and identity leads to thinking about the way broader spaces within the city are organised socially. Here, two linked ideas that have been significant in the past are those of community and neighbourhood. The former has been more central to sociological debate whilst the latter has been more characteristic of geography and planning.

The concept of community has been a multi-faceted one and often ambiguous in its meaning with both popular and more academic meanings. One article, for example, written in the 1950s speaks of over ninety-four different definitions of community. From these, Hillery (1955) abstracted sixteen concepts linked in twenty two different combinations and concluded that only one element was common to all, that they dealt with people. Community has always had overtones of intimacy and a stress upon the nature and type of relationships that are formed between individuals. Considerable controversy has surrounded the definition of the concept and its utility. The concept has been widely used by the public, politicians, and planners as well as by social scientists. The notion of community has both emotive and substantive meanings (Mowbray and Bryson 1981). The concept has had three major usages and associated meanings, some of which merge into each other. These are as a *geographical expression*, as *a local social system* and as *a kind of human relationship*.

Geographical Expression

The first of these relates to clearly delineated territory where boundaries are physical barriers such as hills, roads, rivers, and so on. The people within such a territory would feel a sense of identity as they are clearly marked off from other groups. In this way, the isolated or semi-rural village can be seen as a community. The people within these areas would have a high degree of interaction, partly as the scope for this is limited to those in the local area and this interaction would lead to the establishment of close ties and intimate relationships across a broad range of activities. The populations concerned are often small and have had a high degree of stability with little movement into or out of the locality. The traditional community within much of the literature was of this type and usually within a rural rather than an urban area.

A Local Social System

The difficulty of translating a spatially-based definition of community into the larger and more amorphous urban scene gave rise to a questioning of the necessity for a territorial base to the development of 'community'-type systems of relationships. This led analysts to develop a concept of community as a local social system. This construction seeks to explore the extent to which people living in any particular locality operate within a local system, with locally-based institutions and organisations such as political wards, community committees, sports and cultural organisations, churches and community centres. The emphasis in this usage, therefore, shifts from the territorial boundary to that of the social boundary, as represented in the local social structure. The concern with the development of this type of local social structure has been seen at various times in the growth of community development projects of various kinds within cities, for example, in the British community development projects of the mid-1970s and early 1980s, the Australian Assistance Plan and New Zealand's Department of Internal Affairs community development programme of the same period. A linked idea, which became popular in the 1960s, is that of social network. Bott's original (1957) study of family and social network drew attention to how the internal structure of the family was linked to its broader social environment and pointed to how social networks form around the various members, both individuals and couples, parents and children. This work stimulated other researchers to explore the way that family and friendship networks were interconnected. The question was asked as to whether friends were replacing kin in a more mobile society where family forms were getting smaller and centred around the 'nuclear family unit'. However, what has been shown is that far from disappearing, kinship does remain an important and called-upon source of support. Further such networks were found to be not always based around locality but could span entire cities, regions or countries.

Human Relationship

The third notion of community is that of a form of human association, a type of relationship, one based upon intimacy and face-to-face relationships of a relatively intense kind. Community, or communion as this has been termed (Schmalenbach 1961), is based upon affective ties and emotional bonds, which in turn, can be based either on blood, kinship, or friendship. These bonds that form community are likely to be somewhat precarious in an urban industrial society with high rates of population mobility. Primary relationships are, therefore, often underdeveloped within the city, in comparison with the more settled and stable rural and pre-urban communities.

Community as Ideology

The word community has also had a more ideological/utopian usage within wider public debate. Community here has represented what should be aimed at. We have had such things as 'community development' usually meaning the creation of more integrated and less dysfunctional living arrangements within urban areas or 'community building' and 'community empowerment' which are currently more in vogue. It is meant to recreate some of the collectivity destroyed through the vigorous application of individualistic market processes to western societies. In such discussion, there is a recognition that some aspects of social life have been lost and that this leaves a vacuum and a lack of trust and reciprocity between people, taking away some of the glue that used to keep communities together and allow local activities to take place. The crisis at the level of voluntary associational activities indicates some retreat from collective social life. How much this arises out of changes to families, labour makets and gender roles is still subject to debate and research attention. Rebuilding the older forms of collectivity and mutual support and thus reversing the trend to a greater level of perceived alienation of individuals from society has become a part of the public policy agenda. Clearly, in these types of usage, community is being invested with moral purpose rather than being used solely as an analytical tool.

Reflexive Community

The need for new strategies of community empowerment arising out of the belief that the world has become more alienating for some requires the generation of a more 'reflexive community' built around 'we' rather than 'I' values (Lash 1999). For this to happen, people would need to retrieve their communities and learn again how to share life stories and experiences and create their own sense of identity. The constructing of 'communities' by outside agents and experts is seen as one of the ways that this capacity has been broken down under 'modernity' with its emphasis upon the experts rather than upon the capacities of citizens through their everyday-life worlds. In recreating this sense of identity, information technology, such as desktop publishing and local web sites, could be valuable tools as they have the ability to link people in powerful ways and allow them to interact and develop knowledge about each other and their local place (Ashton 2001). Increasingly, local institutions such as city councils are looking at ways of engaging the citizens through on-line information and chat lines. For example, the mayor of Christchurch, Aotearoa New Zealand has established a city chat line where people can interact with him about city issues. The web sites of cities can also be powerful tools in the creation of local branding and identification, whether these devices increase a local sense of belonging and engagement or whether they are designed for other audiences as part of city marketing strategies is an important question to be explored further in the next chapter.

The development of the St Albans web site (Christchurch) and Amsterdam's digital city (see Box 5.1) are two different uses of new information technologies to encourage greater citizen involvement. In the St

Box 5.1

Information technology and community development

St Albans, Christchurch, New Zealand

- Population (2001): 320,000

In St Albans, a suburb of Christchurch, New Zealand, the community has begun to use new technologies to facilitate communication. The philosophy behind this came from John Wardle, a St Albans haemophiliac infected with AIDS-carrying blood. Knowing he would soon die, he wanted to ensure that his wife and daughter would remain secure. In order for this to happen, he wanted St Albans to be a friendlier place, where people naturally looked out for each other. He felt that simply moralising or passing laws wouldn't work; social attitudes had to change.

With a few others, John Wardle first encouraged people to communicate via a community paper, produced from his desk-top computer and a nearby friend's backyard printing press. Local residents thus began using their own, small-scale technologies, to build community. This monthly paper reaches 5000 households and is supported by local business advertising. It is well loved and has been highly successful in helping to develop a sense of community. Many groups have been formed (for example, art, choir, history, park, residents, youth). Many attempts to mobilise community action have been successful (for example, to get a locally-run park, save a hall, challenge decisions about local-government electoral boundaries), and many have received and given personal help.

The Community Web Development Project, established in August 1999 is the second phase of local residents using technology to enhance local community. This site, using 'virtual space' to enhance 'physical space', is making much progress towards delivering the local information and communication local people say they need and want, by the minute, instead of just by the month.

A recent advertisement in the community paper asking for help with the project elicited over twenty offers of support. Planning now includes a reporter posting daily stories of St Albans people and its environment, a local events calendar, a business specials section listing what is 'cheap today', and a help section that invites people needing and offering help to advertise this. This is an example of a truly community-owned and -operated web site.

Contributed by Hazel Ashton, Community Web Development Coordinator
Web site for project: *http://www.stalbans.net.nz/*
City web site: *http://www.ccc.govt.nz/*

Digital City Amsterdam, the Netherlands

- Population (2001): 734,540

The digital city was launched in 1994 as a way of encouraging greater citizen participation in city government. The web site was to be a place where information about the

Continued

city and its services would be able to be accessed by the public. It was also a way of exploring the possibilities for, and limitations of, the creation of a virtual community. Over its first five years the idea developed into a virtual city growing to comprise a network of small virtual communities with more than a 100,000 regular participants.

The digital city is 'constructed in the image of a real city with "squares" corresponding to different themes or areas of interest (the environment, government, art, sports, Europe, alternative lifestyles, women's issues, music, and so on). Each square offers a space for a number of "buildings" which can be rented by business, non-profit organizations or other providers' (UNCHS 2001a:60). The squares also feature billboards, cafes (chat rooms) kiosks, side roads and bikeways. Each participant can create for themselves a 'home page' – the homes are sited on 'residential areas' situated between the squares and cannot be used for commercial purposes. The digital city, it is suggested, 'has become a true city, dynamic and creative where houses, buildings and squares are constructed, demolished or abandoned every day' (ibid:60).

Participation to date has mostly been by young, well-educated and highly computer-literate people. So the hopes that this will bring about a wider participation of social groups within Amsterdam in local politics has not yet been fully achieved. The project does show how the digital world has the potential to remake social relationships.

Web site for digital city: *http://www.dds.nl*
City web site: *http://www.amsterdam.nl/e_index.html*

Albans case, it was an attempt to create a sense of place identity through the sharing of stories and information. This, it was believed, would create a greater sense of community out of which would come greater and more effective political engagement. In the Amsterdam case, the motivation was to encourage more participation in city affairs through enabling this to be done through on-line discussion and the creation of a virtual city in which people could occupy 'space'.

Analysis of Community

In developing an analysis of the present-day level of community and communal relations within cities, it is necessary to build from these various ideas we have reviewed. Our analysis should emphasize process and acknowledge the tensions, conflicts and power dimensions. Recent syntheses have drawn attention to the key place that boundaries, shared interdependencies and the growth of a common consciousness have played in shaping the meaning attached to community (Pearson 1994).

Boundaries are both spatial and symbolic. As we noted earlier in our consideration of definitions, boundaries can be physical, such as rivers, roads, hills, and so on or they can be symbolic – this is my place, my town, my locality, as there are people here like me. A sense of identification is important and is often fostered by reference to local history and family continuities. The linkage between territorial and symbolic boundaries raises questions about the connections between the social and spatial and also relates to the work done mostly by social geographers investigating the mental maps that people hold of the city (Lynch 1960; Strauss 1961). This work shows that people possess notions of where people like themselves live – those people with whom they would like to be associated. The mental maps are quite often different from the physical maps that could be drawn of a city and, in some respects, are likely to be unique to each individual. Here, the role of analysis would be to see the extent to which people have overlapping images and share networks of social relations.

One variant on the idea of the bounded community is that of the defended neighbourhood (Suttles 1972). The defended neighbourhood is a residential group with a clear sense of boundaries that separates itself off from the remainder of the urban area, it creates an area where residents feel safe and secure. For example, the responses of a population to an actual or perceived threat to their locality such as a freeway construction project, urban renewal or the location of a sex offenders' rehabilitation unit or a halfway house for discharged prisoners can also bring about a closer sense of identity (Mullins 1987). Recently, work has drawn attention to 'Not in my Backyard' (NIMBY) groups who have organised around the preservation of aspects of their locality and the 'last settler syndrome' – now I have acquired access to this area, there should be no further development (Perkins 1988a, b; Dear 2000).

Drawing up neighbourhood boundaries can be done in a number of ways. The first is though the use of restrictive covenants and exclusionary zoning practices. Such restrictions are designed to keep out people who do not conform to the local image. These covenants can stipulate such things as minimum floor space, minimum price of a house allowed on the site, type of materials, and so on. These restrictions are usually employed by higher socio-economic groups and form part of their 'closure strategy' to ensure that property prices are maintained.

A second theme to come through is that of the interdependencies or linkages between the various elements shaping the nature of community structure and relationships and how these linkages enable a common conciousness to form. In contemporary localities, there are at least five possible set of such relationships. These are property, propinquity, ethnicity, gender, and kinship (Hall, Thorns and Willmott 1984; Thorns 1992).

Property relations in the locality are those tied to tenure and represent a possible material base upon which local activity can arise. There has been much research designed to answer the question whether or not home ownership produces real gains for owner occupiers. What this has shown is that gains are not guaranteed and vary depending on such factors as time of entry and exit to the house and the location (Hamnett 1999). The significance of location, tenure and the value attached to property are some of the reasons for the emergence of NIMBY-type social protest focused around maintaining property values and thus locational advantage (Winter 1994). The presence or absence of locally organised social groups indicates that there is a process required to turn the set of objective interests shared by property owners or tenants within an area into an effective social group. The trigger is sometimes the threat to property values, in other cases it may be the result of conscious social actions through, for example, community development strategies, or the formation of local democratic institutions such as in systems of Community Neighbourhood Boards, or tenant management systems within social housing areas. Rent strikes have been one form of social action taken by tenants to defend and draw attention to their concerns (Castells 1983; Damer 1990; Murphy 1994).

Propinquitious relations are somewhat more diffuse and raise the question of the role of territory. Propinquitious relations are usually expressed through local voluntary organisations. Here, the actions of individuals and groups at the local level can increase local identity and pride in the place and this can help to build a stronger degree of collective consciousness. An interesting recent case is the suburb of St Albans in Christchurch. This area is an inner to middle suburb of the city. Three years ago a group of local people protested against the planned destruction of trees and houses by a planned road-widening scheme. The protest began a revival in local identity, which was then capitalised upon through the development of a local paper, distributed free, which began to tell the story of the area through the experiences of the residents. The next move was to utilise modern information technology to build connections across the area through a St Albans web site (see Box 5.1), which became a place for the community to learn about itself and build a stronger sense of identity (Ashton 2000). What this case shows is that the area had become mobilised and the latent community that had existed was now manifest and a means of social mobilisation.

The formation of ethnic sub-communities as a result of migration and the revival of indigenous people is a further potential source of local identification and thus the growth of local consciousness. The success of such events as the Notting Hill Carnival in London, Chinese new-year festivities, Mardi Gras and other such activities now common in many global cities attests to the increasing ethnicity and multiculturalism now present. Such diversity adds colour and life to cities and leads to changes in the dynamics of place-making. With diversity also comes a shift to local politics and to the rise of a more explicitly ethnic dimension to local political life.

Gender and sexual identity has also become an increasingly important base for social organisation (McDowell 1989, 1999; Duncan 1996). In the emergence of gender-based struggles around local issues, new forms of organisation have played an important role in shaping this understanding. In the 1960s and 1970s, women were prominent in attempts to extend the set of services provided within suburbs, particularly those created in the rapid urban growth of the post-1950 period. Such suburbs were places largely of residential property with few employment or shopping and recreational facilities. The burden of this restricted set of opportunities fell most heavily upon women and children restricting them to the physical confines of the suburb through their lack of mobility once the male member of the household had taken the car to work in the morning. It was women, therefore, who provided the impetus and social organisation within the suburbs. They organised play centres, were the main supporters of the parent–teacher associations (PTAs) of the local school and acted as fundraisers for local projects. The gendered nature of social relations is shown by the fact that men tended to have a greater prominence on school management committees that allocated finance and controlled school budgets rather than on the PTAs, which raised the money. In this case, we can see overlaps between gender and propinquity.

Sexual identity has also become a significant focus for urban political activity and place-making. Gay and lesbian groups have established distinctive residential areas within cities, such as the Kings Cross area in Sydney and San Fransisco's Bay area. This has led to the creation of their own distinctive street carnivals and hero parades as one way of affirming and celebrating their identity. Such events have become major money-spinners and a key component of the urban tourism industry. Cities such as San Francisco and London now openly market themselves for gay travellers indicating a distinctive shift in sexual mores.

Neighbourhood

In contrast to the literature and debate about the nature of community, the idea of neighbourhood has always been a spatial one. It has also been closely linked to planning and design. The post-1950s development of the city was essentially suburban with more or less intervention by planners to shape the range of housing and facilities for commercial and recreational use beyond the houses themselves. One attempt to control and shape growth was through the idea of the 'balanced neighbourhood'. The planners here had the aim of creating a place where people could both work and live, so reducing the need for commuter travel and creating more liveable environments. This was supposed to end the separation of work and living created within uncontrolled suburban growth. The weakness here arose from the somewhat top-down nature of the planning. Earlier in this chapter, we drew attention to the fluid and fragmented nature of much of everyday social life. The greater mobility enjoyed by people in the middle and latter decades of the twentieth century, with the expansion of car ownership and the creation of freeway and motorway system across Europe and North America, worked against the planners' idea of neighbourhood balance. People lived in one place and often worked elsewhere across town, and sometimes drove to other towns. For example, in Britain, people commuted from the new town of Milton Keynes to London as it was cheaper to live there and London was reasonably accessible down the M1 or via the rail system. In some countries there were institutional factors shaping this pattern of cross-urban-centre commuting. A further interesting case is that of Holland's Randstad, consisting of the cities of Amsterdam, Rotterdam, The Hague and Utrecht, where the controlled nature of the housing market contrasts with the deregulated nature of the labour market making it more economic for people to retain their accommodation and commute if they obtain a job in another city. This leads to high levels of daily movement around the Randstad by both car and rail (Dieleman and Musterd 1992).

A particular type of neighbourhood that has been extensively analysed is that of the 1950s–1980s suburban neighbourhood. The key distinguishing feature of this particular residential area was its single family houses at low residential densities. The three-bedroom 'bungalow' was the norm with its own plot of land surrounding the house. The creation of this structure provides for the back yard or garden which is often enclosed by fences to ensure 'privacy' and mark out the territory owned by the householders. The ownership of domestic land led to the rise of a gardening culture incorporating elements of recreation and leisure, status and display and 'domestic' production by growing vegetables and fruit (Bhatti and Church 2000). This urban form was most pronounced in North America, Britain, Australia and New Zealand – all societies with high home-ownership rates. The post-1950s' baby boomers were a suburban generation living in separate nuclear-family oriented houses. The typical family for whom the houses were designed was mum, dad and two kids, this being seen as the ideal family unit. The suburbs were seen as great places to bring up the family as they offered clean living in fresh surroundings and were away from the crime-ridden and unhealthy urban centres which were seen as sources of decay and pathology. The nuclear family in the growing suburbia was the new unit of consumption for the growing manufacturing industries, for example, whiteware, televisions, cars, mowers, and phones. Suburbs thus served well the needs of the mass-production consumer goods industries.

Just as in the early days of the industrial city, the development of housing occurred more quickly than appropriate physical infrastructure so infrastructure problems occurred with the growth of suburbia. Here, the physical infrastructure, in the shape of services, was generally supplied such as drains, water, and power. What was much less common, was community-level social infrastructure. The speed of construction meant that houses advanced ahead of such social provisions as shops, community centres, public transport and telephone services. One of the reasons for this lack of services arises from the fact that the developers and the builders were driven, as in the earlier phases, by profits. The level of population required for the development of shopping centres and other services takes time to build up and the commercial interests who provide these resources are not attracted until the population base has reached an economic size. Thus, in the initial years, services tended to be sparse and problematic.

Suburban living was seen to lead to isolation, particularly of women and children, and this led to the growth of 'suburban neurosis'. The more negative images of suburbia contrast strongly with the ideal of the suburban house and family as one that provides a place of domestic bliss. The notion of home has often been idealised and presented in romantic and unproblematic terms. It has been described as the heart of family life – a place of safety and security, of love and affection. What these images fail to recognise is that this may be the case for some but is by no means universal.

Further, there was nothing, it seemed, for the young to do in the 1950s and 1960s. The growth of 'milk bars' and rock-and-roll clubs marked an increasingly commodified teenage leisure market with industries emerging specifically targeted at youth who now had increasing disposable income. This led to cries of moral corruption amongst the rising generation. In Aotearoa New Zealand, for example, a government enquiry was established to assess the degree of moral peril that this new set of teenage opportunities presented (Soler 1989).

By the 1970s, there was an increasing proportion of women moving into the economy and an increasing resistance to stereotyped roles of domesticity. Significant in this change is the growth of the second-wave feminist movement and its deep critique of the bastions of patriarchal society including the single family house in suburbia. Dolores Hayden, an American socialist feminist, in answer to the question, how does the conventional home serve the employed women and her family, answers with one word – badly!

> Whether it is in a suburban, exurban, or inner-city neighbourhood, whether it is a split-level ranch house, a modern masterpiece of concrete and glass or an old brick tenement, the house or apartment is invariably organised around the same set of spaces: kitchen, dining room, living room, bedrooms garage or parking area. These spaces require someone to undertake private cooking, cleaning, childcare and usually private transportation if adults and children are to exist within it (Hayden 1980:170–87).

In such suburban development, little recognition is given to differences amongst households or for varying stages in the life course or to cultural differences. Planning was based firmly on the principle that workplaces and homes should be kept separate. This separation implies that our lives are also compartmentalised along the same lines. It promotes a spurious order, which feminists and other showed was not how everyday life among households was actually organised. The separation of paid employment from the home reinforced a division of labour that implied domestic work was not real work as it was not paid work and it contributed to the invisibility of the contribution women made to the economic and social life of the city and its suburbs (Oakley 1974; Allison 1990).

Summary

The debate over the future shape of the house and home and the relations between women and men draw us back to the wider discussion of how cities are being remade under the more global conditions of the twenty-first century. The linkages we have explored are those between everyday life, community, neighbourhood and the city. The discussion of issues of property, propinquity, gender, ethnicity and family form and relations points to how all these have became more fluid and cross cutting in the latter part of the twentieth century under the changing economic and social conditions which are subsumed under the umbrella of globalisation and the shift to what some analysts would see as a postmodern world. The other powerful current that is impacting upon and remaking everyday social life within the city is that of consumerism and this is what we move to examine in the next chapter.

Further Reading

Home Ownership and Meaning of Home

Dupuis, A. and Thorns, D.C., 1998, 'Home, Home Ownership and the Search for Ontological Security'. *The Sociological Review.* 46(1). This article examines the notion that the home can provide a locale in which people can work at attaining a sense of ontological security in a world that at times is experienced as threatening and uncontrollable.

Saunders, P., 1990a, *A Nation of Homeowners.* London: Unwin Hyman. Chapter 2, 'The Desire to Own', pp. 59–112, provides a good analysis of the desire to own and the ideology and policies underpinning the growth of home ownership. The data is drawn from an empirical study of Britain.

Home-based Work

Kumar, K., 1995, *From Post-Industrial to Post-Modern Society: New Theories of the Contemporary World.* Oxford: Blackwell. Chapter 6, 'Millennial Themes: Endings and Beginnings', pp. 149–201, provides a valuable overview of arguments relating to transformations at the end of the century. A useful discussion of how work is being remade through information technology and how this impacts upon the home.

Gender and Identity

McDowell, L., 1999, *Gender, Identity and Place: Understanding Feminist Geographies.* Oxford: Polity Press. Chapter 9, 'Home Place and Identity', provides a valuable overview of the growing body of literature, which puts gender analysis at the heart of understanding the meaning of home.

Seidman, S., 1994, *Contested Knowledge: Social Theory in the Postmodern Era.* Oxford: Blackwell. Chapter 7, 'The New Social Movements and the Making of New Social Knowledges', pp. 234–80, provides an excellent overview of the growth of social movements around identity politics – gender, ethnicity, sexuality and the challenge they pose for 'modernist' constructions of social knowledge.

Young, I.M., 1997, *Intersecting Voices: Dilemmas of Gender, Political Philosophy and Policy.* Princeton, NJ: Princeton University Press. Chapter 7, 'House and Home: Feminist Variations on a Theme', pp. 134–64. In this chapter, Young explores the idea of home and argues that it provides 'critical liberating potential' because it expresses 'uniquely human values'.

Web Sites

Home and identity

http://www.ihome.com.au/html/have/index.htm
http://www.heritage.gov.au/ourhouse/index.html
http://www.soci.canterbury.ac.nz/rphshome.htm

Information technology and community development

http://www.stalbans.net.nz/
http://home.dds.nl/

6

Consumption and Urban Culture

The drive for ever-increasing and differentiated consumption opportunities to allow people to construct new lifestyles became, for some analysts, the defining characteristic of urban life towards the end of the twentieth century. The new millennium began with a series of parties and events emphasizing the hedonistic, spectacular and playful character of the social world and contemporary urban life. From the first sunrise parties of the new millennium to the jet setters trying to race the dawn around the globe to the celebratory festivals and events, the new millennium dawned with an array of consumption experiences. For many analysts and commentators, this was an indication that the central life interest in the twenty-first century would be based around consumption activity. These shifts have led to a debate about whether the old relationship between production and consumption, seen at the centre of modernist urban life, has now been reversed. Life will be determined by our access to, and use of, an ever-increasing range of goods and services, which will allow more individuation to develop. The consequence of this will be that social differentiation will be around issues of lifestyle and life course rather than work and employment. How we spend our money will be more significant than how we make it. New discourses of consumption have been drawn upon in the debate regarding urban consumption from the field of cultural and literary studies and cultural psychology. Such material has opened out the way to a consideration of a much wider set of processes than those contained within the previous rather productivist treatment of consumption (Featherstone 1991).

Defining Consumption

In identifying the key elements of the debates and analyses of consumption, it is useful to begin with some definition of it. Consumption activity can be seen as any activity involving the selection, purchase, use, mainte-

120

nance, repair, and disposal of any product or service (Campbell 1995:104). In this definition, attention is drawn to the fact that consumption is not just of goods that are manufactured in industrial production but, increasingly in a post-industrial society, of services, knowledge and ideas. This changes the scope of inquiry and moves us to seeing that such things as places, shopping, fashion, eating, drinking, tourism, recreation and leisure activities and sights and sounds become important areas for the demonstration of difference and tastes as well as the 'consumption' of such intangibles as film-watching, art, and tourism sites (Lash and Urry 1994, Urry 1995, Corrigan 1997, Rojeck and Urry 1997). The inclusion of purchase and use draws attention to the question of both the use and the exchange of commodities and the purpose to which they can be put. A house, for example, can be a source of shelter, a way of storing wealth, a place to display artefacts and memories, somewhere to express individual or collective identity, and a place for the construction of family life. The repair and maintenance of the things consumed can also raise interesting questions about lifestyles and the relative importance of areas within the house, garage and shed. Much of this is gendered (Hopkins and Riley 1998). Warde sees consumption as:

> comprising a set of practices which permit people to express self identity, to mark attachment to social groups, to accumulate resources, to exhibit social distinctions, to ensure participation in social activities and more things besides (Warde 1996:304).

What this adds to our previous discussion is attention to the way that what we consume serves as a mark of distinction. The link between consumption and style and status has long been established. The work of Weber (1921), and later Veblen (1934), drew attention to these dimensions of social differentiation as conceptually independent of class (economically-based) distinctions. Social closure, around activities and attributes that endow people with prestige and status, points to what we consume and also the identities we express and seek. Consumption, therefore, raises a series of quite complex questions for analysis and links into the debate about postmodernity that we have previously discussed. In respect to urban life, consumption activities have assumed greater significance as the size of the urban realm has increased and because of the shift of activity from production to consumption. Broadly, the analysis of consumption has been either within political economy or relied on cultural psychology and sociology. The latter has given greater significance to the development of distinctive consumer cultures and a greater degree of agency to the individual consumers and how, through consuming, they craft their sense of identity.

Collective Consumption

Urban studies in the 1970s are strongly influenced by political economy and the debate about urban consumption was centred on the transition from Fordist 'mass consumption' towards a more flexible system of commodity production arising out of the crises in western capitalism necessitating the restructuring of economies to return them to profitability. Here, work was initially stimulated by the research in the 1970s of Castells (1976) into the restructuring of state provision away from 'collective consumption' towards increased levels of private, individual provision. From this, he developed his focus upon collective consumption goods. For Castells these goods are the 'real' object for urban studies. The provision of the various forms of collective consumption, for example, housing, health, and education, were functionally necessary for the reproduction of labour power and therefore for the continued success of the capitalist mode of production (Pickvance 1976).

The understanding of the organisation and reorganisation of collective consumption is then set within a view of the state as 'relatively autonomous', drawing here from the work of Poulantzas (1978). In the 1970s, there were a series of crises affecting industrial capitalist societies. Debate has raged regarding which 'crisis' was the most significant, ranging from that of capital through to that of the state (O'Connor 1973, Pusey 1991). At the beginning of the 1970s, the long boom that commenced in the late 1940s faltered and then moved into recession leading to a period of economic restructuring to try and revive the profitability of capital (Aglietta 1979, Boyer 1988). This took many forms, including the closure of plant in the old industrial core regions and the shifting of activity to the newly developing nations, for example of South East Asia. These shifts creating the 'rust bowls' in the former industrial manufacturing regions and the 'sunbelt' cities of the new hi-tech service oriented development.

The loss of jobs and revenues, which ensued from restructuring, was one factor in producing the urban crisis especially in the large metropolitan centres, along with central government reductions of money for infrastructure development and maintenance (both physical and social). The losses of revenue led to cities reducing their spending in order to balance budgets. Collective consumption goods were the chief casualties in this cost cutting. Castells (1976) considered that such reductions would lead to the growth of urban social movements of resistance to these cutbacks and thus a mobilisation of people against the state, both locally and nationally. This popular movement would become allied to the labour movement and provide a spearhead for a revolutionary reconstruction of society. Castells' (1976) predictions did not eventuate. There was no broad mass movement of opposition generated within the major cities, although there have been sporadic movements focused around particular issues, such as rent and IMF restructuring (Walton 1987).

Political economists have continued to emphasize the significant way production shapes the range and form of commodities available. They see the productive system as being dominant. This leads to the view that the monopoly producers largely create consumer tastes. Advertising thus became a significant factor in determining what we buy, eat, and acquire to help us 'entertain' ourselves. Marx, for example, wrote of commodity fetishism and the way that an emphasis on consumption creates a false conciousness, which distracts attention from the significance of the underlying productive relations within society. This is the 'bread and circuses' argument suggesting that the capitalist class obscures from workers the real conditions of their lives by providing distractions. It suggests that workers are relatively easily conned and implies that all consumption activity fails to effectively recognise the real interests of workers and is simply about increasing the returns to capital through maximising sales and profits (Harvey 1989). This leads, in the present debate, to concerns with the 'commodification' or 'commoditisation' process and the relationship between consumption and class and whether this relationship has in fact been reversed and whether the only basis of distinction is in fact material (Saunders 1990b; Crompton, 1996, 1998, 2000).

Commodification

Commodification is about the process of turning things, which have been produced, into saleable items. Under industrialisation, commodification was principally about the manufacture of new products for sale, the creation of commodities as consumer goods, such as cars, fridges, washing machines, televisions, videos and computers. These commodities required a manufacturing production regime for their creation. Profits under Fordist-production regimes came from the mass-commodity production of standardised products. Profits were increased through extending the markets and ensuring economies were gained from large production runs. The economic crises of the 1970s and 1980s, which led to the restructuring of economic activities, led to a shift from large-scale production to smaller runs based around more flexible methods to create a more varied selection of items for sale. The emphasis shifts to creating differences rather than similarities, standardisation is seen as less important than creating specialised tastes and preferences. Niche markets are sought rather than mass markets. This shift reflects the social and individual desire to be differentiated rather than all wear the same clothes and drive the same car. Such standardisation was seen as associated with centrally-planned regimes such as those of the former USSR and Eastern European state socialist societies. The dramatic pulling down of the Berlin Wall in 1989 and the subsequent disintegration of the USSR, the regime changes in Eastern Europe and the reunification of Germany were all seen to herald a major turning point in the late twentieth century.

The triumph of market capitalism, as the global system, had occurred and the expansion of this system, especially within the wealthier nations, has increasingly depended on the creation of new forms of commodification. The source of the new commodities was seen to lie increasingly in the area of information and knowledge. It was to be about the ability to create new niches for consumption activities that could be marketed and sold, for example, web pages of your baby to display to the relatives and friends is now big business. E-commerce is seen as the way forward for many businesses as it allows for easier access to consumers, is more flexible and opens up the possibility of a global market. It is in the turning of ideas and knowledge, through the use of new technology, into commodities – objects that can be sold and thus consumed – that the new wave of economic expansion and wealth creation is based. This is seen as part of a neo-liberal economic agenda stressing that everything has a value that can be expressed in dollars. The information economy is thus based around turning ideas into commodities, so we 'patent' our ideas. A recent example in Aotearoa/New Zealand was the development of the Pacific Rose apple; a new breed patented internationally so others could not grow this without the consent of and payment to the developers. The breed is valuable to Aotearoa/New Zealand orchardists, as it enables them to keep ahead of their rivals in other parts of the globe. It was discovered, however, that this breed had been obtained and grown in South America. The fact that it was patented allowed international action to destroy the rogue trees and preserve Aotearoa/New Zealand's invention. The incident demonstrates the increasing problem of protecting 'intellectual property' in a world of global communications where information is often easily available via web sites even without having to be a hacker. In education, under neo-liberal regimes, human capital theory has been favoured as governments seek to recover the cost of higher educational investment from students. Governments have to alter the public perception of education as a general benefit to education as an individual benefit in order to legitimately charge those acquiring the higher skills which will then be reflected in increased earnings over their lifetime. This shift in view has allowed the introduction of student fees and loans schemes rather than grants for study in, for example, Australia, Aotearoa/New Zealand, and the UK from the mid 1980s.

Commodification and the City

The creation of the cyberports and science and technology parks (linking industry and universities and research centres), as a route to knowledge-based economies created around research and development and access to the information superhighways, are now seen as the leading form of economic development. A scramble is consequently taking place amongst cities which desire to remain in the first tier of the global economy to acquire these attributes. The focus on the consumption of new commodities has led also to an emphasis upon cultural production – the expansion of the arts, media, film and television-making, with Ireland often quoted as a case where this has clearly been beneficial. Finally, there has been growth in the demand for leisure and entertainment by those who are engaged in the expanding parts of the economies, the so-called service class (Lash and Urry 1987). They increasingly have discretionary income to spend.

Within the urban context there are an increasing range of commodities on offer, shopping malls, cafes, restaurants, leisure districts, theatres, and sports complexes and people watching. There is more differentiation of products and naming and branding, with people no longer drinking just coffee and wearing jeans. They drink flat whites, short blacks, cappuccinos, lattes or espresso. This is reinforced in the popular media. In the film *Pulp Fiction* (1994), for example, there are segments where the characters sustain an elaborate discussion about the relative merits of such coffees. Similarly, the power of the marketers shapes the clothes-wearing public into segments depending on whether they are in Levi's or Tommy Helfinger jeans or Nike or Reeboks shoes. These symbols of involvement in global culture have now spread everywhere and through sponsorship of sports are constantly brought to the attention of the buying public. The Aotearoa/New Zealand All Blacks (rugby), for example, now have their playing strip supplied by Adidas as part of a global sponsorship arrangement rather than by a local Aotearoa/New Zealand company, Canterbury Apparel, and can be seen live only on Sky Television rather than on the public 'free to air' channel.

The urban literature has been divided about how it conceptualises these shifts. Some analysts see them as minor and simply an extension of previous forms of commodification whereas others see them as more dramatic, and representing not simply a continuity but a transformation of urban life. Certainly the move towards consumption as the driving force of the city has resulted in a dramatic change to the visual form of the city. Further, the revival in the emphasis upon the heritage, culture and uniqueness of the city, as part of its search for its images and branding, has resulted in dramatic changes within many cities to the actual landscape.

Explaining these shifts from within a political economy framework has led to an emphasis upon class-based analysis and has largely seen consumption as the 'passive if flexible consequences of production' (Fine 1995). Furthermore, the emphasis has been around creating difference and reproducing inequality. The shift in the distribution of income, associated with the restructuring of work in the 1980s and 1990s, saw dramatic increases in inequality within many developed countries. The gap between the rich and the poor opened out as a consequence of changes to tax regimes and the gap between the pay and opportunities for those who were in the 'service class' as opposed to the servant class'. The gap and the differences in spending pattern's has given rise to a much more differentiated urban culture and a new set of urban wealth-generating activities centered increasingly around satisfying global and local consumption demands. What is created are 'yuppies', on the one hand, with high-spending power who enjoy the new 'café cultures' which have emerged, often in gentrified inner city areas, and the new urban poor, on the other, who are locked into marginal low-wage jobs or who survive on benefits and become short- and long-term clients of the 'food banks' which have become a feature of many contemporary developed cities.

The decline in collective consumption provisions identified by Castells, among others, leads to the growth of a gap between those who can provide for their consumption needs via the market place and those who remain dependent upon state provisions. The latter find themselves facing more targeted regimes and more restricted opportunities as market-based solutions are increasingly favoured. In housing, for example, income supplementation schemes rather than state provided houses have become more popular. The result has been the growth of public squalor amidst private affluence again exacerbating the differences between those in the upper income brackets and those in low incomes and moving in and out of the job market (Ditch, Lewis and Wilcox 2001).

In analysing the growth of consumer activity, political economists have adopted a macro approach strongly influenced, in the urban literature, by the regulation school model of the transition from Fordism to flexible accumulation. In terms of consumption, they have pointed not to the expansion of consumer choice featured in neo-liberal economic models of the sovereign consumer but to the increasing level of monopoly providers who spend money on advertising to shape taste and encourage spending on the commodities that they provide. This suggests that consumption is not so much driven by the consumers as by local, and the increasingly global producers who influence our taste and control our access. The concentration of ownership in such areas as food selling (supermarkets), fast-food retailing (for example, McDonald's, Burger King, Pizza Hut, Kentucky Fried Chicken), and the growth of global franchising arrangements present the potential consumer with a remarkably similar array of goods, regardless of whether they are consuming these in New York, Los Angeles, Hong Kong, Shanghai, Sydney, Auckland, Paris or London (Ritzer 1998).

Consumer Culture

The writer who in recent times has been most influential in rethinking the place of consumption within the realm of social differentiation is the French writer, Bourdieu. In his book *Distinction*, published in English in 1984, he extends the understanding of capital, drawing attention to cultural, symbolic, social and economic capital. The concept of cultural capital has become widely used within educational theory as a means of accounting for differential learning and different degrees of social reproduction. The acquisition of 'cultural capital' – the capacity to take part in the elaborated codes and speech of educational institutions is more prevalent among the middle class giving their children an advantage in the educational process. Elite groups also are the repositories of such capital and guard access to it through elaborate mechanisms to control entry into their circles. In *Distinction*, Bourdieu explores how what we consume contributes to how distinctions between social groups and individuals are created and preserved. Symbolic and cultural capital are used to display taste. To acquire these markers of style is important for social mobility from one status group to another. The markers relate to such features as location in the right suburbs, membership of clubs, societies and professional bodies and owning the appropriate objects and attributes of distinction. In the 1980s, for example, the ownership by the new 'yuppies' of BMWs and the consumption of imported wines in Auckland, Aotearoa/New Zealand, were seen as markers of membership of the newly rich-propertied class. The 1987 crash rendered some of these newly rich just as quickly the newly poor. Others survived and moved on to acquiring new markers of position. In the mid-to the late 1990s, the symbol of the wealthier sections of the population appeared to be the 4 × 4-wheel-drive recreational vehicle (such as the Land Rover or Toyota Landcruiser and Mitisubishi Pajearo). The choice of vehicle here does seem to be more about style and status than necessity as it is difficult to see the need for such a vehicle for commuting on urban roads or shopping at the mall.

From the work of Bourdieu have come two streams of study. The first has been the concern with social and cultural reproduction which has looked at how distinctions are maintained over time, especially between generations (Longhurst and Savage 1996). The second has been developed particularly in the work of Featherstone (1991) and has centred around consumerism and the growing importance of a separate and distinctive consumer culture. In this work, the emphasis is reversed from the work of the political economists and the consumer, rather than being a manipulated and passive recipient of capital's bidding, becomes much more the individual exercising her/his own agency to shape the productive process. Part of the argument here arises from the restructuring of work and class composition. The growth of the service class working in consumption-related employment has, it is suggested, radically transformed the meaning of work for employees. It is now more often based around individualised contracts and performance agreements. Trade unions and extensive working-class-based occupational groupings have been a casualty of industrial and political change. Thus, class no longer serves as the basis of collective consciousness in a postmodern society (Offe 1975, Gorz 1982, Lash and Urry 1987, Hutton and Giddens, 2000) This leads to an inversion of the traditional Marxian understanding of the relationship between production and consumption and class-(employment) based identity and conciousness (Lash and Urry 1994; Crompton 1998, 2000). Bauman (1992) sees this leading to the replacement of work as the central life interest:

> in present day society, consumer conduct (consumer freedom geared to the consumer market) moves steadily into the position of, simultaneously, the cognitive and moral focus of life, the integrative bond of the society. . . . In other words, it moves into the self same position which in the past – during the 'modern' phase of capitalist society – was occupied by work. (Bauman 1992:49).

The other side of the argument looks at consumption in a rather more positive light and sees the changes from mass-commodity to a more flexible and individualistic form of production to have created more choices for people. The postmodern condition for Bauman means coming to terms with ambivalence, ambiguity of meanings and with the indeterminacy of the future. It thus rejects a simple linear notion of progress and looks to a divergence of future conditions shaped by both global and local processes. Here the celebration of difference and contingency are raised to greater significance than the pursuit of standardisation.

Choice, and the freedom and opportunity that this is seen to bring, can improve the well-being of individuals. This in turn encourages the differentiation of culture rather than the blandness of conformity attributed to modernism and mass-commodity production. In the shift towards a knowledge-based economy and a greater recognition of cultural attributes, cultural capital becomes as important as economic capital in determining status and differentiation and thus in shaping social relations. Culture is also seen as more diverse with different 'cultures' associated with different social groups. One analysis, for example, identified the ascetic culture associated with those in the public service, the postmodernist culture of hedonism and excess associated with professional groups and a 'conventional undistinguished middle class culture associated with managerial groups' (Longhurst and Savage 1996:282). Such discussion raises the question of popular versus high culture and how these distinctions are made and maintained. This links back to the work of Bourdieu where he draws attention to the struggle for difference within contemporary social life.

The shifting of the underlying social ethic from the protestant ethic of hard work, asceticism and duty to one which emphasizes fun or pleasure encourages the pursuit of more hedonistic activity and encourages emphasis upon leisure and recreational activity. Work is for income to spend rather than simply to accumulate. The market is thus constructed around encouraging the development of this consumer desire:

> through the mix of feeling and emotions generated by seeing, holding, hearing, testing, smelling, and moving through the extraordinary array of goods and services, places and environments, that characterise contemporary consumerism (MacNaghten and Urry 1995:213).

What this draws our attention to is the engagement of all our senses in the construction and display of goods and services for our consumption in contemporary urban worlds.

Consumers can exert resistance to global capital and disrupt its influence thus exhibiting agency. In the world of popular music and fashion, there are examples of the presence of counter-cultural resistance to dominant or mainstream activity. Here, there is the ongoing incorporation of some, if not all, the resisters. The Greens, starting out as a radical protest group, have over time become incorporated into the governmental system in many European countries. Clothing is an integral part of creating distinction within a society. However, here it is interesting to see that clothing has been both 'trickled up and down' the social ladder. Blue jeans comprise the best case of the trickle up with what was originally an item of work clothing becoming a fashion item now widely worn across the social spectrum. The branding of jeans and the wearing of the 'right' label are part of the development of distinctions through the wearing of clothing.

Another area of significance is that of eating and drinking where elaborate cultures of consumption have emerged which relate to type of food and how they are prepared and sold (Mennell 1985). The consumption of food also draws attention to the role of the family as the single most important unit of consumption. The household division of labour and the gendered nature of this has been a central topic within feminist analysis of consumption. Concern with food and eating links with the other area of growing interest, the body and the images of the body and the requirements that link to the creation of the ideal and demanded body image. Here, the commodification of the body is one of the significant features of the late twentieth century whereby we are encouraged to develop not just a body but to buy commodities to enhance all the parts of our bodies and even replace or enhance via plastic surgery those parts which are in some way deficient. This is no longer just the preserve of women but increasingly men are becoming equally influenced by the need to project the correct image and are also seeking the assistance of a range of products.

The pressure within this system of consumption is towards the privileging of individual taste. This gives a central place to the market and links to the 'sovereign consumer' of neo-classical economics. The individual is increasingly left and encouraged to make their own decisions and arrangements rather than being looked after or provided for by collective institutions (nanny state):

> while in modern society public consumption activities were organised and controlled through the political and social institutions such as laws, regulations, family, social clubs and religious organisations, in contemporary society any control has to be realised through the market's ability to co-opt counter cultural movements or subversive consumption practices (Firat and Dholakia 1998:71).

In the 1990s many of these strands came together around the 'culture of postmodernity' (Featherstone 1991, 1993). The key characteristics were seen as the fragmentation of work and leisure activity and the increasing importance of the symbolic over the substantial. The ideas of Baudrillard (1988, 1998), have been influential here where he has argued that there has been a breakdown of the distinction between the 'real' and the 'imagined' with a growth in what he terms hyper-reality. We no longer know because we have been present and seen and touched, much of the time we see the events through the lens of the television cameras or on film. We shape our view of the world through the constructions provided by the media. We come to believe that the world is constructed as in the movies or on the soaps. The traveller touring Los Angeles on a tourist bus encounters those who see the city through the films and television series that have been made; the characters are more 'real' than the local inhabitants; or those who when they visit New York have to go to the upper part of Manhattan to see the cafe featured on the cult comedy show, *Seinfeld*! The breakdown of the separation of the real and the imagined is part of the more general critique of dualisms present within postmodern analysis.

One of the consequences has been the introduction into urban analysis of the idea that the city is text and as such can be 'read' in a variety of ways to explore the layers of meaning that have been incorporated into its physical and social structure over the decades of its existence. Seeing the city as text allows the exploration of embodied social values. In the past, much of the writing and analysis of the city was gender blind and privileged the male perspective. Writing was centred on such 'dualisms' as the male city – female suburb, or that of the divide between private and public spaces, with the private spaces as largely the female world of suburbia and the male world that of the 'public city'. Recent work has shown how these dualisms are gross oversimplifications and that the world of women has often been one where the divisions were constantly challenged and broken down. In an interesting analysis of the 'tupperware parties' in the American suburbs of the 1950s, it is shown how selling via this strategy served to both empower women through social networking and challenged the accepted boundaries between domestic spheres and the commercial through using the home as the place of sale (Silverstone 1997). Other work has challenged the view of suburbia as a safe and secure place for women and children by drawing attention to the existence of oppression and violence as well as security and stability (Mort 1996, Valentine 1999).

Seeing the city as text has also been incorporated into analyses of urban design and construction, both historically and contemporarily. This approach can be used to explore such questions as the meaning attached to place and buildings by those who design them and those who use them. The builders and developers of urban space very often have a quite different conception of the spaces they have designed when compared with that held by the end-users. They often disrupt and change the design to make it conform more closely to their purposes and uses. The built form can be viewed as a document that contains embedded meanings that need to be drawn out through a variety of readings of the text. The position of the reader thus becomes significant, for example, architect, developer, city planner, city politician, user, citizen and urban analyst. The various readings will reflect the social norms and values of the various readers and their position within the urban power and social structure. This new emphasis draws our attention to the importance of buildings and the spaces around them and the role that they play within the city. The grand avenues of Paris, built as part of the reconstruction, can be seen as celebrations, as places for display and ceremony or alternatively as ensuring the capacity of the state and civic authorities to exert their control – providing unimpeded ability to control the streets, at a time when they were concerned about revolutionary militancy. Urban design has created sites of symbolic importance such as in the design of Canberra, the site chosen for the federal capital of Australia and developed according to a master plan which featured the federal buildings and connecting avenues in such a way as to create a statement about the nature of the Australian state. In the same vein is the design of the centre of Washington DC, also a symbol of federal state power and an arena for display and pageant.

Not only can we read the text of the city as a whole we can also read the text of the houses that make up the city. If we take the example of a house, we can see the built form with its walls, rooms, roof, forms of cladding, and so on, but the house is also a home. The creation of a 'home' requires us to create out of this physical shell a social construction. Culture, time, household structure, gender, ethnicity and class shape what 'home' means. Similarly, we can think of the city as a built environment of land and buildings but the development of an urban social consciousness, the way of interpreting that set of buildings, is a social process about how we create meaning. As such, it would be based around our social relations and interactions, and the ethnicity, class, gender, age, household structure and family forms that are present.

Once we have accepted that the creation of urban meaning is a social construction then we can think about who is and how they are involved. Generally, it is a combination of individuals, households, and social groups involving both the powerful, usually those whose meanings are dominant (hegemonic) and those with less power. Place-making and the construction of place myths is thus a contested process. The significance of 'place myths' is that they can be seen as the 'real' meaning of a place rather than just one possible construction. This confuses our sense of what is in fact real about a place. Here, the power of the media image and the way that we gain our understanding of places such as Los Angeles, New York and London from film and television become crucial to the contemporary construction of place. One powerful informing lens to the major cities of the world are the promotional videos played as passengers descend to the airport terminals that portray the cities, attractions and unique features to the traveller. The production of such images is part of how the marketers construct the city and how it is 'gazed' upon by tourist and others (Urry 1991, Perkins and Thorns 2001).

The decline of class, and thus of productivist-based analysis, also stems from the reconstruction around the market and the individual. The emphasis has shifted in business to a 'consumer solutions framework' driven by market researchers and 'futures managers' within larger commercial enterprises. This approach seeks to persuade customers that they have the capacity to choose and seek their own solutions, guided by the product managers and service providers, to their lifestyle requirements. The explosion of the lifestyle magazines, devoted to the presentation of the latest trends amongst the affluent, have had a significant impact upon urban design, both in terms of the inside and outside of the house and also neighbourhood design and density requirements (see Chapter 9). Within work, there is also the movement to a more individualised system of operation through Total Quality Management and other contemporary management practices such as performance appraisal and pay, and individual contracts and bonuses. These are based around encouraging people to take more control over their lives and working activity so they are 'empowered' in their work. Not all would see these changes in such a positive light and draw attention to the increased level of uncertainty and instability that arises from such an individualised system. Beck (1992), for example, has written of the individualised society of employees in a risk-fraught system of flexible, pluralised and decentralised under-employment.

To explore the implications of these broad changes further for the nature of city life, it is useful to explore in more detail some of the key areas of consumption change. The three that will be explored are those of shopping, theme parks and urban tourism.

Shopping

The shopping mall has special significance in contemporary accounts of the urban and has been seen as the 'embodiment of the postmodern condition' (Campbell 1995). Others have more popularly seen the malls as the new meeting places, as the new icons of contemporary consumerism and even as the 'new cathedrals' of the city (Duffy 1994). A recent Australian writer commenting on the changing nature of the city and the increasingly important role of consuming in the lives of urban dwellers has noted that the:

> art of shopping is central to our self image as consumers . . . in the shops we are offered the illusion of choice (Spearitt 1994:140).

Clearly within a contemporary economy, 'shopping' is a key activity. As most of us now live in cities, it is a key urban activity. Shopping can be seen as a differentiated activity. It is not just about buying things it is also about entertainment and leisure activity. The nature of the shopping environment has changed with the growth of the enclosed mall with its controlled air-conditioned environment and aura of glamour and seductiveness drawing people in to a variety of experiences including the purchase of commodities but also to satisfy other demands – eating, entertainment, meeting people and being seen. It is the site of the contemporary 'flaneur or stroller', who goes to the mall not necessarily to buy, but to be seen as this is the new place of social gathering and the place where you can display your style to others (Wilson 1992, Savage and Warde 1993, Gilloch and Benjamin 1996).

Shopping has become a much more complex and differentiated activity. The present range of different types of shop is likely to include the corner dairy, the petrol station, increasingly moving into the convenience food sales, local shops at street corners or along open streets, takeaways (fast food outlets), open shopping malls from the 1950s and 1960s, department stores (usually in the centre of the city), inner-city malls and arcades, covered malls, and hypermarkets on the edges of the urban area. There has also been the revival of the less glamorous end of the urban shopping market, no doubt as a reflection of the dual nature of the postmodern city, so we will also find opportunity and second-hand shops, cash converters (pawn brokers) and street and flea markets (Zukin 1995).

This list includes the formalised and the less formalised ways of shopping and recognises the persistence of almost pre-urban forms – such as the street traders and street markets. The rise in the informal economy has meant that informal ways of shopping have been revived in many cities with the growth of 'flea' markets and boot and garage sales as ways of exchanging goods either made, imported or surplus to requirements. Many of these exist in a constant battle with public authorities over the regulation and scope of their activities. Furthermore, in some cases, what started as alternative markets have over time become institutionalised and turned into tourist attractions. In Otara, a predominantly Polynesian area of South Auckland in Aotearoa/New Zealand with high numbers of unemployed and a negative public image, a market for food and goods started in a car park early on a Saturday morning mainly for the local population. This has now turned into a tourist attraction and, increasingly, is seen as a positive development which has the potential to draw people to the area (de Bruin and Dupuis 1995). Another example would be the Amsterdam flea market which features prominently in its tourist literature as a place to visit whilst in the city.

The Development of Shopping

Clearly defined commercial shopping districts grew with urbanisation. There was a need for specialist shops to provide for people now in full-time work. They needed others to do things for them such as produce and sell commodities and develop an infrastructure of local shopping to supply the necessities of everyday life, creating the street-based general stores made famous by Ronnie Barker in *Open All Hours*. The network of local stores, pubs, churches and community meeting places formed the infrastructure of local urban neighbourhoods, the urban villages of Gans' study of Boston (1962) and Bethnal Green of Young and Willmott's *Family and Kinship in East London* (1958).

Shopping on a daily basis at the local store, mostly on foot, was based around a division of labour which required someone, usually the wife/mother, to shop almost daily for food. The domestic 'work' of the household was all consuming and the world of women within this structure was centred on the reproduction of labour power through family maintenance, childcare and domestic cleaning.

During the 1950s and 1960s, with the growth of suburbia and the development of more extensive car ownership, there was the creation of the suburban shopping centre. Here, the new innovation was the supermarket which had under one roof the supply of all commonly used items of household use, groceries, cleaning materials, vegetables, dairy products, meat and fish. This begins the demise of many aspects of the traditional streetscape. There has been a huge shift in the retailing of food since the introduction of the supermarket. It has subjected the sale of food to industrialisation through the deskilling of the workforce as the content of work has changed markedly (Fine 1995). Staff no longer have to know about the products as the consumer makes his/her selection on the basis of information and price provided by the marketing and advertising of items. Supermarkets use a variety of strategies to attract customers including the loss leaders, the heavily discounted promotional item, through to the use of 'own brand products'. Selling has been further changed with the introduction of EFTPOS (electronic funds at point of transfer) and scanning which allows improved inventory control and a decreased need for warehousing facilities, as sales are constantly monitored and additional items ordered to maintain stock. This allows the supermarket chains to tailor the stock to local purchase patterns, assisting in profitability. The contemporary store workers in the typical supermarket do not necessarily have any training in, or a great deal of information about, their products. As a result, in respect to the workforce, the emphasis has been upon low-wage and low-skilled and often part-time employees. In Britain, in 1990, 41% of female workers in food and retailing were part-timers compared to 59% who were full-time. Commenting on the level of training in Britain, Jarvis and Prais (1988:34) noted that:

> The reason British shop assistants so often know hardly anything about what they are selling is that no one has ever taught them; and those responsible for

the main British courses in retailing continue to regard such knowledge as less than essential.

Supermarkets have steadily increased their market share of the food trade. Between 1985 and 1991, the proportion supplied by specialist retailers, in Britain, shrank from 21 per cent to 16 per cent. With the supermarkets as the key arena of shopping has come the increased use of the car and the tendency towards the once-a-week large shop. This in turn sets up the need for access to a car and the extension of the shopping hours to accommodate both changing patterns of household employment and access to the household car in those without multiple car ownership. The ownership of the supermarkets has over time become consolidated with a small number of large players dominating the market. In Britain, five companies dominate the market, Tesco, Sainsbury, Gateway, Argyll and Asda. This pattern is repeated across most of the developed countries and cities where retailing along the high streets for food has become less significant relative to the supermarkets and the market has increasingly been dominated by a small number of owners.

One of the earliest malls was established in 1931 in the USA at Highland Park. The concept was of shops away from the street around an enclosed courtyard. By 1946, there were eight such shopping centres in the USA. By the 1950s, the concept had evolved a further stage with the development of the department store as the mall 'anchor'. It was seen as necessary to have something to attract people from an increasingly large area to come to the mall for their shopping so the idea arose of having one super attraction. This was provided by the suburban version of the central city department store which had been a successful inner-city merchandising outlet. These new style malls were beginning to exert a pull over an urban region of up to 25 miles (40 km) from their location. What we see beginning here is a shift from shopping as a necessity to shopping as a pleasure and recreational activity – about meeting people and forming a part of the sense of community or neighbourhood. In this transition, we have moved from the walking city of localised streets to the mall which is a commercialised meeting place of controlled space, owned and operated by a company, who are in the business of selling. Thus, we have seen a shift of activity from a public space, the high street, into a private space, the shopping mall. Further, once these become fully enclosed, it is a space where who has access to the space becomes subject to surveillance and control by those who own and manage the malls. The malls are increasingly organised selling spaces, with a need to get people to come and spend and consume. Thus, there has been a push to move beyond the 'shop' and to generate interest and revenue through the food courts, themed areas and in the provision of entertainment and competitions.

The next step in the development of the mall is the supermall. The enclosed mall, to service a region, builds a set of other activities and experiences around shopping to underline that shopping is not just about the buying of necessities but is also a leisure-time and pleasurable activity. The new formula is the one-stop climate-controlled shopping experience. Food was the first to be added to the mix with the development of the food courts. These introduced an element of the exotic through their multi-ethnic cuisine, delivered through chain restaurants, and the use of the atrium designs and 'natural' vegetation to give the impression of outdoor alfresco dining within the air-conditioned comfort of the mall. By the 1990s, the USA and Canada had over 47,000 malls including the largest in the world at West Edmonton. Here the mall combined retailing with a theme park (Shields 1996). As the malls get bigger and more numerous so there is more competition for customers and more varied 'anchors' have been sought. In the late 1990s and early 2000s, these are likely to include; department stores, chain stores (multi-retailing such as K Mart), multiplex cinemas, sports complexes, museums and art galleries, eating areas, historical reconstructions, themed areas and convention centres (Judd and Fainstein 1999).

The new malls are themed and seemingly diverse, yet tend to share the same characteristics, not just within a particular nation state but across the globe. So whether you are in Toronto, New York, Gateshead, Edmonton, Shanghai, Pacific Plaza on the Gold Coast (Australia), Singapore or Hong Kong, there will be elements of design, contents, presentation and marketing that will be familiar (Miller et al. 1999). Malls have more diversified anchors extending the range to educational institutions as in Hong Kong where one route to City University lies through an upmarket international shopping mall, or the same city's Royal Plaza, a mall linked to a five-star hotel or in Singapore Suntech City which incorporates a mall into a commercial business complex specialising in information technology. They have also spread around the globe with Bangkok now containing two of the worlds biggest malls (Mullins 1999). In the Middle East, a recent mall development in Abu Dhabai has been focused around providing a place attractive to women as they are seen as major purchasers. The 'She Mall' is promoted as providing for the 'whole of life' and has, in addition to shops, a cinema and a health and business centre (Thomas 2000). The spread of the mega mall reflects the growth of the local middle class with discretionary income and the growth of international tourism as a form of economic development.

Much of the marketing is globally linked to franchised activity with the ubiquitous McDonalds gracing many a food court along with Subway, Kentucky Fried Chicken and pizza- and kebab-makers along with a variety of Asian cuisine. Global marketing strategies are now shaping how the 'selling' is being presented. The latest batch shows the influence of the grouping of similar shops, for example, all shoe stores in one area, women's and men's fashions in another, the opening out of areas for display, mall entertainment and for the 'strollers' who come to be seen.

In the 1970s, a new trend that emerged in a number of older cities hit by restructuring and industrial decline was the inner city mall. These new malls were seen as a vital aspect of reviving inner city areas and encouraging the return of both people and activity. In the USA, Baltimore has often been seen as one of the more successful developments. In the 1970s to 1980s, the city undertook a massive downtown redevelopment based on the inner harbour area of the city, which was at this time a 'wasteland along the city's waterfront composed of ramshackled warehouses and decaying wharves' (Levine 2000:129). The Rouse Corporation as part of this development built a $22-million festival marketplace comprising two pavilions of shops, restaurants and markets. One result of this large scale redevelopment was to boost inner-city employment with an 80 per cent growth between 1970 and 1995. However, despite the fact that Baltimore was amongst the most successful US cities to adopt this growth strategy, it has not fully addressed the problems of long-term social and economic decline across the city as a whole arising from its decline as an industrial city (Levine 2000).

Reconstructed inner-city malls are now seen as attractions for both local and urban tourists and a necessary extension to the range of facilities and services provided. In the suburban and outer urban malls, tourism is less significant and here the emphasis has been upon trying to integrate them into the wider community, by encouraging the use of the malls for seniors to do their aerobics and jogging in the mornings before the mall opens for normal retailing. This provides a safe and climate-controlled environment for 'healthy' activity, no doubt followed by the possibility of consumption in the food court, where again the emphasis would be upon the healthy and nutritional nature of the produce. The marketing of the food around the idea that it is natural and fresh has increased with the greater attention to health and well-being in the last few decades. Other ways of achieving this integration are through the promotion of the mall as the new community centre and gathering place, the new civic squares of the late twentieth and twenty-first centuries. Here, the shift of space from the public domain of the open square and public street to the private space of the mall marks a significant shift towards greater privatisation within the urban environment.

Theme Parks

The modern mall, as we have seen, is about shopping and the selling of experiences and encouraging a culture of consumption and fostering desire. It encourages hedonism and pleasure; it seeks to transport the consumer into a world of choice in which the consumer is in control. The creation of the theme park, another major twentieth-century invention, is similarly aimed at creating fantasy and the illusion, of escapism and reinforcing the message that postmodernity is about fun rather than work. The theme park incorporates both nostalgia for the past, with its reconstructions of 'Main Street' with its specialist shops, and the defining historical moments of the community or nation's past. These representations are often only loosely connected to the actual historical record and thus the question arises as to their 'authenticity'. Are they fake and a giant con or do they reflect our past or simply the myths of our past? In settler societies, the glorification of the frontier, such as the Australian outback, and the American West are often featured in their myths. The other motif is transportation into the future, where the world to come is imagined and presented, as at Disney's EPCOT (Experimental Prototype Community of Tomorrow) centre in Florida and, formerly, in Britain's Millennium Dome at Greenwich. What this play on the past and the invention of the future contribute to is the breaking down of the distinction between the 'real' and the 'imagined' worlds in which we live (Baudrillard 1988).

The theme park may have extended from the designated 'parks' such as Disneyland in Anaheim, Southern California, and Disney World in Orlando, Florida, to the city itself (Gottdiener 1997). In his analysis of Los Angeles, Soja (1993) has speculated on whether it is possible to consider the whole city as a giant theme park given its exposure on film and television. On a recent visit to Los Angeles, I took a bus tour of the city and was struck by one passenger from Delaware who maintained an animated conversation (public) with the driver in which he relived his film- and television-watching through the streets of Los Angeles. To him the city represented these programmes and films. They were more real than the present landscape and people. Soja also describes how a new subdivision in Southern California was based around the Don Quixote stories, each of the streets was named after a character or event and, to ensure 'authenticity' and add a 'touch of reality', characters toured the streets in the appropriate costumes (Soja 1993).

Theme Parks – History and Development

The history of the theme park lies in the creation of the world fairs and great exhibitions in the late eighteenth century to celebrate the achievements of industrial capitalism. To the present day, there has been a series of global fairs celebrating technological and scientific achievements and promoting trade between nation-states. One of the earliest of such fairs was the Great Exhibition of 1851 at the Crystal Palace in London. Here, in a specially created building with a glass roof, all the works of industry were presented, displayed and celebrated. All the technological wonders of the age were there for the public to come and marvel at. It spoke of science and progress and of course the robustness of industrial capitalism!

The other strand that links to the creation of the theme park is that of utopian sentiment. Here, ideas about progress were strong as people sought to dream about what the future might and could contain. The utopian socialists of the nineteenth century with their ideas for model factories and communities containing new ways of living and working were the pioneers. In the twentieth century, it was people such as Walt Disney, associated with the entertainment and film industry, who became interested in the imagined future – a future shaped by science and technological inventions and solutions to current problems, such as the mono-rail in Disneyland as the way to solve the urban transportation problems of the congested cities and provide the means of linking the new urban areas together in a series of linked satellites or clusters. Tomorrow Land at Disneyland-Anaheim was the prototype for the Epcot centre and Disney World in Florida that were part of a much grander Walt Disney scheme for future urban settlement. Here, the Disney company owned and controlled its own land and was intent on creating a new community alongside of, rather than under the control of, the state planning system. This they were able to do because of their corporate wealth and power (Fogelsong 1996, 1999). The theme park here was an attempt to take us into the future so we could see what it was like and encourage us to aspire to this vision. In this vision, we find nature being ordered and controlled. It is not a free-flowing space but a very ordered one. There is a strict separation of people and traffic with circulation along organised and clearly demarcated paths. The suggested message is that the urban environment is controlled by the experts, the planners and technologists who provide the context for us to live out our lives efficiently and safely. It is a contrived world rather than one that encourages spontaneity. The endless emphasis on the theme of Disneyland as the 'happiest place on earth' appears to privilege fun and enjoyment, but this is within clearly circumscribed limits and a very orderly environment. The time spent by the patrons in the queues for the few minutes of excitement on one of the rides at the fun parks attests to the elements of control.

The key elements of the theme park as a new machinery for pleasure are seen as:

> evocations of travel in time and space (futuristic element) lilliputianization, physics defying rides, ecstatic relationships to new technology, efficient

organisation of architecture of spectacle and coercion and aspirations to urbanism (Sorkin 1992:394).

At Disneyland, the transport systems that work seamlessly and cleanliness that speaks of a healthy and wholesome environment create the sense of escape from a dysfunctional outside world where the undisciplined complexities within the city prevail. It takes away the unpredictability present in much of everyday life.

Disney World at Orlando in Florida, like the garden city of Howard's utopian book, is located on the urban perimeter with access to the theme park by car for leisure commuters. The park is ringed by accommodation and smart people-movers operate at the edges of the site, but once inside the park visitors are pedestrianised. A clear functional separation of activities, representing a modernist view of planning based upon strict separation of activities, is practised. Internally, the theme park follows the radial pattern moving out from the centre and is arranged in thematic fields or areas such as Frontierland, and Tomorrow Land. The trick of the theme park is to encourage the visitor in the belief that what is being shown is 'just like the world only better' (Zukin 1991, Sorkin 1992). In this sense it seeks an intensification of the present.

Disneyland has now spread beyond North America with the opening of one in Tokyo, in 1983, one in Paris, in 1992, and one now planned for Hong Kong. Disneylands are seen as good generators of employment and tourism development with the proposed Hong Kong site estimated to generate 6000 construction jobs and 18,000 permanent jobs and attract visitors to bolster the local tourist economy. The largest volume of visitors, in 1998, was to the Tokyo Disney site with 16.7 million, followed by Disney World in Florida with 15.6 million, and next in popularity was the original Disneyland at Anaheim in Southern California with 13.7 million, and finally Euro Disney in Paris with 12.8 million. This gave a grand total of 87.3 million visitors for the year to all the Disney sites (*The Press*, 3 November 1999).

Urban Tourism and Place-making

Urban tourism has been linked to the redevelopment and regeneration of the city. As we noted previously, the redevelopment of inner-city shopping malls in buildings, which were often originally the site of industrial activity, has been one of the initiatives for encouraging people to visit and return to the central cities. This, in turn, increases the inner-city resident population and revives the flagging rate base. Other initiatives have been around the re-introduction of trams, the preservation of old buildings and the construction of a new range of attractions including casinos, convention centres, towers and restaurants and entertainment districts (Judd 1999). Southeast-Asian urban tourism has been strongly associated with the 'pleasures of sun, sea, sand, sex, shopping, drugs, food and entertainment' (Mullins 1999:250, see also Lewis 1998). The importance of sex in part reflects the role the cities of Bangkok and Manila played for American service men on their extended rest and recreation leaves during the Vietnam war. At the end of the war, sex tourism was then marketed as part of the tourism experience to the extent that 'male oriented package tours draw large numbers, mostly from Japan' (Mullins 1999:250). The diversification of the tourism product across Southeast-Asian cities has led to the addition of mega malls, the development of historic districts, buildings and heritage and the marketing of the local material culture. In the case of Singapore, in order to market the heritage of the city, some reconstruction was required as much of the original urban landscape had been destroyed to make way for modern high-rise commercial construction. Bangkok has been engaged recently in diversifying its urban development through encouraging a broader range of tourist attractions, including cultural and heritage sites and seeking to establish the city as one of the key financial, business and information nodes within the Southeast-Asian region (see Box 6.1).

Box 6.1

Bangkok, Thailand: consumption spaces

- Population, 2000   6.4 million, 27th largest city in the world

- Population estimate, 2010   7.4 million, 26th largest city in the world

Bangkok is the capital of Thailand and its largest city. It exerts strong primacy – as is characteristic of other Southeast-Asian capital cities (Malaysia – Kuala Lumpur, Indonesia – Jakarta, S. Korea – Seoul, the Philippines – Manila). Rapid urbanisation occurred from the 1950s creating strong inward migration. The lack of a capacity and/or willingness to house this flow of migrants, either by the state or private sector, created slum and squatter settlements on vacant unused land in both central and peripheral areas. Many of the areas became surrounded by later development.

The economic development of the city has centred around two main activities. The first is the fact that it is the centre of the nation's financial, trading, government and communications activities. Here, the city has sought to compete with the other cities of the region – Singapore and Kuala Lumpur – to attract international capital and secure itself a significant place in the Asian region. Secondly, it has developed the infrastructure of

Continued

an international airport and five-star hotels and attempted to improve its traffic problems to position itself with respect to business and tourism activities.

Tourism and consumption activities have been significant in the promotion and image that Bangkok has developed. It is the connection with 'sex tourism' and the idea that it is 'a capital of desire' which has often shaped the media and external images of the city (Lewis 1998). The creation of Bangkok's image as the centre of desire in part relates back to the presence of the US military and extended recreation leave during the Vietnam War. Once this was over, the presence of a well-established sex industry was then marketed and attracted 'male oriented packaged tours drawing large numbers, mostly from Japan, to the sex markets of Bangkok' (Mullins 1999:250). Mullins further indicates that, by the early 1990s, 800,000 prostitutes were working in the Thai sex industry.

Tourism is thus a major factor in shaping the city. To broaden the appeal of the city and to encourage a change of image, Bangkok has sought to develop its consumption activities through the building of shopping malls. Between 1990 and 1994, for example, the city doubled its retailing space and possessed, in 1994, two of the world's five largest shopping malls.

The conflict over land use and the creation of new wealthy sectors oriented towards the global economy have produced pressures upon the areas settled by squatters in the 1960s and these areas have been the scene of ongoing struggles over the continuing rights of the dwellers to stay in these locations (Parnwell and Wongsuphasawat 1997).

The second half of the 1990s brought the Asian crisis that led to the devaluation of the Thai currency and indications that the boom economy was a thing of the past. The future development of Bangkok will depend on the mix of economic activity and the extent to which it can shed its image of the sex and drug capital, a place to satisfy desire, and establish itself as a more wide-ranging 'global' city providing financial and consumer services to a growing, wealthier population within the Southeast Asian region.

City web site: *http://www.bma.go.th/*

Urban tourism is about the remaking of place whereas 'tourism urbanisation' is about the making of cities that owe their existence to tourism. Examples of such areas are now found around the globe. Significant developments have occurred in the Gold and Sunshine Coast in Australia, a region that, since the 1970s, has changed from an area catering mainly for locals to one which is now firmly part of the international circuit. The Costa del Sol in Southern Spain is an area that became popular, particularly with British tourists in the 1960s, and expanded on the back of cheap package deals and cut-price air travel which gave rise to an urbanised strip along the coast. In Southeast Asia there has been the growth of resort towns around the Gulf of Thailand including Pattaya and Phuket, and Bali in Indonesia has been a favoured place for Europeans with direct jet flights to Denpasar. Tourism links to our concern with consumption. Focused on the selling of pleasure, tourism is seen as one of the exemplars of contemporary consumerism.

Tourists escape their everyday lives and, for the period they are a tourist, they are in a different world which often allows them to throw off the constraints and conventions of the everyday and experience different and new sensations. Urry, in a significant analysis of tourism in his book the *Tourist Gaze* (1991), sees tourism as 'imaginative hedonism'. The anticipation of the experience is nearly as significant as the actual. The promotional material encourages this and so does the virtual-reality planning that is now available through new computer technology and the surfing of the World Wide Web. For the tourist travelling to her/his destination, there is a transition from the everyday world to the unfamiliar and potentially exotic location, a transportation in space and time. In understanding the urban tourist, Urry encourages us to see the significance of what he terms the 'tourist gaze'. Working from Foucault, Urry (1991:1) argued that when we go away 'we look at the environment . . . We gaze at what we encounter . . . and the gaze is socially constructed'. The gaze is a concept comprising a way of looking at the world which simultaneously forms what is seen and *the* way of seeing. However, the gaze is not static and is not necessarily constructed by the tourist her or himself but is often constructed for the tourist by the tour operators and local or global industry. Who constructs the tourist gaze thus becomes a significant question to explore. Urry points to the 'array of professionals' who attempt 'to reproduce ever-new objects of the tourist gaze' (1991). Thus, the image-makers are a crucial component of what the tourist sees and does in the city. The guide books and brochures, which are showered upon the tourist at the airport, train station or ferry terminal as they arrive in any major city, provide the entry into the images of that particular city. These images are the representations that the image-makers want us to hold in our heads and the lens they want us to use to see the nature of their city. The tourist thus approaches the city via the images of the place-makers which leads us to an argument about what constitutes an authentic experience. Are there any left, or are all our experiences of contemporary cities as visitors staged events to an extent that most easily accessible tourist experiences are hopelessly and shamelessly fake? (Perkins and Thorns 2001a).

Place promotion is in part a process whereby cities, regions and countries are imbued with new meanings and sold through the agency of advertising, packaging and market positioning (Britton 1991). In this process, the landscapes, social practices, buildings, residents, symbols and meanings of places are potentially available for sale to investors and tourists. Place promotion also includes a representational element directed at local residents. Positive images of places are created by local government agencies and private-sector boosters which are designed to encourage locals to feel good about their home towns and the quality of life that can be had there. Place promotion is a subject about which there has been considerable theoretical debate, much of it centred on differing interpretations of place commodification (Perkins and Thorns 2000b). In neo-Marxist terms, place commodification is related to what Best (1989) calls the society of the commodity and its later transformation into the society of the spectacle (Debord 1983). In the society of the commodity, commodification represents an inversion of exchange value over use value. Objects, in this case places, become commodities when they take on an exchange value over and above their use values and are able to be traded, putting them into the realm of the quantitative. In the society of the spectacle, posited as a way of accounting for the changed empirical conditions of late capitalist society and economy (the period from around 1980 onwards), commodification is a product of a way of living where individuals consume a world made by others rather than producing their own (Debord 1983, Best 1989:29–30). Adherents of this view see spectacle as a complex notion referring, at the simplest level, to mass media society but more deeply to the vast institutional and technical apparatus of late capitalism, which obscures the experience of continuing alienation. The spectacle therefore pacifies and depoliticises and takes the form of a permanent 'opium war' (Debord 1983:14 quoted in Best 1989:29). The narcotics in this case are commodified forms of leisure and entertainment which, while they seem to meet peoples' needs and satisfy them, are in fact a new form of deprivation which take us from Marx's *being into having* to Debord's *having into appearing*. Here, image takes precedence over material objects and 'the universalisation of the commodity form is to be seen as the reduction of reality to appearance, its subsumption to commodity form, its subsequent *commodification*' (Best 1989:32).

Place promotion in these terms blurs the line between illusion and reality. Debord (1983) and his contemporaries extended this theme as they focused their analytical efforts on the nature of the image. They concluded that, in late capitalism illusion overtakes reality and images impose themselves as the tangible and are taken as the real: illusion is authenticated as more real than the real itself (Best 1989).

Place promotion does not therefore necessarily make places meaningless and phoney. Nor does it necessarily create place meanings that are irresistible. Massey (1995:190) offers a useful direction in this respect suggesting that:

> the description, definition and identification of a place is thus always inevitably an intervention not only into geography but also, at least implicitly, into the

(re)telling of the historical constitution of the present. It is another move in the continuing struggle over the delineation and characterisation of space-time.

Place promotion is therefore one of a number of processes at play in the creation of place that must be investigated in specific time-space locations at the intersection of the global and local. Increased commercialisation of a place and its activities, or new forms of commercialisation, will not therefore destroy a place in the sense of making it meaningless; rather it will take the form of a new importation around which local and global actors (including tourists, investors, marketeers, urban planners and managers, politicians and locals), will compete and/or cooperate in the ongoing and emergent construction of the meaning of place (Schollman et al. 2000).

The creation of places often involves conflict and struggle over the appropriation of the images. This can be illustrated in the case of Bondi beach, an urban beach suburb of Sydney. The image of the beach in Australia is one of the outdoors, of the sun, sand and surf, of bronzed bodies and of fitness, of leisure and pleasure in a free-flowing lifestyle. On the beach 'normal' rules are changed and life is governed by hedonism and pleasure. Here, we find a combination of the urban and nature where people can struggle with and overcome nature through their contest with the surf and the sharks! The nature of Bondi as a place within both Sydney and Australia has, however, been subject to conflict in recent years between those claiming to represent the local community and those wanting to develop Bondi as an international tourist attraction. The developers wanted to construct a 'sense of place . . . not for those who live there, but for those who come to see, to consume' (Game 1991:181). The developers essentially wanted to commodify Bondi, to market and sell it as yet another object of the international and national tourist gaze. The locals thus far have been successful in resisting change and so maintaining their 'place' identity against that of the developers. A further set of disputes arose in 1999 when the Sydney Olympic Games Organising Committee wanted to build a beach volleyball facility on Bondi Beach. Again, the locals protested at this invasion into their space and attempted to resist through protest. However, this time they were unsuccessful and the facility was constructed.

Summary

The chapter has explored the growth of consumer activity and the debate surrounding whether this constitutes greater choice or greater delusion amongst the population. Choice is seemingly everywhere. We are encouraged to consume an ever-greater array of commodities and to develop more varied and flexible lifestyles. The shopping mall, theme park and urban tourism are features of the city that link to this greater emphasis on consumption activity. The new urban forms which are thereby generated also reflect the increasing wealth held by some as a result of global and local restructuring, creating a high consuming group who fuel urban change. Not all, however, are part of this consuming society which leads to new forms of urban social exclusion. We will now turn, in the next chapter, to investigate the other side of recent urban change and see how far this has also created new groups of poor and marginalised urban dwellers.

Further Reading

Consumption

Featherstone, M., 1991, *Consumer Culture and Post Modernism*. London: Sage. Chapter 3, *Towards a Sociology of Postmodern Culture*, pp. 28–50, traces the growth of the debate about postmodernism and culture, the rise of a new middle class and the growing importance of distinctions.

Savage, M. and Warde, A., 1993, *Urban Sociology, Capitalism and Modernity*. London: Macmillan Press – now Palgrave Macmillan. Chapter 6, *Modernity, Postmodernity and Urban Culture*, pp. 122–46. This is an excellent review of the key arguments and writers in this area of debate.

Shopping

Spearitt, P., 1994, 'I shop therefore I am'. Chapter 9, pp. 129–140, in Johnson, L., (ed.) *Suburban Dreaming*. Geelong, Victoria: Deakin University Press. The article looks at the development of shopping in Australia and provides a critique of the shopping mall as a contemporary consumption space.

Zukin, S., 1995, *The Culture of Cities*. Cambridge, Mass.: Blackwells. Chapter 6, 'While the City Shops', pp. 187–258. This chapter analyses the different forms of shopping in New York focusing on change in downtown Brooklyn as a case study of how shopping and urban renewal have been connected.

Theme Parks

Gottdiener, M., 1997, *The Theming of America: Dreams, Visions and Commercial Spaces*. Boulder, Colorado: Westview Press. Chapter 4, 'The Themed Culture *and* Themed Environments', pp. 68–97 and Chapter 5, The Las Vegas Casino and Theme Park, and Further Extension of Themed Environments, pp. 98–125.

These chapters take up the theme of the shift from a 'society of producers' to a 'society of consumers' and review some of the new products of consumption available within the urban environment and the associated creation of new 'spaces of consumption' within the contemporary city in the USA.

Zukin S., 1991, *Landscapes of Power: From Detroit to Disneyland*. Berkeley: University of California Press. Chapter 8, 'Disney World: The Power of the Facade/The Facade of Power', pp. 217–50.

This chapter argues that the new landscapes of power have turned the traditional image of centrality associated with cities 'inside out' creating more fragmented cities and that the new landscapes in places such as Los Angeles and Miami are cities built on the power of 'dreamscape, collective fantasy and façade'.

Tourism

Mullins, P., 1999, 'International Tourism and the Cities of Southeast Asia'. In Judd, D.R. and Fainstein, S., eds, *The Tourist City*, New Haven, USA and London: Yale University Press. This chapter is a good analysis of the growth of both urban tourism and tourism urbanisation in Southeast Asia.

Urry, J., 1991, *The Tourist Gaze*. London: Sage. Chapter 1, 'The Tourist Gaze', pp. 1–15. Provides an introduction to the idea of the 'tourist gaze' that became a significant informing idea in the analysis of tourism during the 1990s.

Place-making

Urry, J., 1995, *Consuming Places*. London: Routledge. Chapter 1, 'Time, Space and the Consumption of Place', pp. 1–30 explores the question of how people actually experience social relations and how these contribute to the sense of place that is constructed. Important here are relations of time and space that get reworked dramatically in today's world of new information technologies.

Web Sites

Shopping

http://www.westedmall.com/indexflash2.asp
http://www.suntec.com.sg/index.phtml
http://www.seaconsquare.com/

Theme parks

http://2000.disneylandparis.com/
http://www.tokyodisneyresort.co.jp/
http://www.ratcage.com/disney/parks/disneyland/

7

Urban Social Inequality and Social Exclusion

Introduction

The analysis of urban social inequality and social exclusion focuses our attention on the other side of the contemporary city. In the last chapter, we examined the nature of urban consumption. This emphasized the successful and glamorous side of the city and the increased range of commodities for purchase and activities to engage in for those with the requisite financial and associated resources. The contemporary city has created wealth and poverty, the included and the excluded. There has been the growth of the food banks alongside the new cafe culture. There has been a growth in the relative difference between the wealthy and the poor in most of the developed world's cities, reflecting economic, social and political shifts. The idea of social exclusion draws our attention to those who, for various reasons, have missed out in the changes that have taken place over the last decades of the twentieth century and raises questions about the extent and significance of polarisation, segregation and exclusion in the restructuring of the city and urban life.

In April 1998, a conference was held at the UN in New York around the issues of aging and urbanisation in preparation for the 1999 International Year of Older Persons. The theme for that year was working towards 'a society for all'. At the conference, it was pointed out that, although the 'bipolar' world of the cold-war days had now gone, this did not mean that the present period was one of growing equality between the nations or within the nations. The global gap between the rich and the poor of the world has continued to grow with the gap between the richest 20 per cent of the world and the poorest 20 per cent doubling in the past 10 years. Further, 358 billionaires control assets equivalent to the assets of the poorest 45 per cent of the world's population. In the present world, the largest item of expenditure continues to be on weapons of warfare, about $750 billion per year. The amount of money consumed by illicit drugs follows this (Castells 1998). Such global inequalities bring us back to the

149

question of social exclusion and social integration. The excluding of people from the mainstream of society, within the city and the wider social context, provides the basis for the formation of ghettoes and an underclass of marginal and deprived people. It creates a waste of human potential and can become a destabilising factor upon society.

The purpose of this chapter is to explore the debate and extent of urban social inequality and exclusion. The cities of both the developed and the developing world have their excluded populations. In the developing world there are greater numbers of squatter and illegal settlers who live in makeshift shelters on the margins. These vary from the street dwellers of Mumbai to the favella dwellers of Brazil. In Santa Andre, for example, a district of Sao Paulo, there are 123 slums (favellas) in which approximately 67,000 people are living out of a total population of 620,000. The majority have no basic infrastructure services like water, sewage, drainage, and solid waste collection (Celso and Klink 1999). Further variants are the overcrowded inner-city tenements and those affected by natural and other disasters who erect temporary shelters which in many cases have become permanent – such as the victims of the earthquakes in Kobe, Japan in 1995, and Istanbul, Turkey in 1999 where there has been a failure to create a long-term solution. In these various cases, the occupants have an uneasy relationship with political authorities and limited access to services and amenities and little security over their shelter (UNCHS 1996a, 2001a). A further group would be the refugees from war and ethnic cleansing such as in Kosovo and East Timor.

Within many of cities of the developed and developing world, social inequality is generally associated with spatial segregation, poverty, unemployment and lack of skills, rendering many individuals marginal to the workforce and thus to the necessary income to secure them a place in the mainstream of society. Unemployment and underemployment have been identified as one of the major causes of the urban crisis (UNCHS 1996a, 2001a). The crisis is seen to manifest itself in the deterioration of living standards, lack of adequate social and physical infrastructure, crime, violence, drug addiction, homelessness and overcrowding.

Under the political and economic changes of the 1990s, unemployment has remained as a significant feature of the economies of the developing and developed countries. The cause of unemployment and thus of social exclusion has been increasingly identified as lying in the individual's deficiencies and failures, of education, training, and lack of work experiences. Thus, the 'solutions' have been seen in 'workfare schemes, where benefits are tied to the re-entry into the workforce or into work-related training schemes' (Higgins 1999). Such 'solutions' tend to emphasize the 'private trouble' nature of social exclusion rather than its significance as a 'public issue'.

During the 1990s, there has been a major shift in the discourse of disadvantage away from poverty and inequality to an emphasis upon social exclusion. Levitas (1998) identifies three discourses of exclusion now prominent in the UK and Europe. The first of these is the re-distributional discourse, which focuses upon poverty and inequality and the distribution and re-distribution of wealth. This, however, has been overshadowed in recent debates by the following two exclusion discourses. The second, the moral underclass, focuses upon the moral and behavioural delinquency of the excluded. It broadens out the range of 'excluded' from poverty and low income and thus employment to also include exclusion on the basis of gender, sexual orientation, disability, age, and citizenship status. One result of this has been an increased level of research and debate focused around measuring and identifying all forms and potential forms of exclusion. This may have the effect of submerging the 'problem' under a weight of definitional argument and measurement problems as ever more complex matrices are developed (Quinti 1999). The final discourse is the social integrationist and has a strong following in the EU where the focus is on integration rather than exclusion. Exclusion is understood here as the 'breakdown of the structural, cultural and moral ties which bind the individual to society, and family stability is a key concern' (Levitas 1998:21). However, social exclusion has not been seen in a uniform way across Europe with significant differences in emphasis appearing. For example, in France, the integrationist perspective has been more prominent (Blanc 1998). Blanc also draws attention to the fact that exclusion is not a state but rather entails a process whereby people experience a progressive loss of their identity and involvement with the wider society. An emphasis on process would restructure analysis away from the question of how many are excluded, or in poverty or without a home to questions of how did people become homeless, what was their experience of homelessness and how did they find their way out of this situation? Was this by state policy intervention or was it through their own strategies or through a combination (Anderson 2001)?

Researchers in many countries have studied groups which are seen as marginal – economically, culturally, socially and spatially – in order to document the nature and scale of their inequalities. Political concerns have centred on re-including people into the 'mainstream' of society. The mainstream here stays unproblematic and is assumed to be where all people want to be. It thus has elements of conformist and neo-conservative social ideology, which is resistant to divergence and difference. The concern with re-including also takes attention away from the majority that are treated as an undifferentiated social group, thus ignoring the way in which differences in wealth and position have opened out within European and American societies over the 1990s. The political discourse of the third way also links through to this discussion of social exclusion, as this too is more concerned with individual opportunities than with structural inequalities (Giddens 1998, 2001).

Definitions of Social Exclusion

The key question here relates to who is being excluded and from what in today's cities? The popularity of 'social exclusion' rather than a focusing on income deprivation or poverty, links to the rise of a greater attention to identity politics and the broadening of the understanding of 'exclusion' away from the traditional welfare focus upon poverty and income to also include ethnicity, gender, sexual orientation, disability, and age. Castells defines social exclusion as:

> the process by which certain individuals and groups are systematically barred from access to positions which would enable them to have an autonomous livelihood within the social standards framed by institutions and values in a given context (1998:73).

This definition draws our attention to a number of key ideas. It is about the systematic barring of access so it requires us to look at both structural and individual aspects of our cities. One of the key areas of exclusion is from access to relatively regular, paid labour, for at least one member of a stable household. This relates to housing: for example, if there are only a few people living on the streets without secure shelter it may be possible to see them as making a lifestyle choice but, where there are many thousands, this looks to be most unlikely and suggests that the city housing market is not producing sufficient houses at an affordable price.

The second aspect it draws attention to is that of 'autonomous life', one free from an over dependency upon agencies and institutional control. This speaks to the need to examine the barriers placed in the way of particular social groups from reaching their potential. Social exclusion is the process by which certain individuals are denied access to positions and resources to live a fully participative life. The excluded are those who fall outside the regular, paid workforce and the welfare safety net. Thus in many societies, even wealthy ones, there are the unemployed, the homeless, refugees and those with restricted citizenship rights. Social exclusion is not simply about the denial of material resources but also about political and citizenship rights. It can also be about the absence of gender equality in such areas as land inheritance or jobs, and it can further include restrictions on the participation of the older members of a society in the full range of activities through poor design and planning which does not provide people with a safe and secure environment.

Finally this definition draws attention to the values which are prevalent within the particular social context. The increased recognition given to discriminatory practices and attitudes has been significant in improving the awareness and action against exclusionary practices. Here, issues of segregation and discriminatory employment, along with other human rights abuses, have become more central to local and national political agendas. There still remains, however, considerable discrepancy between the rhetoric of inclusion and the actual practices within the cities of the world.

Social exclusion can take place at a number of levels. It can be about individual access to work, training, buildings and facilities and public and private spaces or it can be about the exclusion of particular neighbourhoods, cities and regions from access to economic and social development. Contemporary global capitalist development is, according to some analysts (Castells 1998), relatively footloose and impervious to the needs of the local population and thus is characterised by simultaneous economic development and underdevelopment. Lee and Murie (1994), see social exclusion as about the extremely marginal groups of people outside the welfare safety net, namely the unemployed, homeless, refugees, and those with restricted citizenship rights, often those who are mentally and/or physically disabled. Programmes of de-institutionalisation have been common through the 1980s and 1990s leading to the former occupants of institutional psychiatric care moving into the community. In some cases, this has been accompanied by inadequate provisions for accommodation by either state agencies or the new 'partnerships' being formed between state and voluntary sector providers which are now seen as the most appropriate solution to the housing care of such members of the community.

Somerville (1998) adds further to our understanding where he draws a distinction between the two meanings of social exclusion that he sees as prevalent. These are: first, a meaning based around the exclusion of the individual from the labour market brought about by the restructuring of economic activity, mainly the shift from the 'Fordist' manufacturing regime of accumulation to the service-based economies characterised by more flexible labour requirements and different skills and employment mixes. These changes have created a group of long-term unemployed and moved the majority of the developed countries away from the idea that they can create 'full employment societies'. The emphasis upon employment changes leads to a concern with training opportunities, reskilling and education to enable the individual to re-enter the labour force and thus end their exclusion and marginality. Here, empowerment comes from the ending of welfare dependency. This has stimulated attention to policies to move people from unemployment benefits to work for the dole schemes.

The second meaning relates to the denial of social citizenship. This can arise from a number of factors. Citizens can be ignorant of their rights and thus do not take advantage of the opportunities which do exist. The solution here is seen to lie in improved education and the creation of institutions to promote improved knowledge and better practices. The setting up of Human Rights Commissions, Race Relations Offices and the establishment of rights in law rather than simply relying on customary practice are good examples. Citizenship can be declined as a result of individuals committing illegal acts. Here, one of the areas of significance relates to immigration status and the marginal status of the guest worker on restricted residency permits and of the 'illegals and overstayers' often encouraged to migrate to supply cheap labour but without any security of position and thus vulnerable to economic and political changes.

The analysis of social exclusion draws attention to the differences between the deserving, those who therefore legitimately require help, such as those who are evicted through no fault of their own, and the undeserving, those who 'waste' their money and thus default on the rent. This draws our attention to one of the long-running debates within the field of urban social exclusion, that about the intentionality of the excluded, and thus whether they should be assisted back into the mainstream social world. The position adopted reflects how the causes of exclusion are viewed, particularly whether they are seen as the result of individual or structural failures.

Causes of Social Exclusion

The causes of social exclusion differ with respect to the analysis carried out and the theoretical perspective adopted. One view is firmly based around individual failure and supply-side factors such as education, skills, motivation and attitudes leading to a policy response which emphasizes the targeting of resources to improve the individual's capacities. Such policy responses engender a discourse of exclusion which emphasizes the personal characteristics and problems of the unemployed and homeless and which seeks solutions aimed at changing these, so rehabilitating or re-incorporating the individual back into the mainstream of the society. The British Government's social exclusion unit's policy on welfare to work, for example, divides society into two groups, the excluded and the included (Marsh and Mullins 1998, Marsh 2001). This is suggested as a way of allowing resources to be targeted more precisely to those in need. What this division achieves is

> an overly homogeneous and consensual image of society, . . . in which inequality and poverty are pathological and residual rather than endemic (Levitas 1998:6),

and it leads to minimalist solutions. Further, such approaches can also create poverty traps through the way the abatement and targeting regimes are put in place. The Aotearoa/New Zealand Accommodation Supplement, introduced as the sole housing assistance measure in 1991, and the UK Housing Benefit or some of the 'workfare' schemes that have been introduced to move people from long-term dependency on unemployment benefits and back into the workforce all have somewhat similar effects and create poverty traps of varying magnitude (Ditch, Lewis and Wilcox 2001). There has also been the attachment to the new policy regimes of a strong moralistic rhetoric – such as that found underlying the proposed code of social responsibility advanced by the National Government in 1998 within Aotearoa/New Zealand. The code emphasized the responsibilities of the individual and family rather than those of the government or wider community.

In contrast to this emphasis on individual failure is the analysis which points to structural and external factors. Amongst such factors are global economic change and the restructuring of the job market, and spatial development, which means that not enough jobs are available, however ready for work the local population is, in any particular region. Evidence is growing that the restructuring of the 1980s and 1990s, carried out by governments pursuing the neo-liberal economic agenda of greater individual freedom and competitiveness within their economies, has created greater income and wealth inequalities both internally within societies and across the global economy. A recent study on income and wealth (Joseph Rowntree 1995) for example, shows that income inequality has grown strongly over the 1980s and 1990s in the UK, the USA, Australia, and Aotearoa/New Zealand. Recent comment in Australia, for example, drew attention to the widening rift between the urban and rural population and, within the urban population, the growing concentration of wealth in Sydney. The Australian Tax Office in January 2000 released figures showing the top ten most wealthy postcodes within Australia. At the top were the affluent Sydney harbour side areas of Darling Point, Edgecliffe and Point Piper where average annual income jumped ten per cent in 1999 to A$83,645 compared to the average of the rural areas of A$19,388. Further, of the top ten postcodes, eight were in Sydney, and two were in Melbourne. The group of countries with the greatest shifts in the distribution of wealth in the 1980s and 1990s are all ones that carried out major structural changes to the operation of their economies in the direction of economic liberalisation (Rowntree 1998). One of the consequences of this path of economic reform was to create greater internal differentiation and increase the number of people excluded from the mainstream. Thus, in each of these three societies, the number at the margins has increased giving rise to greater unemployment, homelessness and poverty. The majority of those experiencing these pressures are found within the larger cities.

Urban exclusion is the other side of the contemporary city. It is about who are included/excluded, about urban marginality and the rise of an underclass (squatters and street dwellers). Informal workers in a barter or exchange economy rather than the paid, full-time labour force are a further component of such an underclass. The shifting boundary between state and market relations has been influential in creating the conditions for the growth in these excluded groups.

Issues of inclusion and exclusion are then a mix of economic, social and political issues (Burchardt, Le Grand, and Piachaud 1999, Byrne 1999). The solutions are being increasingly sought through new forms of political arrangements. The so-called third way (Giddens 1998, 2001) is being advocated, one which relies neither upon the state or the private sector alone but is a new form of partnership which also includes NGOs and other community-based groups in a new form of active citizenship. Such ideas are reflected in the Habitat Agenda where it talks about an enabling strategy based on the principles of partnership and participation (UNCHS 1996a). Social research does raise some warnings about the possibilities of such partnerships within a world constituted around market-based wealth generation.

Patterns of Social Exclusion

In this section, the focus will be upon five aspects of urban social exclusion, which have attracted attention; socio-spatial separation/segregation, poverty, homelessness, crime and gentrification.

Socio-spatial Separation/Segregation

The analysis of the socio-spatial patterns across the city has been central to urban analysis from the earliest work of the Chicago School through to the more recent work associated with those working within the managerialist, political economy and postmodern perspectives. The uneven nature of the resource distribution and the separation of wealthier and poorer areas has been a common theme in this analysis, as has the creation of ethnic subareas and communities. In some cities, the latter form highly excluded 'ghetto' areas. Each city tends to have something of a unique pattern of distribution reflecting such things as the geography of the city and its history and culture. The present spatial inequalities are invariably a reflection of past political, economic and social practices (Lee 1999). Over time, areas within cities do change their population composition and the activities contained within them, for example, through gentrification and urban renewal. One very significant aspect of spatial separateness is that of how the 'boundaries' between areas are formed and maintained. Here, a range of possibilities exist varying from actual physical barriers such as the Wall that divided Berlin from 1961 to 1989, to legal devices such as zoning regulations through to the existence of forbidding reputations which both attract and repel particular groups of city dwellers.

Neighbourhood boundaries can be set through the use of physical barriers. The work here of Marcuse (1989, 1995) is of value where he describes New York as the 'quartered city'. By this he means a city of distinctive subareas, socially separated through the action of inclusion and exclusion by powerful social groups and actors. He identifies five types of area. They are the dominating city of luxury-housing enclaves, the gentrified city of the business and professional 'yuppies', the suburban city of single-family housing, the tenement city of renting and the abandoned city left for the poor and homeless. Carrying through the metaphor of inclusion and exclusion, he further describes the 'walls' that demarcate the different areas of the city. These he sees as the symbolic boundaries separating out the city and demonstrating the differences between the powerful and the powerless. He sees five types of wall in New York. These are firstly, the 'barricades' that people erect to protect themselves. Such 'walls' have increasingly appeared in cities in recent times with the growth of fragmentation in social relations and thus the breakdown in communal social life. People seek a sense of security behind the 'barricades' of garden fences, security lights and alarms and through keeping guard dogs. The walled enclosures clearly separate those within the walls and those without and create a sense of 'us' within and 'them' – the potentially dangerous and untrustworthy outside. Secondly, are the 'stockades' which are seen as the wall of aggressive superiority characterising the gentrified city. Thirdly, the 'stucco walls' shelter the more exclusive residential areas creating areas that are considered safe as they are separated from the rest of the city. These areas, at their most extreme, can be gated and provided with security personnel or based on electronic entry through swipe cards or they can rely more on symbolic access restrictions through land-scaping and signage indicating that you are entering a particular territory. Boundaries around areas can be further reinforced through planning regulations, building restrictions and zoning practices (Huxley 1994, Luymes 1997).

Two recently constructed suburbs in Perth, Australia, illustrate this process. Mt Claremont and St John's Wood are physically and socially separate new housing areas sold to residents on the basis of an exclusive image. Prospective buyers are informed that they will know who is in the suburb, and an image of social exclusion is promoted against the back-drop of the city as a place where security cannot be guaranteed. In St John's Wood, each cul-de-sac has its own demarcating wall separating it off, helping to create the image of safety and seclusion and exclusiveness. Image change was important for developers here as they were building on the site of a former psychiatric hospital. Hillier and McManus (1994), in their study of this development, conclude that the image created re-inforces the idea of the home as haven, as a refuge from the rest of the city. A similar picture of restricted access to residential development to promote exclusiveness is given by Johnson in her study of Roxborough Park near Melbourne. Here, the developers claimed to be creating a dif-ferent sort of housing-development area that would be ecologically sustainable, affordable and would be based around the creation of community (Johnson 1994b). The rhetoric of the development was about building a community and this was to be achieved through a design for a 6000-strong neighbourhood and the development of sociability. When, however, an extended family of Sikh Indians wanted to buy land on behalf of an absent brother and establish a medical centre in one of their houses rather than in a designated service centre, the rigidity of the zoning and culturally prescribed nature of what constituted the desired community was revealed (Johnson 1994b:297).

This brings us to the fourth of Marcuse's 'walls', the 'ramparts' which are the 'fortifications surrounding the citadels'. This is the corporate office tower that has come to dominate the downtown business districts of the city as finance, insurance, and real estate interests have become promi-nent. Such towers shadow the streets of most global cities and encroach into the 'public spaces' of the street and proclaim their control over the landscape. Finally, there are the 'prison walls' which define the ghettos (Davis 1991, 1995). Such analysis points to the fact that spaces within the city are clearly divided and segregated on the basis of class, gender and ethnicity and that they reflect relations of power.

The gated residential developments with security systems to control entry and egress, which emerged first in parts of the USA, are now spread-ing to other countries as part of a response to the fear felt by many in the community, of crime and violence to people and property. In many developed countries, the rates, especially of property offences, have risen and the clear-up rate has fallen leading to many turning to privatised security systems with alarms, as the solution to crime. The most extreme form is the gated community. These communities not only control security, however, they also have quite developed internal control systems which ensure that all residents uphold the 'normative' standards set. These often relate to the physical arrangements of space and the range of social activities permitted (Knox 1993, Blakely and Snyder 1997). A further variant, reflecting both the ageing of western societies and the increasing concern about property and personal security, is the 'retirement village'. These are, in effect, 'gated' communities for a particular demographic group and create a further factor in the way space has become segregated.

Analysis of contemporary Sao Paulo has shown how residential restructuring has created sharp social distinctions within the inner city between the poor and the rich leading to the need for increased levels of security around the enclaves occupied by the wealthy (Box 7.1).

A further way that boundaries can be demarcated is through the activities of gangs marking out their turfs or territories. One indicator of this, in the contemporary city, is the use of 'tagging', the spray painting of

---

Box 7.1

Sao Paulo, Brazil: an example of a 'walled' city

Recent research into Sao Paulo in Brazil shows how urban restructuring, incorporating the city into the global economy, has led to the city being restructured around tertiary economic activities.

This has given rise to 'de-industrialisation' and substantial changes to the workforce. One consequence has been population redistribution in the inner areas bringing back the middle and upper classes to live in apartments. At the same time, poorer people have been forced out of the residential areas on the perimeter as these also have been improved. The result has been the juxtaposition, in the centre, of the very wealthy and the very poor. This leads to a more diverse and fragmented inner-city population that has, in turn, heightened fear amongst the wealthy regarding their personal security, leading to the apartments they occupy becoming isolated enclaves with armed private security guards, new surveillance technology and supporting vigilante operations (Caldeira 1996).

A similar pattern of increasing polarisation between the wealthy and very poor in the city centre has occurred in Rio de Janeiro as a consequence of de-industrialisation and the growth of a more service-based economy (Riberio and Edward Do Lago 1995).

buildings and fences to indicate that the area is part of the territory or turf of a particular gang (Ley and Cybriwsky 1974). Rivalries and disputes can erupt into periods of open hostility and conflict, often over such things as drug dealing, until the patterns of control are re-established. The maintenance of such territories can be with the collusion of the law-enforcement authorities as the existence of clearly delineated gang turfs can help to maintain stability.

A final method of demarcation is through the development of a forbidding reputation which clearly deter strangers from entering the area. Such areas are often associated with particular ethnic groups, for example, the South of Brisbane or Redfern districts of Sydney with their high aboriginal populations, or Harlem and the Bronx in New York with their Black and Latin American populations. Sometimes these reputations have entered the local urban folklore and persist long after the reasons for their emergence have dissipated, as Damer's study of the Gorbals, a once notorious area of Glasgow, has shown (Damer 1974, 1990). Defended neighbourhoods, as a form of community, are as much an example of how order and social control are managed in the contemporary city as of how they are about developing closure around a particular district and set of people within the city.

Poverty

The analysis of urban poverty has had a long history within urban studies and was one of the driving issues in the early debates about city life and the impact of rapid urbanisation. As we saw in Chapter 2 from the early work of Engels, Booth and Rowntree, in Britain, urban poverty was placed firmly on the research and policy agenda in the second half of the nineteenth century. The work of Booth, for example, linked poverty to income, occupation, residence and overcrowding. The causes of poverty were as much structural as they were individual and therefore needed structural solutions, which in turn required the level of income going to the poorest to be improved, but by how much? This led to an ongoing debate about whether this should provide relief from absolute or relative poverty. Absolute poverty was seen as the capacity to survive and have sufficient shelter, food, clothing and work.

Table 7.1, drawn from the UN global report prepared for Habitat 2 gives some indication of the global scale of the problem of poverty and its enduring nature. Here, it is shown that this is both an urban and a rural problem and that rates are greater in the developing than in the developed countries. For example, in 1985, 29 per cent of Africa's urban population was in poverty, in Asia (excluding China), 34 per cent and in Latin

Table 7.1 Extent of absolute poverty: selected countries

Country or Region	Urban	Rural	Nation	Date
	Proportion of the population below the poverty line (%)			
Africa	29.0	58.0	49.0	1985
Botswana	30.0	64.0	55.0	1985/6
Cote d'Ivoire	30.0	26.0	28.0	1980/6
Egypt	34.0	33.7	33.8	1984
Gambia	63.8	57.7		1989
Ghana			59.5	1985
Morocco	28.0	32.0		1985
Mozambique	40.0	70.0	55.0	1980/9
Swaziland	45.0	50.0	49.0	1980
Tunisia	7.3	5.7	6.7	1990
Uganda	25.0	33.0	32.0	1989/90
Zambia	40.0		80.0	1993
Asia (ex. China)	34.0	47.0	43.0	1985
Bangladesh	58.2	72.3		1985/6
India	37.1	38.7		1988
Indonesia	20.1	16.4	17.4	1987
Korea (republic of)	4.6	4.4	4.5	1984
Malaysia	8.3	22.4	17.3	1987
Nepal	19.2	43.1	42.6	1984/5
Pakistan	25.0	31.0		1984/5
Philippines	40.0	54.1	49.5	1988
Sri Lanka	27.6	45.7	39.4	1985/6
Europe				
France			16.0	1990
Germany			10.0	1990
Hungary			15.4	1991
Ireland			19.0	1990
Italy			15.0	1990
Poland			22.7	1987
Spain			19.0	1990
United Kingdom			18.0	1990
Latin America	32.0	45.0		1985
Argentina	14.6	19.7	15.5	1986
Brazil	37.7	65.9	45.3	1987
Columbia	40.2	44.5	41.6	1986
Costa Rica	11.6	32.7	23.4	1990
El Salvador	61.4			1990
Guatemala	61.4	85.4		1989
Haiti	65.0	80.0		1980/6
Honduras	73.9	89.2		1990
Mexico	30.2	50.5		1984

Table 7.1   *Continued*

Proportion of the population below the poverty line (%)

Country or Region	Urban	Rural	Nation	Date
Panama	29.7	51.9		1986
Peru	44.5	63.8		1986
Uruguay	19.3	28.7		1986
Venezuela	24.8	42.2		1986
North America				
Canada			15.0	1990
USA			13.0	1990

Note: These are all estimates based on data from a household budget, income or expenditure survey and are based on the concept of an absolute poverty line expressed in monetary terms. The figures for different countries are not necessarily comparable since different assumptions will have been made for setting the poverty line. (NB: comparisons between these countries should be avoided, as different criteria were used to set poverty lines)
Source: For countries in Africa, Asia and Latin America, Hamid with Foud 1993. India: Planning Commission 1993. Zambia, Ellen 1993. For countries in Europe and North America, Townsend 1993.

America, 32 per cent. The large numbers of rural poor in all these regions is also one factor creating urban migration, as the unemployed and underemployed population move to find better opportunities. The rich European and North American countries have much lower rates, around 10 to 22 per cent, and these countries have generated the most heated debate about the question of relative as well as absolute poverty. However, in most developing countries it is absolute poverty that is the focus of attention. For example, recent UNESCO-sponsored research into city development and poverty found that the improvement of basic environmental conditions, such as access to clean water and adequate disposal of waste, were two keys to improving city life and eradicating poverty (Box 7.2).

The debate about whether to focus upon absolute or relative poverty has been a deeply contested terrain with the absolute position being dominant at times and, at others, a greater willingness to embrace the 'relative idea'. Relative poverty moves the definition outwards from the necessities of life to include the material and other supports necessary for a fully *participative* life. Townsend, one of the most influential writers in this debate argued that:

Individuals, families and groups can be said to be in poverty when they lack the resources to obtain the types of diet, participate in the activities and have

Box 7.2

Poverty and city development

UNESCO-sponsored research into city development and poverty eradication focused upon a series of urban sites in developing countries. Two of these are:

- Yeumbeul-Malika, a neighbourhood within the Dakar conurbation, estimated population: 150,000

- Jalousie, a neighbourhood in the suburbs of Port-au-Prince

In both cases, the projects were designed to improve environmental conditions through sewage disposal and access to clean drinking water. To improve the material base of the people, the projects were also concerned to promote income-generating activity. The existence of poverty here arises from a cycle of deprivation, which includes a lack of skills and work, and health problems arising out of the living conditions where large numbers are squatters with inadequate shelter.

The Jalousie project, in its first phase, had to start by working to improve the built environment through a series of practical projects that:

- improved the road and pedestrian network;

- built a retaining wall,

- a footbridge over a ravine cutting the neighbourhood into two parts,

- a football ground to enable recreation;

- introduced street lighting,

- street furniture made by local craftsmen and

- created murals by a local artist.

Through the engagement of the local people with community organisations, a spirit of participation was encouraged leading to greater empowerment of local community members.

What these and other 'poverty eradication projects' show is that poverty eradication is a multi-dimensional process, as poverty is associated with a whole range of associated institutional and environmental problems.

UNESCO Cities Project web site: *http://www.unesco.org/most/*

the living conditions and amenities which are customary, or at least are widely encouraged and approved in the societies to which they belong. Their resources are so seriously below those commanded by the average individual or family that they are in effect, excluded from ordinary living patterns, customs and activities (Townsend 1979:32).

The debate has not followed an identical course in all countries and has been linked into wider discussions of the nature of the welfare state and public provisions. In the late 1980s and 1990s there has been, in many countries, a resurgence of the 'absolute' position as part of the restructuring of welfare states and the desire to move people from dependency on state benefits. The focus of much urban research into poverty has been upon defining the poverty base line, which has led to the search for reliable indicators and so-called 'objective' measurements of poverty based on such factors as minimal food cost for the survival of the individual or household. Into the debate, therefore, have reappeared the concepts of the 'deserving' and the undeserving poor as neo-liberal governments have sought to reduce the level of welfare dependency and move people from benefits back into the workforce.

As part of this shift, the causes of poverty are more likely to be located in individual failures than in structural deficiencies such as the lack of jobs created within the economy. Having redefined poverty within the city as primarily an individual failure, it is then possible to see solutions based around re-equipping the poor and the marginal so they can re-enter the mainstream of city life. The return to the deserving and the undeserving distinction allows for a return to a moralistic debate which stigmatises many of the poor as shiftless and indolent and the author of their own disadvantagement. The growth of urban poverty in the 1980s and 1990s is further demonstrated by the rise in the numbers of homeless in the major cities of both the developed and the developing world.

Homelessness

The debate over homelessness follows, in many respects, the one over poverty and has been characterised by the same concerns to identify those 'deserving of help'. These are usually seen as those made unintentionally homeless – through no fault of their own. Again, we see the strong influence of individualistic explanation for the rise of homelessness and the preference for psychological rather than sociological theories to explain the numbers of homeless. The issue of definition has also figured large in debates with a shift from an absolute definition to the concept of a continuum of housing need stretching from a position where people have no roof over their heads and live on the street as 'rough sleepers' or pavement dwellers through to those living in overcrowded and insecure dwellings where they have no tenure security and where the accommodation often fails to comply with minimum standards (Watson and Austerberry 1986, Somerville 1992). This would include those squatting illegally and those who live in a variety of shanty and illegal dwellings on vacant land within, on the edges of and beyond the city. These dwellers often have limited access to such services as clean water and adequate sanitation. Debate has raged over the number of homeless people. Daly (1996a, b), in a three-country study of Canada, Britain, and the USA, shows that all three had substantial numbers of homeless people. Further data from Quigley, Raphael and Smolensky's (2000) recent review of North American and European research, indicates that concern over the number of homeless grew in the 1980s and various estimates were made as to the size of the problem. In Europe in the 1990s, the European Federation of National Organizations Working with the Homeless suggested a figure of up to five million for Europe and, at about the same time, advocacy groups in the USA provided a figure of three million for the USA (Matthew 1992, Daly 1996b). Public agency figures tend to be much more modest, with, for example, the Federal Ministry for Housing and Urban Development in the USA estimating 500,000 to 600,000 homeless in the mid 1990s (Daly 1996b:16). In the less developed world, figures are substantially higher (UNCHS 1996).

One way of conceptualising homelessness is to think of it in terms of the distinction between private troubles and public issues (Mills 1956). Generally, the more psychological explanations favour the view that it is primarily a private trouble whereas the sociological are more likely to see it as a public issue. Hoch (1986), for example, draws a distinction between the liberal position, which sees the homeless as sick and victims of social and economic systems, therefore requiring assistance to re-empower them so they can overcome their current exclusion. This suggests a policy response based around programmes of re-education, retraining and counselling and other forms of individual social support. The Conservative position on the other hand tends to see the homeless as deviants and vagrants who need to be contained and regulated. This view stimulated the growth of shelters in the USA under Reagan in the 1980s to keep the homeless off the streets. This strategy speaks less to the causes and rehabilitation of the homeless and more to their containment. This is the solution opted for by cities when faced with glamour events and their need to project a positive image. Thus, in Atlanta, at the time of the 1996 Olympics, 10,000 homeless people were moved from the streets and Sydney engaged in the same strategy for the 2000 Olympics (Searle and Bounds 1999). Similarly Auckland cleared the homeless from the domain, a central park, during the 1999 Asia Pacific Economic Co-operation (APEC) conference in the city as the leaders were meeting in the park and, for both visual and security reasons, they wanted the homeless to be invisible. Containment and discouragement strategies such as modifying park benches to prevent sleeping and sprinklers that randomly spray parks to prevent squatting do not address the cause, only reduce its physical presence (Davis 1995).

The dominance of psychologically informed explanations has led to the widespread assumption that mental illness is a major contributing factor to the level of homelessness in the 1990s. Here the de-institutionalisation of the care of those with mental illness and the shift to community-based care are often cited as being significant factors. Quigley, Raphael and Smolensky (2000) examined the de-institutionalisation hypothesis and suggested that this cannot be the driving force for homelessness in the USA. Furthermore, their research suggested that at least half of the de-institutionalised from the mental health system became re-institutionalised in the criminal justice system taking them out of the possibility of homelessness. Of the 100,000 homeless in the 1980s, they indicated that less than one third could be attributed to de-institutionali-sation. The majority were there due to low income and the lack of affordable housing. Clearly, where de-institutionalisation has taken place without adequate community-level support or adequate accommodation forthcoming, housing stress is likely and this can exacerbate the levels of homelessness.

The reverse argument has not been as extensively investigated, whether homelessness arising from income deprivation, causes or contributes to mental illness. Further, the discourse of psychiatry is almost silent on the impact of the economic and social context within which the homelessness occurs. As we have seen in other chapters, the extensive changes to the economies of various countries under restructuring, and global processes, have created winners and losers in the job market, have led to income re-distribution which has favoured the better-off and to new groups of urban poor who are unable to afford accommodation and thus swell the ranks of the homeless. The impact of these changes has been uneven across all social groups with those at risk including sole parents, battered women and children, abused youths, the disabled, the frail elderly and workers and their families where jobs have disappeared. At least some of the home-less are there through structural changes over which they have had little or no control, rather than through individual personality deficiencies or illness. This suggests that the way to address the problem is through poli-cies to increase opportunities for work, to provide supplementary bene-fits to those on low incomes or to look at ways of reconstructing the job market to provide better-paid jobs.

In an interesting analysis of the voices of the homeless, in the 1980s, Culhane and Fried (1988) provide valuable insight into the process by which people become homeless. Their work shows the significance of structural factors and the way in which people can become trapped into a homeless situation. Two of the 'voices from the street' in their study tell of homelessness as:

a gradual thing . . . spending some period of time with friends, and really very rapidly, very quickly wearing out my welcome there. So that was a slow process, and all the time money was moving away from me. I was spending and nothing was coming in. Looking for jobs and job interviews, and food, and trying to maintain my clothes (Culhane and Fried 1988:177).

The first speaks of the gradual drift into homelessness which it was very difficult for the individual to arrest as each stage took him further away from the possibility of re-engagement with the 'normal' world of work and opportunity.

My business went bankrupt and my whole life fell apart. I guess there was no question, even though I started sleeping in the car, and on very cold nights staying in Third Street shelter in New York City, I still didn't consider myself homeless until the car was vandalized, my clothes stolen and I was completely broke – I was without clothes, any material possessions – I was absolutely naked in the world – I ended up in a psych ward (Culhane and Fried 1988:177).

The second voice again draws attention to the cycle of dis-advantagement, which set in place once the business failed and the capacity to survive in an American city began to deteriorate. Money, secure shelter, clothing and the capacity to look for and find work and a new start became more and more difficult resulting finally, in this case, in the hospitalisation of the individual. The final example is one featured in a local Aotearoa/New Zealand newspaper. In 1998, the Nelson *Evening Post* carried the following headline: 'Help denied homeless man'. The story went on the explain that 'the Department of Social Welfare's Motueka Branch refused any sort of help for a hungry homeless man because he did not have an address'. Clearly, in Aotearoa/New Zealand society in the late 1990s, if you did not have an address you were a 'non-person' as far as officialdom was concerned. This demonstrates the problems faced by the 'excluded' to reintegrate themselves back into society.

These three examples raise the question as to whether homelessness is an individual matter or one reflecting wider social conditions. Is the lack of secure and adequate housing at a price that can be afforded then one of the root causes of the problem? In many developing and developed countries the way the urban land and housing markets are constructed contributes to the supply and cost of housing. In most cases, the needs of the poorest are not a high priority and reliance is often placed on such strategies as 'trickle-down effects'. Here the replacement of middle- and upper-income housing is considered to free up housing for the poor and those entering the market for the first time. Markets though seldom work according to such models and due to ownership patterns and monopoly practices may fail to yield low-cost housing. The level of government intervention and provision then becomes crucial. Here, the 1980s and 1990s have been characterised with debates about the value of different forms of intervention, especially that of direct provision, such as state-built housing as opposed to consumer subsidies, by way of housing vouchers and demand-side allowances to increase the choices available to the poor and to reduce their marginality and thus to improve the degree to which they are able to compete in the broader housing market (Yates and Whitehead 1998, Yates 2000).

A further aspect to this debate has been the one about housing rights and the question of the extent to which governments should enact a statutory right to housing for their citizens. The debate was a central feature of the 1996 UN conference on Human Settlements, Habitat 2. In the end the Habitat Declaration falls short of supporting a statutory right to shelter favouring a restatement of the 1948 UN declaration of human rights which includes a reference to housing and asserts that housing is a human right. What this leaves open is of course, how that need will be met. In section 44 of the Habitat Agenda there is the statement that 'since the adoption of the United Nations Declaration of Human Rights in 1948, the right to adequate housing has been recognised as an important component of the right to an adequate standard of living' (UNCHS 1996). No consensus as to how adequate housing for all was to be achieved in practice emerged at the conference. In countries undergoing rapid urbanisation, one of the tensions that arises is that regarding migration and whether restrictions need to be placed on the movement of people from the rural areas to the cities. A consequence of rapid rural-urban migration is the creation of squatters and homeless people who have few rights within the cities that they have migrated to. Many end up in the kind of circumstances of Mr Chen in Nanjing (Box 7.3).

There have however, been countries that have invoked a form of statutory right to housing. One example is the UK which enacted the Homeless Persons Act in 1977 that required local government to house certain categories of homeless people 'if no accommodation was available . . . which that person could reasonably occupy' (Whitehead 2000). The act focused upon the unintentionally homeless in local authority areas. This policy was, under the Conservative Government of the 1980s, somewhat contradicted by the Right-to-Buy policy as this encouraged the sale of council (public) housing stock as part of Margaret Thatcher's policy of popular capitalism. Sitting tenants were able to buy their state houses at attractively discounted prices (see Murie and Forrest 1988). Since the stock of publicly-owned housing has declined the ability of local government to meet their obligation and to provide long-term solutions for the home-

Box 7.3

Nanjing, China: urban homelessness

In the *South China Morning Post*, in April 2001, a story, under the headline 'China's Poverty Time Bomb', was carried about a Mr Chen, a squatter in a former army barracks in Nanjing, a city of 2.8 million people in China's new economic zone. The city was currently experiencing an economic boom which had created increased levels of inequality. Mr Chen was one of about 100 million rural dwellers that had moved – often illegally – to the cities. Without legal rights to housing and work, they had become the urban homeless.

Mr Chen's story was of a family who were forceably sent out to the country in the late 1950s for political reasons. After his parents' death, Mr Chen returned to the city of Nanjing and tried to obtain residency rights – this he failed to do and so for the last 15 years he had lived in a disused army barracks as a non person on the margins of the city with a couple of dozen others – fellow migrants from the countryside.

Mr Chen, like many urban migrants, came back to the city for a mixture of both push factors (rural poverty) and pull factors (perceived urban opportunities for work, money and life-style advantages). However, the institutional structures did not allow him rights to work or housing as he was deemed an illegal migrant. Hence, his situation of long-term poverty and homelessness (*South China Morning Post*, Wednesday 18 April, 2001).

less in their area has been undermined with the result that many of the homeless are provided with short-term accommodation in local private hotels and boarding houses. This initially solves the problem of people without any shelter but fails to address the long-term problem of an inadequate supply of cheap housing for rent, especially in the larger cities.

In the late 1990s, the homeless in the UK were divided into three groups for policy purposes; those in housing need who were given priority for accommodation, those for whom the government did not take direct responsibility, the non-vulnerable single people and couples (voluntary homeless) and lastly the roofless. This latter group generally also contained those who had experienced violence in relationships, drug and alcohol addiction and abuse, mental health de-institutionalisation and street kids. The estimate for the late 1990s is that these three groups comprised 494,000 of which on any one night about 1600 would be rough sleepers (Whitehead 2000).

The debate about the statutory right also links through to the earlier discussion about the undeserving or deserving 'homeless' and which group should be assisted by the public purse.

Crime

Urban crime is another aspect associated with social exclusion. Table 7.2 shows that crime is very much a fact of life in the world's cities of more than 100,000 population. The highest rates were recorded in Africa (76 per cent) and South America (68 per cent) and lowest in Asia (44 per cent). Within these regions, particular cities have also varying rates. The data show that the most prevalent form of urban crime is that against property – vehicles, burglary, and theft. A trend over the past two decades has been one of an increasing level of more violent crime against the person. Here, the overall rate was 19 per cent but this varies considerably across regions and across cities within regions. In 1990, Sao Paulo had a murder rate of 35 per 100,000, Rio de Janeiro, 60 per 100,000 and Clai in Columbia a rate of 87, and Washington DC of 70.

Increasing levels of urban violence lead to a greater sense of insecurity for many urban people decreasing their use of local facilities such as parks, squares and urban transit systems, especially at night. The solution often sought to this problem is that of increased surveillance and the use of security systems linked to the police, private security companies or other agents of control. However, in many of these countries, there is also an increase in police violence and loss of faith in the justice systems. For example, in Sao Paulo in the early 1990s, the military police killed more than 1000 suspects (Caldeira 1996). A further reaction is the shifting of activity away from the public places of the street to the more secure and controlled environment of the mall.

In the USA, the use of the shopping mall rather than parks for jogging

Table 7.2 Victims of crime over a 5-year period (% of population)

	Theft/Damage of vehicles	Burglary	Other theft	Assault/other crimes of personal contact*	All crimes
West Europe	34	16	27	15	60
North America	43	24	25	20	65
South America	25	20	33	31	68
East Europe	27	18	28	17	56
Asia	12	13	25	11	44
Africa	24	38	42	33	76
Total	29	20	29	19	61

Note: *includes mugging, aggravated theft, grievous bodily harm, sexual assault
Source: UNCRI 1995, drawing from UNCRI and Ministry of Justice of the Netherlands international survey of victims of crime (1988–94) based on a sample of 74,000 persons in 39 countries; UNCHS 1996a

grew significantly during the 1980s and 1990s as they are considered safer and more secure places to exercise. A further aspect of this desire to be secure is the creation of fortified enclaves where wealthier urban residents can protect themselves from urban crime (Davis 1991, Knox 1993). In the USA over the 1980s and 1990s, there has been a strong growth in 'gated communities' which sell themselves on the fear of crime and the desire for privacy and security within a lifestyle without fear (Luymes 1997).

Explanations for the increasing levels of urban crime also draw from both structural and individual-level explanations. The inadequacy of income, the high levels of unemployment, poor housing, insecure tenure, limited opportunities for legitimate social and economic advance and the development of the drug trade have all been suggested as part of the explanation. Others have sought explanation at the level of the individual and in family and community failure and point to the instability of life for many in the cities where dysfunctional families are unable to care for and control their children.

Gentrification

The growth of gentrified inner-city areas has influenced the local population and resulted in displacement. The trend towards greater inner-city living began in the late 1960s and early 1970s. The move back to inner areas by middle-class professionals put pressure upon the property market and led to the renovation and renewal of the property, which in turn raised the market value and led to a wider set of social changes. Former working-class terrace housing, for example in Sydney's inner suburb of Paddington became fashionable and the former working-class residents were squeezed out over the 1970s and the land values rose and the property prices soared (Kendig 1979). A similar chain of events took place in Melbourne over the same period within the inner city suburb of Carlton. London was another site of change, which attracted research attention in the late 1960s and 1970s, with Ruth Glass coining the term, gentrification, to describe this particular pattern of social and spatial 'improvement' and redevelopment (Glass 1955). Since the 1970s, the phenomenon has been identified in many European, North American and Australian cities (Smith and Williams 1986). It has focused on the process of physical renovation of the housing stock and the associated change in the social composition. Middle-class buyers in these areas progressively replace the existing working-class population. In the 1980s and 1990s, a new round of 'gentrification' has been identified linked to the restructuring of the urban workforce which has brought a greater number of service professionals into the inner city, creating an increased demand for inner-city accommodation. This has been supplied by a combination of new con-struction, conversion of former commercial premises, such as in the lofts and warehouses of Greenwich village in New York and the refurbish-ment/renewal of inner-city residential accommodation (Zukin 1982; Rose 1990). The impact of new wealthy residents upon the rents in a district was shown when former President Bill Clinton chose to set up his Office in Harlem in August 2001. One of those protesting at the opening was quoted as saying that 'poor black men and women will not have a home in Harlem any more because rents will be going up' (*The Christchurch Press* 1 August 2001).

Warde (1991), in reviewing this latest round of gentrification sees it as comprising four processes. The first was the resettlement and social concentration that generated the displacement of one group of residents with another of higher social status causing new patterns of social segre-gation. This process was similar to that of the earlier round of gentrifica-tion noted in the 1960s and early 1970s. The second was the transformation of the built environment through renovation and building that highlights distinctive aesthetic features and the emergence of specific types of services. This aspect arises from the nature of the population involved which contained a high proportion of 'new service professionals, with many connected to the design, marketing and promotional industries. The third, flowing from this, was the concentration of people with an assumed shared culture and lifestyle or at least shared class-related, consumer preferences. They emphasized lifestyle and were status- and position-conscious with access to discretionary income, often through being two-earner households. These households were quickly dubbed 'yuppies', young upwardly mobile professional and 'dinkies', dual income no kids'. Finally, the economic reordering of property values created a com-mercial opportunity for the construction industry and an extension of private ownership of domestic property leading to an increased level of interest in inner-city development and the willingness to invest in a variety of new forms of accommodation, including the conversion of offices and warehouses to residential use as well as the building of new structures.

Alongside the renewed interest has come a theoretical debate as to the cause of this revival in gentrification. The debate has centred on the famili-ar consumption production divide. The result is that the focus is either upon the gentrifiers, the actual individuals moving back to the inner-city areas and their associated cultural and consumption patterns or on the process by which gentrification occurs. This latter orientation leads to the analysis of such features as the land market, financial institutions, devel-opers, builders and local regulatory authorities.

The consumption-based theory of gentrification has featured the rise of the service class and the lifestyle with which it has become associated. It is shaped by the new post-industrial world, where manufacturing has declined and been replaced by new forms of work, particularly in the information economy, finance, real estate, culture and entertainment industries. For these groups, location in the centre became more attractive, due to access to restaurants, cafe bars, theatres and other sources of entertainment. As this new group of gentrifiers moves in, the existing population is 'forced' out due to rising house and land prices and rents. They thus form socially distinct sub-communities within the central city area with high consuming power and differing political interests and orientations to the former working-class occupants. The area thus undergoes both a spatial and socio-political change. Attracting more residents of this kind to the inner city is politically popular with city authorities as it gives a boost to rate income and helps to stimulate inner-city business activity required to prevent the downtown declining and losing out to the suburban malls in the battle for retail and entertainment provision.

In the latest round of gentrification, women have also been a more significant group in their own right and as part of dual-income partnerships. There are now a much greater number of high earning women in the new 'service class' and with the changing nature of household formation, many more women are seeking inner-city accommodation themselves and see apartments in the city as more attractive than living in the suburbs (Rose 1990). Although, the consumption-based explanation identifies, reasonably well, who the gentrifiers are and what social changes are produced in the composition of and lifestyles within some inner-city areas, it does not necessarily explain which localities will be gentrified and which will remain untouched.

The alternative line of theorising has come from the work of neo-Marxists; particularly influential has been the work of Neil Smith (1996). In this work, the focus is upon the supply of urban space and who produces the built environment and thus the changes that have occurred to the housing stock and the occupants over time. Central to this analysis is the housing and land market and the mortgage and real estate industry. Here, economic rather than cultural forces are generally seen as being of greater significance. A key explanation for Smith and others became the 'rent gap theory'. Hamnett (1991) explains this as

> a matter of financial returns to landowners on their property. As a district deteriorates, the rent obtainable from letting houses falls and the value of the land for new development is minimal. Hence existing landlords let properties deteriorate even further because they never get returns on investment

in maintenance. At a certain point it becomes profitable to change the use of the land.

Rent Gap Theory is therefore a way of explaining why housing is available in particular areas of the city at particular times. It argues that shifts back to the centre of the city are as much about movements of capital as they are about movements of people. It does not explain, however, who moves so much as where people move.

Explanations for 'who moves' have been strongly influenced by notions of choice and have been shaped by the consumer-sovereignty model. In this model, decision-making is seen to take place at the level of the household, which is treated as an autonomous decision-making unit. From this, it is concluded, that the supply and allocation of housing is a reflection of the wishes and desires of individual households. The consumer is seen to exercise a dominant role in shaping the housing market. Choices are seen to be influenced by 'push' factors, negative aspects of the individual or household's current location, and 'pull' factors, positive aspects of the new location. The individual then goes through a period of searching, using a combination of formal (agents, newspaper and real-estate advertising, and now web sites) and informal (friends, family, neighbours) strategies until they finally make their 'choice'. The upward shift occurring in the inner city, through gentrification, is seen to create vacancies in other parts of the city which allows the 'displaced' to find alternative locations within the overall set of housing opportunities within the city. Urban housing mobility analysts talk about filtering and building new capacity at the upper end and, through redevelopment, allowing people to move into the vacant properties and so move up and down the 'housing ladder' or vacancy chains. It is assumed here that many urban residents have conscious long-term housing strategies or careers, which they seek to carry out over their life course. Such clear intentionality is often disrupted by the instability that is now increasingly common in people's life courses as a result of the 'flexible' job market and relationship changes. Jobs are now more likely to consist of a series of contracts of varying lengths rather than a permanent career. Further, the increased rate of household dissolution and re-formation increases housing mobility and can result in a number of different housing paths being followed rather than a single career path over which capital is carefully acquired through strategic moves. The replacement of the concept of career by the idea of the 'housing journey' may be more appropriate. Many individuals are likely to encounter an increasingly diverse range of housing and job experiences and have to make many adjustments to their location, not all of which will be positive in terms of area or meeting their needs.

Increased levels of uncertainty suggest that not only choices but also constraints need to be considered in the analysis of housing movement. Clearly, what gets built, how the state regulates the land and housing market at national and local level and the economic capacity of the household will all impact on the ability to choose. When factors such as age and stage in the life cycle, household structures, residential history and previous tenure experience are also taken into account, it becomes clear that the simple idea of the sovereign consumer is a myth. The move of the gentrifiers into the central city areas is the result not just of their choice but also is affected by a set of limiting factors or constraints, many of which the individual or household has little or no control over. Gentrification is thus not just about capital accumulation or life-style choice. It is important, therefore, to understand the linkages between the economic and cultural factors in inner-city and suburban change (Beauregard 1990).

Summary

The analysis of urban social inequality and exclusion has shown that the global changes to cities that have taken place over the last decades of the twentieth century have been uneven in their effects. The restructuring of urban life constantly recasts the winners and the losers. It creates and maintains patterns of inequality. The persistence of spatial segregation, poverty, homelessness, urban crime, and neighbourhood change through gentrification, has been documented in this chapter. The analysis of these factors has been set within a debate about the 'worthyness' of those who have been marginalised by the structural changes. There have been attempts to explain the continuing presence of poverty and homelessness as the consequences of individual failures or choices. This leads to the view that policy needs to be constructed around enabling the re-entry of the individuals into the social and economic world that exists in the city. The alternative view adopts a more structural position that sees the need to change how economic and social opportunities are structured and wealth is generated. This brings to the fore issues of urban control, planning and governance. These will be addressed in the next chapter.

Further Reading

Social Exclusion

Levitas, R. 1998. *The Inclusive Society? Social Exclusion and New Labour*. London: Macmillan – now Palgrave Macmillan. Chapter 1 'Three Discourses of Social Exclusion' presents an analysis of debates within Europe around the question of social exclusion.
Somerville, P. 1998. 'Explanations of Social Exclusion Where does housing fit in?' *Housing*

Studies. 13(6). This article also reviews the general debates and then focuses in on the housing-related aspects of the social exclusion agenda.

Poverty

UNCHS. 1996a. *An Urbanizing World: Global Report on Human Settlements*. Oxford: Oxford University Press. Chapter 3, 'Social Conditions and Trends', Section 3.2, 'Poverty,' pp. 107–22, discusses definitions and the extent of poverty across the cities of the world.

Homelessness

Culhane, D. and M. Fried 1988. 'Paths in Homelessness: A View from the Street' in Friedrichs, J., ed., *Affordable Housing and the Homeless*. Berlin: Walter de Gruyter. This chapter is one of the few available that gives a view of the experience of being homeless. Provides some of the voices of the homeless of the USA.

Daly, G. 1996b. *Homeless: Policies, Strategies, and Lives on the Street*. London: Routledge. This book is a comprehensive comparative analysis of homelessness. Chapter 3 provides a good overview of the evolution of homelessness in three advanced societies – Britain, USA, Canada.

Crime

UNCHS. 1996a. *An Urbanizing World: Global Report on Human Settlements*. Oxford: Oxford University Press. Section 3.3, pp. 123–25, provides useful data on urban crime and violence across the various cities of the world.

Gentrification

Smith, N. 1996. 'After Tompkins Square Park: Degentrification and the Revanchist City'. King, A., (ed.) *Re-Presenting the City*. Basingstoke: Macmillan – now Palgrave Macmillan. Neil Smith has been one of the leading writers on gentrification. In this chapter, he explores some of the recent development in New York City.

Warde, A. 1991. 'Gentrification and Consumption: Issues of Class and Gender'. *Environment and Planning D, Society and Space*. 9. This article provides a good analysis of the main theories of gentrification.

Web sites

International focused sites re. world poverty/homelessness/exclusion

http://www.unesco.org/most/
http://www.unesco.org/most/bphome.htm
http://www.unchs.org/istanbul+5/statereport.htm
http://www.jrf.org.uk/
http://www.bestpractices.org/
http://www.gruppocerfe.org/eng/reti/default.htm
http://www.unrisd.org/cgi-
bin/initlst2.pl?searchname=../engindex/cop5/forum/base/initlst.htb

Australian Housing and Urban Research Institute

http://www.ahuri.edu.au/

Housing gateway database

http://www.colorado.edu/plan/housing-info/

US and UK government sites

http://www.hud.gov/news/index.cfm
http://www.cabinet-office.gov.uk/seu/

8

Planning and the Urban Environment

Introduction

The theme of this chapter is that of urban control and therefore it considers the issues of planning, urban governance and social movements. The wider theme of transitions is also incorporated in that how we both think about and seek to shape and control the patterns and nature of urban growth have changed over the past century. During the first two thirds of the century, urban growth pressures and the dominance of a broad modernist planning agenda were two of the most significant features shaping these patterns. Resources were not seen as especially limited and, if they were, the applications of science and technology would enable 'progress' to take place and would provide more efficient ways of creating and maintaining the cities. The 1950s and 1960s were decades in the developed world in which mobility became increasingly centred on the motor car. It allowed for individual and family travel so encouraging the spread of the urban population into suburbia. The linking of the suburb to the city and cities together across the nation was to be facilitated by the construction of freeways or motorways. The freeways spread, as had the railways in the late nineteenth century (Kellet 1969, Blair 1974). The road lobby and the energy industry, especially the major oil companies, together with the contractors and road builders became significant political pressure groups advocating an increase in construction as the solution to the developing congestion within the cities. The transport planners became a key group. Motorway systems were planned across Western Europe, based on inner and outer ring roads and key links between major centres. London had its motorway 'box' designed at this stage to enable circulation around the city and the same concept was then exported to many other cities. Auckland in Aotearoa/New Zealand, is another city that has a motorway system designed in the late 1960s by Buchanan, a leading British urban planner.

The battle for dominance in the transport field between road and rail and between public and privatised provision was generally won in favour of the private and the road.

It was not until the 1960s that the issue of whether growth was positive and could continue in an unbridled way began to be questioned. This was first through the work of those who drew attention to the problems that population growth posed for resource consumption and the associated environmental impacts of an increasing number of people on the planet (Carson 1962, Erhlich 1968). The environmental scientists and activists, who identified the risks associated with an increasing use of resources as cities spread across previously open landscapes, joined this concern. The associated questions of pollution and disposal of urban waste became increasingly urgent ones as cities grew into megalopolises incorporating millions of people in gigantic urban regions. Infrastructure problems have hit the headlines in many parts of the world as cities struggle to deal with the supply of key services such as water, electricity, transport and waste removal and disposal. Within this increasingly stressed and complex urban environment, the question arises as to what is the role of urban planning and how has it been reshaped over the past decades to reflect the new social and environmental understandings? How have processes of government been changed? What resistance has taken place and what social movements have contributed to the new ways that have been adopted to shape the city in the twenty-first century?

Broadly, urban planning has gone through three phases over the course of the last century. It was initially seen as part of the agenda of the social reformers as a necessary part of addressing the physical and social problems that had been created by rapid urbanisation. This led to a system of bureaucratic rules administered by local government and enshrined in a set of town planning statutes. The second was a growing critique of planning through the 1970s and 1980s from both the left and right of the political and intellectual spectrum. The critique argued that planning, rather than a mechanism for social change and an improved quality to the urban environment, was inherently conservative and more about maintaining the power and position of planners than meeting the needs of urban communities and diverse populations (Simmie 1974, Angotti 1993). The 1970s and 1980s thus saw a considerable loss of faith in the planning process. Planning lost its previous legitimacy and struggled to find a rationale or scientific base for its operation (Gibson and Watson 1994). The third phase, in the 1990s, saw a partial recovery in the place of planning with the emergence of the new agenda of sustainability and the move to place the nature of environmental concerns at the centre of planning (this will be taken up in the next chapter).

Planning and the City

Origins of City Planning

The origins of town planning lie in the response to the early modern industrial city, which was the product of rapid urbanisation in the nineteenth century, especially in Europe and North America. It arises out of a debate some have characterised as about 'salvation by bricks', where there was a belief that social problems could be solved through redesigning the city (Greed 1999:3). Thus the direction of change, right from the beginning, was seen to flow from design to the social rather than the other way round. The design professions and those trained in surveying and engineering have, therefore, dominated planning. The reformers of the nineteenth century were concerned to address the problems of urban squalor, poverty and inadequate housing which they saw as a result of insufficient control over the urban development process. Widely used then, and more recently, was the medical metaphor in describing the city and its woes. Cities *choked* our lives, were sources of *illness*, they were *diseased, pathological places* and they *bred* crime (De Swaan et al. 2000). Planning was thus a fusion of scientific rationality and political and administrative practice.

It was not until the twentieth century that the first set of explicitly planning Acts were put in place (Cullingworth 1972). In the UK, the first Town Planning Act was passed in 1909 and focused upon health and housing conditions. Two factors were seen as significant in causing disease and poor physical health. These were the lack of sunlight, because of the crowded tenements, and the lack of clean water because of inadequate sewerage and draining. These factors were targeted and identified as areas where action could rapidly bring about improved well-being. The early planners were drawn from the ranks of the civil engineers and their activity was based around creating an improved physical infrastructure that would then enable a better quality of life to ensue. The British Town Planning Act, 1909, established a planning system based on administrative control and sought to integrate land-use planning at local and national level. This, by the mid twentieth century, led to the creation of a Ministry of Town and Country Planning in 1947 which can be seen as the culmination of a process whereby land-use planning became an increasingly recognised part of local government. Two key Commissions were the Barlow (1943) and Reith (1945). What they advocated was urban consolidation and control of suburban expansion through the establishment of 'green belts' and a system of new towns to take overspill and those displaced by urban renewal and war-time destruction. Eight such new towns were originally planned; more were added later in the 1960s. By the 1960s, however, they were not just about solving the problem of London's growth, the original focus, but that of other large conurbations (Schaffer 1972, Clapson 1998). Further, they were to serve as stimulants to regional growth as part of wider social and economic planning prevalent at this time.

In the late nineteenth century in San Francisco and New York, zoning ordinances were introduced to enable the regulations of housing standards and the use of space. In 1909, legislation was passed giving municipalities the right to engage in city planning. Among other state and national laws at this time were: 'Housing codes and zoning to regulate construction; civil service legislation that curtailed patronage; protection for women; development of fire codes; laws setting reserve requirements for banks; licensing laws for professionals; laws regulating disposal of sewage and garbage as well as food processing in restaurants; and laws regulating hours and working conditions'(UNCHS 2001d). Thus in both Britain and the USA, legislation was enacted to moderate the harsher impacts of urban growth and created an ordered urban environment. Somewhat different planning systems resulted with the US system based more around legal rather than administrative rules.

Another planning innovation was the new towns. These first emerged in the 1920s in the USA, and unlike those in the UK, were developed by private rather than public developers (Allen 1977). Under Roosevelt's New Deal, in the 1930s, a further attempt was made to generate state-initiated new towns. This idea again surfaced in the 1960s under the Johnson Administration's Great Society programme. In this, public-sponsored new towns were again suggested to help address the 'problems' associated with US cities, such as crime, overcrowding, racial tensions and poor housing, but such plans were once again defeated by the strength of the private development lobby.

In the UK and the USA both the intertwining of planning and the system of governance is a central theme along with the presence of political conflict around the activities of the planners. This raises the question of who do planners represent? Is it the politically and economically powerful, or the marginalised groups? Do they have a professional practice that separates them from the political process? The desire, by planners, to claim technical/and or administrative expertise as the basis for the legitimation of their actions has been strong. This can be seen in their claims to professional status and in attempts to control the nature of planning education and accreditation. The response to these dilemmas in the 1960s saw the rise of 'advocacy planners', mainly in the USA, who explicitly saw planning as a political activity. Such planners chose to leave the planning bureaucracies and work for the 'planned for' to produce alternative solutions to urban problems (Goodman 1972). This sharpened the political nature of planning and showed it as a contested terrain where advocacy and action groups of various kinds were increasingly key players.

Planning has sought its legitimation through its technical and scientific expertise. It was based around the idea that it was possible to produce logical, coherent and systematic arrangements for urban development. This would enable planning to stand outside of politics and produce design-based solutions. This was appealing to local body politicians or local councillors as it allowed them to claim scientific validity for their decision-making process. Geddes, (1949) one of the earliest proponents of planning, argued for the 'survey before plan' approach. The survey would involve the analysis of the physical and social requirements so that the final plan would be one incorporating physical and social infrastructure. Planning thus represented something of a challenge to the unfettered market forces that had been the dominant shapers of the city. The land and rent market were identified as the drivers of growth, thus they had to be restrained through administrative and legal rules to ensure that they took into account wider objectives. One of the problems of this approach was that planning became influenced by a series of 'ideologies' or design imperatives which set up controversies about the shape and pace of urban growth. There were pro-growth and anti-growth movements, there were those who advocated urban consolidation and those who were for the garden city and suburb, who saw spaciousness as healthy and those who saw this trend as destructive of the environment.

Comprehensive City Planning via 'Master' Plans

In many countries, 'master plans' were developed in the second half of the twentieth century to cope with both redevelopment and slum clearance and the continuing growth of some urban regions, usually at the expense of others. The desire for an orderly pattern of development was a central underlying concern. Such plans usually entailed some form of limit to the spread or 'sprawl' of the larger cities and a strategy for 'decentralistion' either through deliberate planning decisions or through putting in place a set of incentives. Many of the same logics were applied in all cases (Kidokoro 1995). One example is that of Seoul (9.9 million population in 2000) in South Korea. South Korea is a country dominated by its capital city. Despite the successive five-year plans developed by central government from 1960 to 1990, Seoul continued to outstrip other cities in its rate of growth with its population quadrupling over this period (Hong 1996). The planning system adopted through this period was one comprising a number of instruments designed to both limit Seoul's growth and provide incentives for relocation. New construction of factories was restricted and new industrial parks were promoted through three ten-year plans. By the 1992–2001 plan, a shift had taken place away from an emphasis upon regulative measures to an emphasis on 'economic channeling based on new congestion charges and quota systems' (Kim and Gallent 1998:10, Newman and Kenworthy 1999). In this they are reflecting the global shift within planning to more market-based strategies utilising pricing systems for the allocation of scarce urban space. Singapore is another Asian country to attempt to control urban congestion through the use of a charging system on cars entering the central city at certain times of the day. A further example would be Melbourne's new city link road system to improve traffic circulation to and around the Central Business District which is based on an electronically collected toll system.

Garden City – New Towns

The garden city/suburb was a particular feature of 1920s' and 1930s' development in the UK and North America. It owes its origins to the work of Ebenezer Howard and the Christian socialists and utopians of the late nineteenth century. Howard, in his book *Tomorrow A Peaceful Path to Real Reform*, published in 1898, advocated the idea of entirely new towns, which would combine urban and rural living. These new communities would be ones with balanced development, not solely residential, but also with a viable industrial and commercial base. A green space around existing cities was, he thought, desirable to prevent aimless sprawl and allow the creation of his new self -contained communities. The work of Howard and others who took up this theme of urban consolidation and development of garden cities and suburbs, reflected an anti-urban bias that has been present in some planning traditions. The big city was seen as a place that was hard to control, a place where crime flourished, where the health of the population was threatened and where political radicalism could flourish in conditions of deprivation and poverty. The solution was to move the population out to healthier air and more spacious building in the suburb where the best of the city and country could be combined. This move could also be associated with the transition to owner occupation thus reducing social radicalism and creating a more responsible citizenry.

The 1950s', 60s' and 70s' version of this was reflected in the new town movement and the desire to create within them balanced communities (Herbert 1963, Dennis 1968, Cresswell 1974, Clapson 1998). The new town towns created in the UK were an attempt at social engineering. They were to be complete communities and so included not just housing but also employment, services and community facilities to encourage sociability amongst the new population. The idea of balance and sociability by osmosis can, in retrospect, be seen as somewhat naive and insufficiently cognisant of the variety of deeply ingrained social distinctions and differences within UK society. Class, gender, ethnicity and life-cycle factors among others are central to patterns of sociability. Simply assuming that sociability would arise from propinquity was too simple and, as many studies showed, was not the result. Further, patterns of mobility also affected the 'balance' and commuting distances expanded with the improvements in the speed of transport so that some new towns, such as Milton Keynes, had substantial numbers who travelled daily back to London rather than living and working in the new town.

A strongly idealised notion of community and neighbourhood underpinned this period of urban planning. This assumed that stability and balance would be achieved over time. A maturation would take place. The analogy was not dissimilar to older evolutionary models found within the early twentieth-century work of the Chicago school. What such models took attention away from was the role of political and other forms of power and control and allowed a naturalistic discourse that supported a laissez-faire approach to neighbourhood planning (Suttles 1972). The other strong influence was that of the design professionals. Calling upon their expertise and their design capacity, they suggested that the key to successful urban solutions to growth and dysfunctional living was a greater emphasis upon useful design of the physical environment.

City Planners

Architects and landscape architects have had a significant influence on urban design. Schuman (1991) draws attention to the models of architecture that have prevailed over the period from the 1950s. The first model, he describes, is where architecture is the lamp that lights the way to a nobler and more satisfying world via both the built and the visual environment. The second is where he sees the architect as holding up a mirror. Here, the design is seeking to reflect and comment upon the world. This would link closer to the ideas of postmodernists who see professionals not so much as creators of taste and style but as reflectors, as people who help in the identification and expression of trends. The issues of power and control are significant and link into the wider debate about governance. Should urban design be a top-down process in which some groups in society decide what is appropriate for others or is it going to be about bottom-up design – where the planning takes place with and alongside the community concerned. The emergence of advocacy planning and guerilla architecture brings social movements and urban design together and raises the question of empowerment and the role that social movements have and continue to play in the development of the city. In this reading, planners take on the role of advocates for the marginalised and powerless and set up an agenda revolving around the highly political questions of who plans and who benefits. Here, what is often invoked by planners and the planned for is a notion of the public good. This, however, is a contested terrain rather than one which is necessarily agreed.

Planning and City Design

The design for positive living could be created. There were various design solutions advanced from Le Corbusier's 'cities in the skies', solving the problems of urban growth through the development of medium and high-rise buildings to the social engineering of Skinner's Waldon Two (1976). The 1950s to 1970s illustrate both the worst and the best of the visionaries. There were garden suburbs designed to give higher quality urban space around the houses. Not all saw these providing an advance on previous living arrangements. There were, for example, studies lamenting the passing of the more intense streetscape of the older 'urban villages' (Young and Willmott 1958, Gans 1964). The suburbs created over the 1950s and 1960s, in response to demographic and migratory pressure and increasing affluence, were largely the products not of the architects and visionaries but of the speculators and developers (Sandercock 1976, Ball 1982). Many suburbs lacked facilities and amenities and so resulted in new tyrannies of distance being created as people became isolated in their distant suburbs. Feminists also have drawn attention to the stereotyped gender roles implied in suburban designs based around the single-family home and how this generates 'domestic work' of childcare, cleaning, and cooking, which falls disproportionately upon women (Friedan 1963; Hayden 1980; McDowell 1989, 1999; Johnson 1994a; Duncan 1996). Feminist analysis has shown that for many women the problem is not being either in the world of work or that of the home but now increasingly attempting to manage the 'balancing act of trying to maintain a presence in both' (Gilroy 2000:3).

As Hayden has noted 'dwellings, neighbourhoods and cities designed for homebound women constrain women physically, socially and economically (1980:S171). The design challenge is to create a practical combination of work and living space which will foster career homelife balance. Some solutions relate to the wider provision of childcare to enable choices and also to the creation of more flexible work practices. Design-related solutions have been advocated by some feminists, these have included the building of kitchen-less apartments, where the tasks of cooking, cleaning and childcare might be more easily shared (Hayden 1980). One model incorporating some of these features is Scandinavian Co-Housing where the tasks, which usually fall upon women, are done through collaboration amongst all the members of the housing project (Jaques 1999, Sangregorio 2000).

The high-rise solution was extensively followed in North America, Europe and many other parts of the globe as the answer to urban growth and the accommodation of growing numbers of urban dwellers in restricted spaces. Hong Kong has one of the highest urban densities in the world. As space has always been at a premium, the high-rise solution has been widely practised in the public and private housing sectors. In the public sector, the Hong Kong Housing Authority currently houses 2.5 million people comprising 39 per cent of the population. The current stock consists of 704,000 flats in a variety of designs stretching over the period from the early 1950s when the first blocks were constructed in response to a fire that destroyed much of the low-cost housing existing at that time. The original blocks were of a slab construction with only one room per household and shared toilet facilities. Although still small by Western standards, with approximately 6 square metres per person, the designs and facilities have been considerably enhanced since the 1950s. The blocks have, however, got progressively higher with the latest ones now up to 40 floors high.

The downside of the many of the multi-storey designs was identified as anonymity and a vulnerability to crime, particularly as the labyrinth-like nature of some of the large blocks made it easy for those committing crime to escape. This, together with residents' lack of knowledge of each other, promoted a fear of strangers in such places. Consequently, over time, a critique of this form of urban living emerged, creating a new planning strategy based around re-designing the high-rise blocks. This new strategy was founded on a set of 'design logics' which sought to remove the anonymity and insecurity of these buildings but this necessitated high levels of maintenance and 'management input' (Dunleavy 1981, Coleman 1985, Power 1993).

Critics saw that the human scale was lost in the development of high-rise apartment blocks associated with the re-development and slum-clearance schemes of the 1950s, 1960s and early 1970s. Many of these projects were constructed by the state or its agents, as part of large-scale social housing schemes (Power 1993). In Melbourne, Australia, high-rise development was undertaken by the State Housing Commission for rental. By the 1990s, many were occupied by the newest migrants to the city. Such blocks are often seen as 'problem areas', where design has limited the development of social relations, and so have suffered from a high turnover of tenants, large numbers of vacancies, vandalism, graffiti, and feelings of insecurity amongst the occupants.

It was not just high-rise 'housing estates' that attracted attention, the large suburban public housing estates constructed in the 1950s through to the 1970s were also problematic. These areas were built for low-income households and thus contained a disproportionate number of those with social and other problems. As the state sought to shift stock from the public to the private sector through the 1980s and 1990s in many countries, the remaining areas of public housing became 'residualised' and the population even more concentrated around those with low incomes, often beneficiaries of the state, and those with psychological and other social problems. Such estates acquired 'forbidding reputations' and the fear of crime and harassment of the dwellers have become major areas of concern to public-housing authorities. This leads to high turnover rates as people seek to move on to the private sector and home ownership thus increasing the administrative costs to the public authorities and also creating considerable population instability.

Coleman in *Utopia on Trial* (1985) has made some of the strongest claims regarding the impact of design on social behaviour in her study of high-rise council-owned estates in the UK. Her study systematically examined the prevalence of graffiti, litter, vandalism, and crime rates and came to the conclusion that these varied directly with the nature of the design. Design could produce social disorganisation. The most likely designs to have this effect were the high-rise tower blocks linked with walkways as these created lots of unsafe spaces where people could be mugged and threatened (Caudrey 1986). Other research, however, has shown that she over-emphasizes the impact of design and pays insufficient attention to both the nature of the management of the apartment blocks by the Local Housing Authorities and the social composition of the residents in the blocks (Power 1993). The problems of high-rise buildings can, however, be overstated. Burke (1988) on the basis of analysis of research in Victoria suggests the negative aspects have been exaggerated and have become part of an ongoing urban myth. Data shows that many high-rise estates do in fact have high degrees of tenant satisfaction and waiting lists of prospective tenants wishing to live in these areas.

New Forms of Planning

What emerges is the connectedness of planning, design and marketing in the contemporary urban environment. A key question debated has been that of what is the best way to distribute scare resources? The neo-liberal agenda of the 1980s and 1990s has placed renewed emphasis on the market as the allocator of goods and services, including, land, buildings and urban infrastructure. There has been a move away from the idea of planning as intervention and control of entrepreneurial activities. The new emphasis is upon private-sector-led regeneration and change. This means reducing planning to a:

> service function for the corporations and its ancillary management class whose behaviour under market discipline is causing the problem planning must seek to address (Low 1999:1).

Low here is drawing attention to the fact that investment decision-making is not particularly place sensitive or necessarily concerned with the long-term development of a city or region. Each of the developer's decisions is shaped by the market niche within which they are operating, and is measured against their financial objectives and returns. This clearly makes an overall coordinated strategy much more difficult to achieve. Further, the shift to market-based solutions leads to a greater emphasis upon marketing and customer solutions. Planning is seen as one 'commodity' and is increasingly provided by private-sector-based rather than public planners. Under these conditions, a different set of underpinning values and imperatives comes into play. As Dear notes:

> Planners who continue as agents of the state can shelter under a mantle of legitimacy afforded them by their elected officials, and even claim to act in the public interest. In contrast, planners who are agents of private capital are responsible only to the bottom line of business profitability (Dear 2000:125).

Consumer choice (sovereignty) is central to the market model. In the urban market place, the position of the suppliers of the various commodities is determined by their market share so they compete vigorously for customer support and loyalty. To gain this they increasingly seek to persuade the customer that they are here to offer them 'solutions' to their living requirements rather than having to take a standardised product. The customer is encouraged to now adapt and 'customise' it to meet their needs. Local authorities, under this competitive pressure, are concerned to maintain their market share and ideally expand their economic opportunities. So part of the 'planning' becomes marketing of the city or place promotion. Selling the city through branding and logos and re-imaging become significant activities. The market here is not just local, within a particular nation-state, but global. This creates intensifying global inter-city competition.

An example of this more market-driven planning was the introduction, under the Thatcher Government in the UK, of a series of initiatives to reduce the role of local authorities in urban development and encourage greater private-sector initiative. The two key changes were the establishment of Enterprise Zones and Urban Development Corporations in the 1980 Local Government Act. Enterprise Zones were designed to provide more favourable development conditions for entrepreneurs through tax breaks and the simplification and speeding up of planning law. Urban Development Corporations were made up of non-elected members drawn principally from those with property and business backgrounds (Duncan and Goodwin 1988, Thorns 1992).

For such advocates, the fall of the Berlin Wall in 1989 and the resulting collapse of the Eastern Socialist states and the shift within these to 'market'-based economies was a clear sign that rational planning based around state-organised five to ten-year programmes was dead. Instead such states should move to the creation of the appropriate fiscal frameworks to allow economic growth, urban resurgence and redevelopment. The private sector was to be the engine of growth, in partnership with central and local government, NGOs and CBOs. This is consistent with the hollowing out of the state and the shifting of activity from within the state to the voluntary sector or private commercial-based organisations. The emphasis is not on service delivery and community development but upon efficiency.

By the end of the 1990s there were signs that the strength of the neo-liberal agenda was waning. In the USA, there was renewed support for the Federal Housing and Urban Development Department, after a period where its future had appeared threatened (Gotham 1998, Wachter 2000). A significant factor here was the publication of the *State of the Cities Report* (Department of Housing and Urban Development 1997) that re-focused attention on urban change and how this was opening up a new poverty divide within US cities. There were many urban places getting left behind, where unemployment and underemployment were concentrated. There were areas of increasing disadvantage, crime, poverty and decay. It was concluded that these areas required not just housing improvement but also a programme of neighbourhood renewal. The solution was to be found through a move to empowerment zones and enterprise communities where partnerships would be sought between the state and the private sector to regenerate the whole area. The market was seen as having failed to solve the problem of declining neighbourhoods and thus new forms of intervention were required. The solution adopted here has parallels with that introduced by the Major administration in the UK in 1994. This programme of Single Regeneration Budgets was a move away from the strident rejection of planning which had characterised the Thatcher years and a sign that markets were not capable of delivering all requirements. The new approach focused around the question of how to re-integrate problematic places into the mainstream of the urban economy. It was linked to the growing discourse centering around social exclusion and inclusion.

A further sign of change is provided with the release of the 'Rogers Report' (Urban Task Force and Rogers 1999) on how to achieve an urban renaissance (Box 8.1). The task force, established by the Blair Government in the UK, was directed to 'identify the causes of urban decline in England and recommend practical solutions to bring people back into our cities, towns and urban neighbourhoods (p1). The report suggests that since the industrial revolution towns and cities have been spoilt by 'poor design, economic dispersal and social polarization'. The report thus moves back to a more interventionist agenda and away from the belief that the free market alone will create optimum conditions for city development. For the writers of the report, the future course should be one where towns and cities are more compact and connected – meaning here improved transport links to lessen car dependency and associated pollution and the maintenance of the necessary infrastructure to enable existing urban places to continue to be viable. The way they see this agenda being achieved is through the leadership of local government authorities and the creation of effective partnerships between citizens and communities. Further connecting with the social exclusion agenda, the report acknowledges that the management of urban areas needs to take account of the fact that there continues to be 'council estates and other deprived neighbourhoods' that will require special attention.

Alongside these changes there has been the growth of a new movement within planning theory centred on the idea of 'deliberative planning' (Healey 1998). This form of planning draws from the idea of collective rather than purely individual involvement in the planning process and in some ways is an extension of the public participation in planning debates of the 1960s and 1970s. The model is based around citizens meeting to discuss their environment to identify concerns and then work together for solutions. The advocates of this form of planning suggest that it is necessary to look at ways to shift the previous arguments about participation and consultation, which mostly reflected objections and a reactive approach to ones of incorporation and the seeking of jointly negotiated solutions. The involvement of citizens in these new processes of planning would build consensus around options and a new course of action to solve environmental, housing and neighbourhood planning issues (Healey 1998). It would also permit 'social learning' and so engage the support or buy-in of the locality into the solutions and thus give it a greater chance of success (Forester 1999).

A further challenge to rational scientific planning as the basis of urban design came from the postmodernist critique of design and an emphasis upon difference, variety and a more vernacular style. Postmodernists see

Box 8.1

Towards an urban renaissance in the UK: report of the Urban Task Force, June 1999

A significant report on urban planning and urban development by the Urban Task Force under the guidance of Lord Rogers was published in 1999. This sets out some of the key facts about Britain's urban population and sets an agenda for an 'urban renaissance' based on 'practical solutions to bring people back into our cities, towns and urban neighbourhoods'.

Urban factfile

- Urban areas in England account for 90 per cent of population, 91 per cent of economic output and 89 per cent of jobs

- The public sector spends over £200 billion a year in English towns and cities and on the people who live there – almost 60 per cent of total UK public expenditure

- Government projections estimate that 3.8 million extra households will form between 1996 and 2021 – a 19 per cent increase

- One in four people living in urban neighbourhoods think their area has got worse in recent years, compared with only one in ten who think it has got better.

- More than 90 per cent of the urban buildings and infrastructure that will exist in 30 years time has already been built.

- Car traffic is predicted to grow by a third in the next 20 years. Average commuting time is 40 per cent higher than 20 years ago.

- Unemployment in inner cities runs at more than double the rate elsewhere.

- 40 per cent of inner-urban housing stock is subsidised 'social' housing.

- Around 1.3 million residential and commercial buildings are currently empty.

The report discusses issues such as:

- recycling land and buildings;

- achieving excellence in leadership, participation and management;

- delivering regeneration;

- designing the urban environment and

- making the connection – transport links and other infrastructure for cities, towns and neighbourhoods to function as strong economic and social units.

Web site for report: *http://www.regeneration.dtlr.gov.uk/utf/renais/1.htm#1*

Source: Urban Task Force and Rogers 1999

differences not as something to be removed and standardised, but rather to be celebrated and encouraged. What constitutes postmodernism, we have already seen, is a matter of considerable argument. However, within architecture and urban design there is an agreement that this shift, from the mid 1960s, has brought about a wish to open up:

> the immense variety and richness of things, materials and ideas that the modern world inexhaustibly brought forth. They breathed fresh air and play-fulness into a cultural ambience which in the 1950s had become unbearably solemn, rigid and closed (Berman, 1982:32).

Jencks further sees postmodernist architecture as an attempt to 'communicate with both the public and a concerned minority, usually architects' (Jencks 1984:80). He also suggests it opens the way to a more participatory design that has 'rejuvenated architecture'. At the beginning of the twenty-first century, the influence of the postmodernist critique has a number of quite significant impacts upon urban design. It has encouraged the trend towards a greater recognition of diversity with the rejection of 'master narratives' and 'master plans' for cities and a increased preference for local solutions and the view that there is no one best way to accomplish objectives. Thus, planning education entered something of a crisis in the late 1980s and 1990s. What was to be the underlying rationale that gave it its identity? Was it a reflective critic of 'modernism', by which was usually seen as all the worst features of the 1950s to the 1970s, such as the large-scale development of housing, the extensive use of unadorned designs stressing functionalism, and the control of activity through rational segregation between people and traffic and work and residential areas (Watson and Gibson 1995). The outcome of the challenge has been either reactionary, with an affirmation of the status quo and tradition leading to what has been termed neo-traditionalism which tends to be expressed through the revival of community ideologies as part of a new set of moral rhetoric about social inclusion, or resistance which, in contrast to the first, looks for a programme of political change which addresses issues of power and seeks to 'deconstruct' and to explore rather than conceal social and political practices and thus empower those currently without power. This takes us to the question of urban governance (Dear and Wolch 1987, Levitas 1998, Dear 2000).

Urban Governance

Globalisation, and the growth of global cities linked together through flows of information, travel, property markets and financial transactions, pose new problems for national and local systems of governance. Has the nation-state been in some ways supplanted by the city-state? Are the ways that decisions are made about economic development and land use still the prerogative of locals or are they now made by the TNCs? Many commentators have raised these questions as they seek to establish the form of urban decision-making and governance emerging in a more globalised urban world. Cities have had trans-border connections for much of the last century encouraged via such international organizations as the International Union of Local Authorities founded in 1913 (Scholte 2000). Town twinning began in the 1950s and spread rapidly so that outside most towns a road sign will proudly display an array of towns connected through 'twinning'. This usually leads to cultural and other exchanges and may lead to economic development. By the end of the century, further global linkages between cities have been forged through a series of international organizations including the UNCHS (Habitat Programme), Agenda 21 initiatives as an outcome of the 1992 Rio Earth Summit 1992, and the formation, in 1990, of the International Council for Local Environmental Initiatives which now has 337 municipalities represented in 57 countries.

The growth of these networks provides a way for cities to promote and achieve their economic and political objectives independently from national governments and thus potentially increases their capacity to follow independent strategies. The existence of international federations also provides an opportunity for local governments to become global players rather than just national ones and some cities have seized this opportunity to enhance their competitive position and attract new forms of investment. These actions in turn impact upon the local planning and political decision-making process.

The identification of planning and urban development, as essentially a political and economic process that is increasingly both about global and local issues, draws attention to wider questions of urban governance. Planning from its origins has been associated with state practices. Planning became part of the administrative and management structure of the city. It assisted in the allocation of physical and social resources. As such, planning was involved in the debates about re-distribution and inequality. During the 1950s and 1960s, Social Democratic states practised urban planning as they considered it was a central tool to ensure greater equity of access to goods and services. Spatial inequality was recognised alongside social inequality and was seen as something that could be addressed through design and management-type solutions. The separation of the planned-for and the planners emerged as a point of tension and an ongoing debate has occurred as to how the 'public' should be involved in decision-making (Healey 1998). Numerous public participation exercises have been held to seek 'community input' into planning processes and most countries have instituted some form of legal framework for objection and appeal to land-use planning decision-making.

How city growth is shaped by the political and planning institutions is not something which has only one outcome but is the result of a process involving different levels of governance and forms of mobilisation. The case of Toronto is illustrative of some of these processes and the form they have taken has resulted in the city following a different growth and development path to that of a number of North American cities where planning and political controls were looser (Box 8.2).

Box 8.2

··

Toronto Canada: the role of politics and planning

● Population: Greater Toronto Area, 1996, 4.62 million

The greater Toronto area is made up of a number of administrative areas, the largest of which are Metro Toronto with a population of 2.38 million and the City of Toronto with 654,000.

The Canadian population is concentrated along the border with the USA and, within each Province, one city – the state capital – exerts a strong influence. For example, in 1991, 61 per cent of the Canadian population lived in the metropolitan areas. Ontario, within Canada, accounts for 36 per cent of the total population of the country. Toronto is Canada's largest metropolitan area.

The story of Toronto over the twentieth century has been one of a gradually expanding urban area within which the 'city' of Toronto has become a smaller part. Over the first half of the century, manufacturing played a dominant role in the life of the city. In 1911, 35 per cent of the labour force was employed in this sector. By 1961, this had fallen to 30 per cent (Thorns, 1993), showing a slow decline.

Since 1961, restructuring has taken place with the economic life of the city shifting to financial and business services and, with this, the strong development of high-rise office towers within the CBD.

Growing suburban populations in the wider metropolitan area during the 1950s and 1960s led to the emergence of political struggles between the interests of the new suburbs and the central city. A way of dealing with this was sought through the establishment of a Metropolitan Authority (Metro Toronto) in 1953. This authority was made up of 12 representatives from the city and 12 from the suburbs. The creation of this new authority was a major factor in the subsequent planning and development of the region and has been described as the 'most notable municipal experiment in North America (Lemon 1984, 1985).

A metropolitan planning system was thus put in place in the 1950s when the city was starting to expand. Unlike many North-American cities, Toronto grew in an orderly way

Continued

---

and has avoided the blight in central areas that have occurred in other large cities as they expanded, de-industrialised and shifted to a finance, business service and information economy in the 1980s and 1990s.

Toronto also did not rely totally on private cars for circulation but developed and integrated a public transit system comprising both subways and buses with the first subway opening along Yonge Street in 1953, followed by University in 1963 and Danforth in 1966. Subways and associated public transit operations, by the end of the 1960s, were carrying 70 per cent of all downtown workers.

From the 1970s, the balance within the Metropolitan area shifted back to the central area which became progressively more important than the suburbs due to:

- shifts in employment from manufacturing into finance and business services as Toronto became the most significant financial centre in Canada;

- gentrification of inner neighbourhoods and redevelopment of inner areas into offices and apartments;

- Social restructuring of inner city populations with higher proportions of younger people and of those in professional and managerial occupations;

- political shifts which have been reflected in city and metro politics and planning (Frisken et al. 2000).

The Toronto case shows the influence of the local political culture on urban development and city structure and the way that a more orderly pattern of urban development can be created through an active planning system and considerable development in urban infrastructure.

City web site: *http://www.city.toronto.on.ca/*

Alongside of these developments, there has also been the radical restructuring of state activity under the aegis of the neo-liberal revolution. This sought to decrease the level of state involvement in service provision and reduce red tape and bureaucratic forms of decision-making in favour of more market-based ones. It also favoured decentralisation of decision-making on the grounds that those closest to the activity were able to make good decisions. Under the influence of public choice and agency theory, the model of governance adopted tended to privilege accountability and transparency. Cross-subsidisation was seen as bad as it distorted distributions and hid the true cost of activities thus preventing sound investment decisions. Many western governments therefore reduced their public service and required local governments to adopt a more business-like structure to guide their operations. In Aotearoa/New Zealand, the Local Government Amendment Act 1989 reduced the number of local authorities through amalgamation and required new forms of strategic planning and accounting. These were further reinforced in a 1996 Amendment. The result has been local authorities taking, as their core planning document, the strategic plan which requires them to develop a mission statement, goals, objectives, and a business plan. The 1996 amendment added a 'strict economic allocation model' which required them to address the question of who pays and who benefits from services and related activities. A ten-year financial strategy and capital works plan were the final requirements. Under this new system, the city administration took on a more corporate structure with the city manager as Chief Executive Officer (CEO) and new divisions for financial control, policy and strategic planning and environmental planning and services (Perkins and Thorns 2000b, 2001c).

The contested nature of planning, given that it deals with the distribution of real resources, has been central to arguments for change to the process. Some critics have suggested that the planning system has been captured by pressure and lobby groups who have thus been able to shape it to their advantage rather than it being a neutral and rational process of allocation of resources across the city. There has also been a growing debate about the nature of representation, especially the tension between citizen and representative democracy, whereby the citizen transfers the right to make decisions to elected politicians for a period of three to five years. In the era of information, technology and instant information, there are calls for a reassessment of this division and calls for citizen referenda on key issues. Information can be made available via the Internet and web sites, citizens can debate in both cyberspace and in face-to-face encounters so why not allow them a greater engagement in decision-making. What we see here are challenges to the power and position of entrenched political and economic interests, which thus are likely to face resistance.

In a recent study of citizen participation in the development of a an urban growth strategy for Wellington, Aotearoa/New Zealand's capital city, it was found that over the period of the programme, the Wellington City Councillors became less enthusiastic and involved in the process. The process involved 2000 Wellington residents and 100 organisations in developing a vision for how the city should develop by 2020 to create a more sustainable city. The programme was one of participation rather than partnership with the City Council. Blyth (1999) concluded from this study that the process resulted in more than consultation but less than partnership.

The 1990s have seen shifts in the planning and governance of cities. In part, this is the result of the growing inclusion of environmental issues and the debate about a sustainable future arising from the global concerns of Rio and Agenda 21. The increased understanding of the globe as an interconnected social, economic and ecological system has raised the question of how all these interests can be effectively represented in urban decision-making. Is it, for example, possible to create a system that spans both the social and natural world and so involve animals and plants in the decision process? This has led some to argue that we need to generate a 'parliament of things' (Latour 1993) to replace our current limited system based around the current population. These issues will be examined further in the next chapter.

To conclude our discussion of urban planning and control it is useful to reflect on the nature of urban resistance. The story of the second half of the last century could be told from the position of the powerful, suggesting changes are always initiated at the level of government. Such a story would be incomplete. Struggles over the use and abuse of the built environment have been very much part of the narrative.

Urban Struggles

In the 1960s, there were a series of anti-freeway protests which rippled around the world and indicated a growing disenchantment with the 'roading solution' to urban congestion and travel (Mullins 1977). The threat to the existing urban infrastructure posed by redevelopment and construction of motorways created urban protest groups which had some success at halting or altering plans. It showed up the potential range of conflict within the urban setting, for example, that between the inner city and outer suburban residents. The first group favoured less traffic in the central areas to reduce congestion, parking, pollution and the preserving or enhancing the local environment whereas outer suburban residents were now concerned with improved access to the centres, reductions in travel times and increased parking opportunities to facilitate their commuting. Cities are faced with contradictory agendas. Some have tried control via taxes on those entering the centre at peak times, car pooling, subsidising public transportation, bus only lanes, increasing road and petrol taxes or combinations of these ideas. Urban analysts drew, from the various urban protests, a range of groups differentiated according to their durability and the degree to which they were interested in short-term resistance or longer-term social change. The earliest analyses were based around class politics whilst the more recent analyses have shifted, along with the social movements literature generally, to identity politics as their focus (Frankel 1994, Seidman 1994).

Urban struggles in the early and middle years of the twentieth century were generally associated with class struggles over the distribution and re-distribution of resources. Social movements were the route to political power. The trade unions and tenants action groups joined forces to fight rents and landlords to improve living conditions. A series of rent strikes in Glasgow in 1915, 1920, 1927, initiated by the Glasgow Women's Housing association, were aimed at keeping down housing cost and encouraging a greater state involvement in housing provisions (Castells 1983, Damer 1990). This struggle links place, gender and class together in a political struggle for change. The greater involvement of the state in housing from the 1920s and 1930s was one outcome of the pressure that the rent strikes created at national and local levels. The focus of much urban protest became, through the extension of the welfare state and subsequent restructuring, the state and its agents. In the 1970s, with the fiscal crisis of the capitalist state and the consequent need to restructure activities, a round of cuts to public provisions occurred across most capitalist states. The result was increased social protest such that some analysts saw this as the likely route to more profound social change (Castells 1977b). The extent of collective response was muted through the pace and scale of change and the fragmenting of old political and social alliances under the impact of both economic and cultural globalisation. A particular variant of the resistance to restructuring and change were the IMF riots in a number of developing countries as a result of the imposition of structural adjustment programmes by the IMF as a necessary accompaniment to the receipt of loans (Walton 1987).

In the 1980s and 1990s, the restructuring of the local and national state provided some sites of resistance and a growing recognition that globalisation and the more market-based and privatised system of economic relations did not render locality redundant but restructured localities in interesting ways. A series of studies pointed to the continuing significance of place and local social relations and solutions to global change. Urry, for example, suggests that:

> As production capital assumes international form capitalist society manifests increasing fragmentation of classes on the local level and therefore political behaviour is characterised by the heightening importance of local social movements not based upon class (Urry 1981:455).

Greater attention has been drawn to the local level, as the place of political decision-making, by the moves towards greater decentralisation that have been part of the debate about governance and the shifting of decision-making away from the centre. The practice here shows contradictions. There has been the rhetoric of empowerment and public participation but this has not always been linked to the redistribution of resources or the capacities and resources to allow people to be effectively involved in decision-making. The opening-out of local agendas, in the planning arena, for greater public participation do not just bring into play 'progressive' social movements. Research here has identified the NIMBY groups, who have generally been seen as favouring the protection of the status quo practising resistance politics (Dear 1992). Such groups develop an initial consciousness around a point of local defence or protection activity associations and so are very often categorized as 'reactionary' in their actions. Judgments such as these need to be carefully considered as they may simply reflect a differing value system being expressed. All participants in urban social action like to consider that they represent the 'true' voice of the community. In an increasingly individualised and fragmentary world, creating consensus or agreement over courses of action may be more difficult now than in the past.

Examples of resistance abound in urban life. Within residential areas, many are formed around the development of activities seen to depress property values and bringing in undesirable activity. These can include activities such as skate board parks for teenagers, half-way houses for those who have been de-institutionalised from psychiatric care institutions as part of moves to community-based care, the building of prisons and remand centres and the development of commercial activities likely to cause changes to noise levels, traffic flows and polluting activities. The shift from resistance to local landlords to forming a city-wide tenants protection association or the move from resisting local developers to forming a wider environmental protection group or joining with Greenpeace or Friends of the Earth can take the individual from their local concerns to global ones.

The other side of the politics of localities has been the rise of more fluid and decentred forms of urban action. The rise of identity politics around gender, sexuality, ethnicity, age and disability has weakened the class-based nature of former urban movements and created a more fragmented landscape of urban resistance which often works at the level of individuals. The nature of struggle here is guided by the presence of legal remedies. Increased litigation occurs as people seek solutions though the courts, challenging decisions and claiming rights, often contained in constitutional protections for minorities and other marginalised groups. The shift from broad collective social action to rights-based action is part of the re-alignment of the state under a neo-liberal agenda. Such an agenda seeks to reduce the direct intervention into people's lives by the state. This again is something of a paradox as the rhetoric has been consistently about greater individual freedom and opportunity to make decisions. In many cases, however, the state has maintained considerable centralised power, exercised though through different mechanisms than in the period of the dominance of the social democratic state from the 1930s through to the 1970s.

Urban resistance in many cities has formed around the conflict between global and local agendas. The incorporation of cities into the global economy exerts new pressure upon land values and uses and may thus force locals out of these areas. Struggles have developed around this displacement. One example would be the locality of Klong Thoey in Bangkok (Berner and Korff 1995). This locality emerged as a squatter slum in the 1960s as a result of rapid urban growth and migration into the city and an inability of the city to provide housing. The area occupied was close to the harbour but, as an area of swampy ground, was unattractive for commercial development. However, over the next twenty years, the city grew and incorporated the area bringing improved transport and drainage and increasing the attractiveness of the location. By 1990, 20 per cent of all new construction in Bangkok was in Klong Thoey and of this 40 per cent was for housing and 60 per cent for commercial and high-rise office accommodation. This change placed considerable pressure upon the original squatter population and highlighted the competition between living space and the needs of the local population for housing and the more profitable uses created by Bangkok's increasing integration into the global economy. The resistance to slum clearance was enabled by the entry to the area, in the 1970s, of young well-educated people who engaged in social work and helped facilitate neighbourhood development, initially amongst the young people. Over time, Klong Thoey became a symbol of resistance to urban change that disregarded the locals. The strength of the locals became recognised by the city administration and resulted in those evicted being resettled on adjacent land on a twenty-five year lease (Berner and Korff 1995). The case illustrates the way that it is still possible, where local communities and neighbourhoods build social cohesion and a clear strategy, to alter the outcomes of urban development successfully and create more acceptable solutions for the present residents, thus modifying the impact of globalisation upon their locality.

In the 1990s, the problems generated by the retreat of the state and the emphasis on greater individualism gave rise to concerns for the integration of people into the city (Allmendinger and Thomas 1998). According to some analysts, the fragmentation and greater fluidity of urban life are part of a greater degree of globalisation which is leading to the destruction of community and the institutions which provided the glue of society, such as family and community life. The Klong Thoey case provides some degree of optimism and shows that the power of human agency still exists. The recognition of this has led to a counter ideology emerging in the latter part of the twentieth century, that of social capital and the need to restore 'community' as an integral part of creating a new sense of social responsibility to allow the fighting of social decay as witnessed by urban crime, unemployment, educational failure, racial and ethnic tensions (Putnam 1995). Such a strategy requires the rebuilding of interpersonal links from the ground up and the development of new, more cooperative political processes. Here, the power of information technology could be a valuable part of the recreation of local resistance where this allows for improved information flows and the building of networks. Such networks may begin as virtual ones but the creation of successful forms of urban mobilisation is likely to involve the formation of real networks of friends and neighbours, creating a strong sense of local identity.

Summary

The chapter has examined the place of urban planning within the development of the city. Planning is part of the control and governance structure of the city. It is part of urban management and, as such, often associated with the desire to impose order and mitigate the excesses of market-based economic decision-making. It reflects a social interventionist tradition that had its roots in the nineteenth-century reformists and social engineers, motivated by a desire to improve the quality of life and overall well-being of citizens. In the late twentieth century, under neoliberalism, the emergence of postmodernism in architecture and design, the critique of the enlightenment view of knowledge, and a far greater focus upon individualism, variety and difference has emerged. This in turn has created a more fragmented and varied urban landscape and has given new emphasis to arguments about control of urban development. A crucial question has been that of the legitimacy of planning and urban control. The previous rationale for planning lay in its claims to expertise based on science and evidence, giving it a way of moving from the present to the future. This largely consisted of extrapolating from the present. Therefore, the theoretical models tended to become associated with the entrenched economic, political and social interests of the day. The disruption of this agenda via the environmental challenge of the late 1980s and 1990s has led to the restructuring of the debate on urban planning and futures around the 'sustainability agenda'. The next chapter examines this agenda to assess whether this can form a basis for a twenty-first century urban project.

Further Reading

Planning

Angotti, T. 1993, *Metropolis 2000: Planning, Poverty, and Politics*. London: Routledge. The book takes up the analysis of the place of planning within the political structures and decision-making. It identifies, in chapter 5, the various roles that planners and designers have adopted with respect to urban form.

Dear, M. 2000. *The Postmodern Urban Condition*. Oxford: Blackwell. Chapter 6, 'Deconstructing Urban Planning', pp. 117–39 analyses the nature of planning from 1945 to the 1990s.

It argues that planning is about power – about achieving outcomes that serve the purposes of powerful agents within society.

Urban Social Movements

Damer, S. 1990. *Glasgow; Going for a Song*. London: Lawrence and Wishart. Chapter 5, 'The Depression', provides an analysis of working-class movements and struggles surrounding rent increases, documenting the significance of class-based movements at this stage in Glasgow's social development.

Dear, M. 1992. 'Understanding and Overcoming the NIMBY Syndrome'. *Journal of the American Planning Association*. 58(3). This paper examines the rise and role of NIMBY groups within the city indicating the power of the property interests within urban life.

Governance

Scholte, J. 2000. *Globalization: A Critical Introduction*, Basingstoke: Macmillan Press – now Palgrave Macmillan. Chapter 6, 'Globalization and Governance', pp. 132–58, deals with the challenges to nation-states that have arisen as a result of globalisation process. It examines how supraterritoriality has promoted moves towards multi-layered governance within which cities have acquired new significance.

Web sites

http://www.city.toronto.on.ca/
http://www.planning.org/
http://www.brook.edu/
http://www.greenbelt.org/
http://www.smartgrowth.org/
http://www.soci.canterbury.ac.nz/suphome.htm
http://www.regeneration.dtlr.gov.uk/utf/renais/

9

The Sustainable City

Introduction

The analysis of global urban development in the last couple of decades has been greatly influenced by the 'sustainability debate' and the increasing recognition that we are all part of one eco-system (Therborn 2000). This debate focuses upon the interplay between the environment and the natural resources it contains – water, energy, soil, air – and the pollution and consequent corruption of the eco-system that has taken place through industrial and urban development. A recent idea that has gained currency in the debate is that of the 'ecological footprint' which is the calculated amount of ecologically productive land needed on a continuous basis to supply a population with all its resources (goods, services and energy, and so on) and to assimilate all wastes (Parliamentary Commissioner for the Environment 1998:2). The use of this concept is an attempt to provide integration across the natural and social environment. In much of this debate, 'sustainability' is seen largely as a matter of bio-physical processes and the social and the cultural facets of the city and the social actions and political institutions which have emerged over time are seen as secondary to the natural or derivatives from the bio-physical environment.

Inequalities of power and position, especially distribution issues and access for all social groups, are of major importance in the analysis of urban change and the provision of a desirable path for future development. This raises the question of the relationship between issues of social justice and those of environmental sustainability. They also draw back our attention quite firmly to the fact that we are now living within a global world, one where new risks have arisen as a result of the speed with which both material objects, ideas, microbes and all other forms of life can be transferred across distances previously acting as barriers. Bio-security has become a major concern for food producers such as Aotearoa/New Zealand. Yet, despite their surveillance, transmission has occurred of species and diseases which have affected the local ecology.

A recent example is the Veroa Bee Mite, which has the potential to severely damage both Aotearoa/New Zealand's honey production and its native bird life through the impact of fewer bees upon the pollination of native plants and trees. Concerns about the quality of food and the range of 'additives' turning them from 'natural' to modified products is an area of debate which is hotting up at the global and local level as scientists develop new forms of gene technology and thus the capacity to clone and modify our human genetic make-up and that of our food and broader environment. Many will see this as just an extension of a long process of change. It is the speed and the global spread of change that makes the present age one of greater risk. Gene technology is one example, among many, of the global spread of new risks which pose a threat to the 'natural' environment, to the continuation of the present 'bio-diversity', and thus to the survival of human life upon the planet.

The quest for sustainability therefore reflects a wide set of global concerns about the future of life on the planet. On 18 November 1992, for example, some of the world's leading scientists from seventy countries signed an urgent warning to the world's political leaders. It stated:

> The environment is suffering critical stress . . . Our massive tampering with the world's interdependent web of life – coupled with other environment change which is inflicted by deforestation, species loss, and climate change – could trigger widespread adverse effects, including unpredictable collapses of critical biological systems whose interactions and dynamics we only imperfectly understand. Uncertainty over the extent of effects cannot excuse complacency or delay in facing the threats.
>
> A new ethic is required – a new responsibility for caring for ourselves and for the Earth. We must recognise the Earth's limited capacity to provide for us . . . We must no longer allow it to be ravaged. This ethic must motivate a great movement, convincing reluctant leaders and reluctant governments and reluctant peoples themselves to effect the needed changes (EOLSS 1997).

Some of these ideas have been given voice through the rise of environmental movements, green politics and a series of global fora through the 1980s and the 1990s.

In the final decades of the last century, therefore, there has grown up a strong argument that the future of the city can only be assured if a more 'sustainable' approach to urban development is adopted (Blowers and Pain 1999, Polese and Stren 2000). The city, as we have previously observed, is where most people will be living in the present millennium. It has been argued that, in order to accommodate this increase and ensure that the conditions of urban life, both social and environmental, do not deteriorate, a substantial shift in our thinking about the nature of the interconnections between the social and the natural worlds will be required. Part of this shift is the acceptance that the world is now a 'global place' where there is a need for the recognition of ecological 'risk' and where all our actions are interconnected. So too does the solution to local urban problems require the realization that we are part of a global system. As Giddens has pointed out:

> For thousands of years human beings worried about risks coming from external nature – from, for example, floods, bad harvest, plagues and other natural disasters. They worried about what nature could do to them. Relatively recently – in the short period of history we are discussing here (last 20 or so years) – we started worrying less about what nature can do to us and more about what we have done to nature (Hutton and Giddens 2000:5).

The postmodern challenge to the epistemological foundations of 'enlightenment knowledge' has served to create greater uncertainty with respect to 'technological solutions' and the capacity of conventional science to understand and explain the world. There has been a revival in indigenous knowledge and a greater appreciation of the wisdom contributing to previously disregarded social and ecological practices (UNESCO 2000). There has been a growing recognition of the need for an architecture and design of houses and settlements that reflects a genuine 'indigenous voice' rather than imposes a western style of design and a greater appreciation of the value of traditional design and building materials. A recent example is the emergence of an 'aboriginal architecture' debate within Australia (Haar 2000).

What this shift in thinking has done is to create a new set of discourses, which are now beginning to shape discussion about city development. These can be broadly subsumed under the label of 'sustainability'. As we will see, this then becomes a problematic terrain, as the understandings folded within this term are quite diverse. The language may have changed but there is still the question of the extent to which change has been made in actual social, economic, political and environmental practices and, thus, how far we have moved from rhetoric to action.

In this chapter, the aim is to explore the emerging debate about urban sustainability and therefore what a 'sustainable city' would represent. The structure of the chapter is, firstly, a discussion of the growth of the 'urban sustainability' argument and an attempt to identify its key components, secondly, a critique of some aspects of this debate with a view to clarifying the underlying set of concerns which need to be addressed and, finally, a couple of case studies of contemporary urban development which seek to represent aspects of the sustainable city. These will feature the Aotearoa/New Zealand Resource Management Act 1991 that has provided a new basis for city planning, and the idea of New Urbanism and Smart Growth, which emphasizes urban consolidation rather than wasteful suburban sprawl. What gets incorporated into policy-making and decision-taking is often 'sustainable management' focused around natural resource preservation and excluding the social equity dimensions of the broader sustainable development agenda. Much of the debate downplays or fails to recognise that the city is a social and political construction. It is often a site of struggle and conflict and thus the role of social movements in shaping the city needs to be recognized (Castells 1983, Brodie 1996).

Sustainable Development

The idea of sustainable development has become accepted as the guiding principle for contemporary development. It is generally defined using the fomulation found in *Our Common Future* (the Brundtland Report of 1987) as:

> development that meets the needs of the present without compromising the ability of future generations to meet their own needs (World Commission on Environment and Development 1987:43).

Right from the beginning of the debate, however, there was an underlying major conflict between 'environmentalists concerned to safeguard the bio-sphere, and proponents of economic growth concerned to increase and expand production' (Polese and Stren 2000:15). The concerns for sustainability have generated a number of prescriptions for action. The Brundtland Report is perhaps the most notable and resulted in the following prescription for sustainable development:

> the pursuit of sustainable development requires:
> - a political system that secures effective citizen participation in decision-making;
> - an economic system that is able to generate surpluses and technical knowledge on a self-reliant and sustained basis;
> - a social system that provides for solutions for the tensions arising from disharmonious development;
> - a production system that respects the obligation to preserve the ecological base for development;
> - a technological system that can search continuously for new solutions;
> - an international system that fosters sustainable patterns of trade and finance and

- an administrative system that is flexible and has the capacity for self-correction (WCED 1987:65).

Sustainable development in this interpretation is thus a holistic concept which looks to create a new pattern of ecologically informed and sensitive social and economic development which recognises not just the immediate needs of the present occupants of the planet but also the longer term needs to ensure that human settlement can survive in a way that enables an improved quality to life across the globe. Agenda 21, with its explicitly social chapter, was produced at the Earth Summit in Rio de Janeiro (1992) as a programme for action to create more sustainable development. Here, the need for political and economic arrangements to protect the natural environment and produce goods and services and for political practices ensuring social equality, fairness and living arrangements that are socially and bio-physically sustainable was emphasized.

The Rio summit was followed by several other events including the Global Conference on Sustainable Development of Small Island States in Barbados, 1994, the International Conference on Population and Development, Cairo, 1994; the World Summit on Social Development, Copenhagen, 1995; the fourth World Conference on Women, Beijing, 1995 and the second UN Conference on Human Settlements, Habitat 2, Istanbul 1996. The sentiments of Rio were reiterated in the Istanbul declaration in June 1996 at the end of Habitat 2, the last of the series of UN global conferences at the end of the last century:

> This conference in Istanbul marked a new era of cooperation, an era of solidarity. As we move into the twenty-first century, we offer a positive vision of sustainable human settlements, a sense of hope for our common future and an exhortation to join a truly worthwhile and engaging debate and challenge, that of building together a world where everyone can live in a safe home with a promise of a decent life of dignity, good health, safety, happiness and hope (UNCHS 1996:2).

The vehicle to achieving the changes necessary to implement the declaration rested on the creation of new partnerships between the state at both a national and local level and third sector NGOs and CBOs and private sector capital. This new formation at the local level would lead, it was suggested, to the greater empowerment of communities.

Progress towards achieving the objectives set out in these global fora has been slow and the plus five series of meetings now being held (for example, the Social Conference +5 was held in 1999 and Istanbul +5 was held in New York in June 2001) has indicated that shifts in ideas and debate have been greater than tangible action on the ground. In many situations, the way that 'sustainability' has been assimilated into national policy has resulted, at best, in partial responses, which have favoured technical solutions based around a more deep-rooted incorporation of 'environmental science' into the urban development process. In these responses, there has only been a limited embrace of the social justice dimensions of the idea of 'sustainable development'.

It is now claimed that the concept of sustainable development has become an internationally accepted model of environmental development policy (Institute for Social-Ecological Research 1997). A recently-initiated Management of Social Transformation UNESCO research project has, as its aims, to:

> initiate and intensify – on an international scale – a fundamental and problem oriented debate on the concept of sustainability within the various social sciences (ISOE 1997).

This need attests to the continuing difficulties in defining what is actually meant by sustainable development, particularly how its ecological, economic and social dimensions are to be brought together.

Figures 9.1 and 9.2 represent the view underlying much of the discussion about 'sustainability'. Figure 9.1 represents the current view of the world where economic and development policies are not sufficiently in tune with the earth's natural systems and carrying capacity. Thus, the present policies are 'unsustainable' meaning they will lead to a degradation of the natural systems which will lead to resource depletion, pollution, health problems and deterioration in urban life. Globally, this scenario leads to global warming, climate change, ozone depletion and a series of environmental effects posing an increasing threat to a number of world cities, especially those based in coastal regions. The alternative scenario is shown in Figure 9.2. In this case, the model is based around 'sustainable development'. Where biodiversity is privileged, there are enlightened institutions and natural resource use recognises inter- and intra-generational equity.

The sustainable development project is thus centred on a view that economic and other development policies, including urban ones, should be based on:

> six principals of sustainability, namely: inter-generational equity; intra-generational equity; risk aversion strategies; conservation of biodiversity; internalisation of environmental cost; and enlightened institutions (EOLSS 1997).

Figure 9.1 Elements and consequences of the global crisis

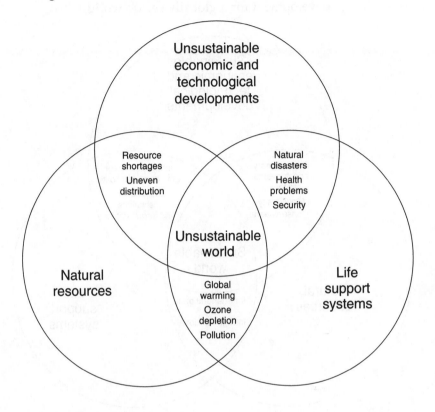

Source: EOLSS 1997

The sustainability debate is thus about long-term rather than short-term, often market, cycles and it's about the way these things can be integrated. It is about horizontal and vertical equity and recognition that actions within the present generation have implications for the successive generations, thus cycles of development need to be both longer and recognise their global impact. It is no longer possible to look at one nation's development in isolation from that of others. The debate is also strongly shaped by 'systems thinking' which sees everything as linked; it looks at how the world is integrated and often draws upon organic analogies. Debate is strongly environmentally determined with an emphasis upon the need to recognise and maintain present biodiversity. The danger to particular species is increasingly being identified with the need to take measures to ensure that whole categories of plants and animals do not become a thing of the past. The creation of biosphere reserves has been

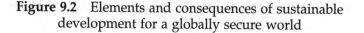

Figure 9.2   Elements and consequences of sustainable
development for a globally secure world

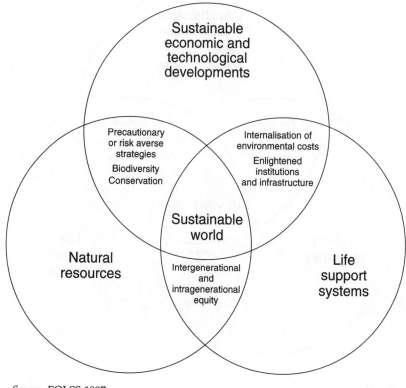

Source: EOLSS 1997

part of the agenda of international organisations where conservation
values have become more prominent. This can be seen, for example, in the
UNESCO Man (sic People) and the Biosphere programme and in the
creation of World Heritage Areas to ensure the preservation of areas of
unique natural habitat such as South Westland in Aotearoa/New Zealand,
an area of virgin rainforest. One problem with some forms of conservation is that it is focused on removing humans from the reserves so maintaining the natural habitat. People are also part of the planet and solutions
which do not incorporate the human and the natural are thus likely to end
in failure. This brings the debate around to the necessity for 'enlightened
institutions', these would recognise the interconnectedness of the human
and the natural in ways that allow mutual recognition and give agency to

both (Latour 1993). Social analysts have been wary of some of the claims from the sustainability debate which are reminiscent of the ecological determinism of past urban theory that suggests that if only we could fix the environmental bottom lines, mostly reflective of natural resource concerns, the rest would fall into place.

A problem shown by this construction is that there is a denial of much of our collective experience from urban history which indicates that cities are, in addition to being natural and physical environments, also social and political constructions. They are arenas of conflict as well as consensus and agreement about the priorities for urban life. Under industrial capitalism, the dominance within cities has already been noted of the property and financial sector which sees land as a tradeable commodity and, as such, generates and distributes wealth unevenly, creating one of the sources of urban inequality and one of the loci of power and influence. Market demand for property and profits extracted from development through land and property speculation have often fuelled urban growth and shaped development of, and the preference for, peripheral expansion or urban consolidation (Sandercock 1976, 1998). Trade-offs between national, regional and local government and developers has often been a key factor in suburban and roading decisions and the relative balance between private (often car-borne) travel and public transport systems, for example, the recent discussion within Victoria Australia over the expansion of freeways rather than investment in rail, and other forms of public transit. A recent *Age* (21 August 2001) newspaper article suggested that the Victorian Government had sold out to the roading lobby and moved away from an integrated approach to transport development. What urban history indicates is that there has been disintegration as well as integration and often very little of the 'functional integration' implied in the 'system'-based ecological models.

Eichler, in a recent discussion of sociology's current limitations, draws attention to its failure to recognise the importance of the linkages between the bio-physical limitations of the earth and current patterns of social organisation. She points out that the natural environment has been profoundly affected by human activity and makes the claim that environmental problems at their core are social problems. Within the 'environmental literature', however, they are often presented as technical ones' (Eichler 1999). This is a timely reminder to us that what we need to analyse are not just the ecological and chemical factors but also the social and the political factors that are destroying the urban environment. In the end, change will be brought about through the conscious activity of citizens. There is a strong link between environmental deterioration and the constant drive to increase wealth and commodity production.

This brings the debate back again to the process of governance and the significance of enlightened institutions. For Satterthwaite (1999:6) the:

> key issue is not sustainable cities – but cities where built form, government structure, production systems, consumption patterns and waste generation and management systems are compatible with sustainable development goals for the city, wider region and whole biosphere.

Further, Satterthwaite notes that very often the focus is on 'ensuring human activity keeps going' (1999:7) and, that preservation of the existing set of arrangements takes precedence over any real attempt to change to a new basis of understanding.

Two agendas have been identified. The so-called brown agenda which is about the improvement of old urban industrial sites in often run-down central or inner-city neighbourhoods. In these cases, the site is often polluted so development involves the clearing, cleaning and renewal of the actual site as well as either the refurbishment of buildings and or rebuilding either residential, recreational or commercial activities. The Olympic site for the 2000 Olympics at Homebush in Sydney was one such site and the claims for the location in Sydney were partly expressed around the fact that this choice would enable a renewal project to go forward which would allow derelict and once-polluted land to be restored to use (Searle and Bounds 1999). In contrast, the green agenda has ecological sustainability as its central platform. This agenda sees the important change to be that of planning on the basis of the bio-region, and, within these 'natural' rather then 'politically' defined areas, they would embark on a process of reducing wasteful consumption and, through conservation and recycling policies, attempt to create a renewable resource-based community. Also likely to be featured are policies to bring back nature to the city in the form of more open space and the reintroduction of native plant species.

A further tension is between the developed and developing countries in terms of the agenda to achieve sustainable development. Rather than a focus upon the 'green agenda' for many developing countries, the key issues are the eradication of poverty, disease and the obtaining of the essential basic urban infrastructure such as clean water, disposal of sewage and other wastes and the creation of reliable sources of power. Thus, they see issues of biodiversity, protection of the ozone layer, forests and rare species as connected closely with urban development to improve the overall quality of life of citizens (Polese and Stren 2000).

For social scientists, who have been critical of some constructions of the debate regarding sustainable development:

sustainability poses a far more serious challenge to many of society's most basic beliefs and analytical concepts than most mainstream planners and policy makers have been prepared to contemplate (Rees 1999:28).

Following the 1992 Rio conference the tendency in many countries has been to see sustainable development as essentially a bio-physical problem of management whereby the environmental scientists would help develop new codes and regulations to afford better environmental protection through pollution and emission controls which would help to stabilise and then reduce the overall problems which the earth summit identified. To move beyond this limited view, which simply requires an adaptation of the existing system of monitoring and control, and embrace the more radical notions of sustainable development requires a recognition that this change is about both environmental issues and social justice which challenges political and economic interests which are well established within the current economic order.

As Becker et al. have noted, the arena of sustainability in its entirety is a:

contested, discursive field which allows for the articulation of political and economic differences between North and South and introduces to environmental issues concerns with social justice and political participation (Becker, Jahn, Stiess 1999:1).

The issue of the North/South divide with respect to urban sustainability issues is significant when set against the fact that most of the growth in urban population will come from the South, for example from Africa (south of the Sahara). Further, some forms of aid have taken the form of exporting to the South older technology which does not conform with the more stringent pollution controls now existent in some of the northern countries. This does little to solve 'global problems' although it may ease the cost of more stringent controls in the northern economies.

Further, Becker et al. argue:

Seeing this requires a move from seeing the debate about preservation to one of social change and transformation. (Becker et al. 1999).

In some readings of sustainability, what is identified is what we have to do to 'preserve' what we currently have rather than moving to the second, and more fundamental question, of what must be changed for the global readjustment that would be necessary for the world to exist in ecological and social harmony. This raises the further question of whether this is either practicable or possible? This question points to the need for a critical reflection upon what constitutes sustainability in both theory and practice.

Critique of Sustainability

The notion of sustainable development as noted earlier arose from a variety of international fora beginning with the World Commission on Development in 1987. Since then it has rapidly assumed a central place in development theory and the debate about the future of the city. According to Wood (1993:7 quoted in Wall, 1997:43) the sustainable development variant of this development theory has gained so much support because:

> It appeared that sustainable development was an idea whose time had come, reflecting a convergence of scientific knowledge, economics, socio-political activity and environmental realities that would guide human development into the twenty-first century.

It had become the mantra of the 1990s and was associated with the rise of globalisation, the dominant discourse of international urban debate. It was a powerful rallying point for a variety of social actors including those who wanted radical change and those who wanted to be able to fashion a way of conducting business as usual within a changing world. As Wall (1997:43) paraphrasing Wood (1993:7) noted, sustainable development has the capacity to empower more than just the dispossessed. One important reason for the idea's rise to prominence was because:

> It lends legitimacy to the free-market economy, belief in trickledown econom-
> ics and the benefits of technological progress. It offers a wide range of oppor-
> tunities for action at all levels, and new institutions, policies and programmes
> which may be initiated under the guise of sustainable development provide
> significant opportunities to expand power bases, acquire additional resources
> and enhance prestige on the part of bureaucrats and administrators.

Wall's position suggests that the growth of the 'sustainability' agenda may in fact be serving quite diverse political interests. This is demonstrated in the way that the discourse of sustainability has been developed in different countries and within different national and international agendas. One of the results has been the dilution of the term to confine it either as sustainable management or within a bio-physical technical scientific frame which excludes the broader social and economic dimensions.

A further set of problems arises from the lack of specificity in the use of the term 'sustainability'. A recent British report on the language of sustainability has noted that 'there is little understanding of the current language used to communicate sustainable development' . . . and that it needs 'unbundling to facilitate understanding before the "name" will have meaning' (DTER 1999). Luke has also drawn attention to the present ambiguity lying within the term when he asks:

> Sustainable for how long? A generation, one hundred years, one thousand years? Sustainable for whom? Present generations, all future generations, all species of this generation, all species for all future generations?; Sustainable at what level? Families, cities, nations, globally, economies?; Sustainable under what conditions? Present western standards of living, small subsistence communities, some future 'Star Trek' culture?; What ought to be sustained? Personal income, social and cultural diversity; GNP, bio-diversity, individual consumption, personal freedom and choice, material frugality (Luke, 1995:21–2 quoted in Kerr 1997:2)?

Clearly, there is a wide area of possibility for inclusion within the term and also areas of wide divergence amongst the advocates of sustainability leading to some commentators considering the term itself of little value. Regardless of the definitional questions, there is a wide appreciation of the need to look at alternative styles of urban development within a global world where increasing resource constraints are being recognised.

One of the key points of contention then turns on whether this is a problem which can be resolved through technological means or whether it requires more fundamental change. Rees (1999) notes that technological expansionism clearly occupies centre stage in the eyes of most government and official organisations, and sees a link with neo-classical economics and the steady state paradigm of growth. The discussion has thus identified what can be termed weak, where the challenge to broad social change is muted, and strong versions of sustainability. The latter point to the fact that this state cannot be achieved without a far-reaching change to most aspects of social and economic activity. The suggestion here is that a particular reading of sustainability has captured sustainable development as a set of ideas, as it has been applied with respect to cities. This set of ideas, consistent with the views of some environmentalists, suggests that as long as natural environmental bottom lines are established, ensuring the protection of the natural and environmental systems, then the social, economic and cultural will largely look after themselves. Such an interpretation is favoured by neo-liberals as it provides a way of embracing sustainable development as sustainable management and clearing the way for continued economic development consistent with respect for the natural environment's systems and resources. It thus allows the challenge of the WCED 1987 and Rio Earth Summit in 1992 to the nature of capitalist growth to be neatly deflected. The more radical reading of WCED and especially Agenda 21 from Rio, with its social chapter, thus gets sidelined.

In these terms, urban policy is often now constructed around a form of environmental determinism, ecological bottom lines and individualism, thus denying the importance of the social, cultural and political side of development. Such myopia was also present in the 1920s and 1930s in the Chicago school of urban analysis. The model they advocated was based on plant ecology and the impersonal competition of the land market based largely on neo-classical economics and the work of Ricardo (Kilmartin, Thorns and Burke 1985). Thus the explanation that they generated of city structure was largely a result of unconscious processes focused on biological or psychological rather than social or political processes (Dickens 2000). As a result, there was little room in the analysis for the influences of Chicago's political and planning system – its planners, managers, mayors and real estate professionals; nor were community groups and social movements, representing the interests of migrants and more established citizens, factored into the model. In a similar way, the debate about sustainability has a nasty habit of starting with a broad agenda but moves quickly to forms of ecological or environmental determinism that rely, for their explanatory power, upon impersonal processes, and thus provide severe limits upon human agency (Perkins and Thorns 2000b, 2001c).

Environmental determinism is the triumph of rational science as it denies the realities of political power and the complexities of human social relations. The adoption of sustainability, particularly the sustainable management and ecosystems thinking, as a starting point for developing social and city policy has considerable limitations. These ideas are based on biological metaphors and therefore give privilege to natural science and associated technical responses to environmental problems (MacNaghten and Urry 1998). They are conservationist in a natural environmental sense, and also tinged with political conservatism when seen from a social policy perspective. It certainly comes as no surprise that these ideas have become popular in association with the rise of neo-liberal politics.

What gets lost in the debate about sustainability as it has transposed itself into policy-making is often the 'social'. The existence of, and the role of, the community and collective actors in social life is largely denied. We are either left with bio-physical explanations or economic rationalism – ecological bottom lines or market process. Partly, this arises from the seemingly widespread loss of faith in, and commitment to, planning by governments at either national or local levels. Such an approach is seen to be reminiscent of state centrism, of regulatory and inflexible bureaucratic practices and a series of both residential design, planning and environmental disasters.

Having now examined the theory and debates surrounding urban sustainability in general terms, it is now useful to turn to a more grounded analysis through the exploration of two case studies. These will illustrate how the ideas just discussed have been translated into actual urban planning and management and provide a way of further testing the relationship between the shifts in rhetoric and their impact upon the actual process of city development.

The Aotearoa/New Zealand Resource Management Act 1991

In 1991, Aotearoa/New Zealand carried out a radical reconstruction of its planning system. Its essentially British-style Town and Country Planning legislation was repealed and replaced by the Resource Management Act. It has been argued that this legislation led the world in the development of a new form of statutory environmental planning and management (Memon and Gleeson, 1995), as the Resource Management Act focused on the sustainable management of the bio-physical environment. While this claim maybe overstated, the ethos and provisions of the Resource Management Act have attracted considerable international attention. Within Aotearoa/New Zealand, much debate to date has centred on statutory interpretations (for example, the meaning of various sections of the statute), procedural matters (for example, the operation of the Environmental Impact Assessment process), and, given the Act's emphasis on the bio-physical environment, the influence of the legislation on various aspects of natural environmental management (for example, air quality, natural hazards and water quality) (Hughes 2000, Memon and Perkins 2000). In contrast to the Resource Management Act's emphasis on bio-physical environmental management, one of the distinguishing features of the statute is its very limited focus on urban planning generally, and on social planning specifically, and this too has been a source of analysis (Perkins et al. 1993, Memon and Gleeson 1995, Perkins and Thorns 2000b).

The reforms emerged out of the radical agenda of the third Labour Government and were shaped by their wider set of reforms for the state sector. These were founded on increasing the role of the private market, extending choice and privileging the individual consumer (Boston, Dalziel and

St John 1999; Kelsey 1997). Planning was seen as a bureaucratic process that intruded too extensively into the market place and thus increased the cost of development through delays as the application passed through the local government system. A more 'efficient' system, that would produce an improved allocation of activities within the urban and rural environment, was desired. Also, the solution was, consistent with the consumer-sovereignty model, to be based around private property rights. During the process of developing the legislation, considerable lobbying took place both by developers and by environmentalists. The environmentalists were primarily concerned about the protection of nature, protected national areas, indigenous forests and wetlands and endangered species. The solutions were sought in the application of science in order to provide improved knowledge of the eco-systems and market forces, and greater efficiency in distribution and adaptability. The effectiveness and efficiency criteria being used here, upon which costs and benefits are to be judged, are not specified in the legislation but reflect the dominance of the economist's model of efficiency.

The legislation was passed at the end of 1991 and edited out any reference to sustainable development or commitment of future generations, largely on the grounds that this would limit too greatly opportunities for economic development and investment. The Act replaced all previous planning acts and also a large number of the boards that had previously held responsibility for natural-resource control and conservation. The Act, in the end, had only one objective; this was to promote the sustainable management of natural and physical resources. By focusing on 'effects' rather than prescriptions, the act was intended to provide environmental bottom lines. Once such lines were established, market forces could be more or less left to create the best and most efficient use of the resources available. One assumption underlying the paradigm used in the Act is that it is possible to develop precise natural environmental standards, which are separated from political and value considerations, and which constitute a static 'environmental bottom line' (Craig 1998). This is questionable. The shift to the bio-physical basis of the new Act has instead encouraged a new set of expertise and a new discourse about the shape of the city. The concentration on the natural and bio-physical has removed the previous identification of urban and rural planning as separate and distinct activities. Cities do not appear as units to be planned, all decisions are shaped by a broadly environmentalist framework – but one which is partial as it largely excludes economic and social questions. Unlike the previous planning regime, the question of social equity is avoided.

The authors of the statute based it on the idea of sustainable management – a restatement of the sustainable development idea – but one excluding significant social, political and economic planning concerns.

Sustainable management within the Resource Management Act, 1991 focuses on managing the bio-physical environmental effects of human activities and represented an

> uneasy legislative compromise between environmentalists' demands for a more holistic approach to resource management and the agenda of neo-liberal interests who have long wanted greater flexibility in planning practice to facilitate investment (Le Heron and Pawson 1996:251).

As part of this change in the emphasis of local-body planning activity, the Local Government Act 1974 was amended, in 1989, to facilitate the reorganisation of the boundaries and administrative tasks and responsibilities of territorial local authorities. This pushed them firmly towards a corporate model of organisation and gave them greater encouragement to involve themselves in economic development and employment promotion. This has stimulated place promotion which has emphasized the generation of new logos and city slogans to capture their locational advantages and separate out their claims from those of other competing urban centres, leading to a growth in 'boosterist' politics (Logan and Molotch 1987; Hall 1993, 1997; Levine 2000; Perkins and Thorns 2000b).

One consequence of the new approach has been to define human social and community life naturalistically, as part of bio-physical eco-systems. This is reductionist because it ignores the significant urban social theoretical understanding that cities are a significant product of human culture. As Aasen (1992:7) has pointed out:

> cities are in fact not natural organisms: they are artificial, cultural constructions. If we treat human communities as part of ecosystems, we ignore the complex social and economic processes which produce and maintain cities and . . . preclude the question of our cities and other aspects of our constructed [and social] environment from the serious consideration which they deserve.

Partnership building thus requires us to recognise its political nature and the fact that it is not a neutral activity but one that is embedded in the structures of political and economic power. To incorporate citizens fully into decision-making may well require considerable change to how current decision-making is being conducted. In this respect, there are signs of the growth of citizen's action, which has made a difference.

The Aotearoa/New Zealand case shows how the broader debate regarding sustainable development became modified and then enshrined in a piece of legislation. This then shaped both the discourse and practices of planners and others within the cities and created a new set of planning documents and constraints. These were heavily influenced by ecological systems thinking and limited attention to social and political aspects of urban growth and change. The tension between the market interests of the developers and the ecological interests of the environmentalists was not resolved in the original legislation but papered over and this has continued to be a source of tension and conflict in the administration of the Act leading to pressure for amendments.

Auckland links our discussion of the legislative changes with Aotearoa/New Zealand and the growth of the new urbanism/smart growth agenda in the USA. (See Box 9.1). Both of these initiatives are linked to the broad sustainability debate that has been examined. What is interesting is the way that particular cities have picked out aspects of these current debates and incorporated them into their policy and planning frameworks. Auckland is facing a range of 'sustainability' issues and, increasingly, is seeking the solution in greater intensification and improved urban design to combat the 'wasteful' use of space in the past.

BOX 9.1

Auckland, New Zealand: A sustainable city?

- The urban region consists of four cities whose population (2000) is as follows: Auckland (391,000), Manukau (290,900), North Shore (192,000), Waitakere (176,400).

Total (urban region): 1.05 million

- 27 per cent of the total New Zealand Population is contained in these four cities

- Population: (2021, estimate): Auckland (492,000), Manukau (380,000), North Shore (242,600), Waitakere (229,800).

Total (urban region): 1.34 million (21 per cent estimated increase)

The Auckland urban area is the largest population concentration in New Zealand and has exerted considerable influence on the country as a whole with strong migration into the urban area in the second half of the twentieth century from the rest of New Zealand and overseas. Migration from Europe and the Pacific area dominated until the 1980s to 2000, when increased flows came from the Asian region, resulting in a much greater range of cultural groups represented in the population.

Growth of the city in the second half of the twentieth century was rapid, strongly suburban from the 1950s to the 1980s and heavily reliant upon private transportation and assisted by the construction of an urban motorway system beginning in the 1960s. This now provides a 'spine from the south to the north'. However, the increased population and high car ownership is increasingly causing congestion and occasionally 'grid lock' on the system.

Continued

In the last two decades, more and more attention has been placed on 'infill', increasing residential densities in inner- and middle-ring suburbs and the redevelopment of downtown offices into residential apartments.

Shifts in housing and residential development cause tensions across the region as the various local authorities have different perspectives on the desirability of centre v. peripheral expansion.

Questions are now being raised about the 'sustainability' of this urban region of low-density dispersed settlement.

Indicators of the social and economic fragility of the urban area include:

● crises in the water and electricity supply;

● problems with the transport system (public and private);

● decreasing housing affordability relative to the rest of the country;

● significant disparities in social indicators relating to health and education across the urban area;

● growth in urban crime and personal safety issues;

● a significant number of unemployed and long-term beneficiaries, in part, as a result of the restructuring of the economy in the 1980s and 1990s leading to a loss of industrial jobs especially in South Auckland (Saville-Smith 2000, Auckland et al. 2001).

Solutions recently advocated have drawn upon the 'smart growth' model.

City web site: *http://www.akcity.govt.nz/*

New Urbanism/Smart Growth

The growth of the new urbanism movement within architecture in the USA (Duany, et al. 1992; Calthorpe 1993) was spurred by a rejection of what they saw as the deficiencies of modernist functionalism which had created sprawling suburbia in the USA. This was seen as a failed form of development. It not only gobbled up valuable land at the urban fringe but also had produced suburbs which did not encourage sociability or civility. The people were isolated and design encouraged separation rather than connectedness. Garages filled the streets and houses were turned away so reducing the opportunities for spontaneous interaction. People congregated at the mall rather along the 'main streets'. This all led to the isolation of suburban housewives and children in the suburban house which became a prison as much as a haven, creating the 'problem' of suburban neurosis (Friedan 1963, Hayden 1980). Further problems were traffic congestion and pollution, and the loss of the ability to build community on an experiential sense of place (Katz 1994, Congress for New Urbanism 1996, Southworth 1997, Southworth and Parthasarathy 1997). Further, the functional separation of activities into designated zones had broken down the interrelation between public and private life, the world of work and home. At the centre of new urbanism is the design of the neighbourhood, with a defined centre, a variety of dwelling types, shops and offices to supply 'weekly needs' a primary school, playgrounds, and a variety of pedestrian and vehicular routes, narrow streets and shading by trees to slow the traffic, and some form of self-goverment. The ideas of new urbanism draw from images of traditional American small towns and the idea of the village and community and speak of a need for a more 'traditional urban form'. Its supporters promote traditional urban neigh-bourhoods where houses have porches overlooking the pavement, en-couraging interaction with passers-by. The main street replaces the mall as the focal point and service centre. The idea is to develop mixed-use neighbourhoods where there is housing for all phases of life and for various income groups, together with shops and services and community facilities. New urbanists are thus often described as neo-traditionalists in their attempts to rework the past into present designs and to link these to calls for the creation of strong communities to replace the soulless suburbs and the dysfunctional suburban world of sprawling low-density housing satirised in films and novels about American suburban life.

In the academy award-winning film, *American Beauty* (2000) Lester and Carolyn live in a 'picture perfect house in the suburbs, with manicured lawn and white picket fence. Carolyn spends her spare time pruning her roses, her gardening clogs colour-coordinated with her pruning sheers, Lester keeps the house neat and tidy' (*Economist* 24 March 2000). The reality is different from the picture-postcard images and the film suggests that the only way to 'find fulfillment is to subvert the suburban conven-tions'. The prevailing images of American suburbia used here are still ones based more on myth than the reality of suburban life as shown by social researchers. The life of the 'suburbanite' has become increasingly diverse. Change has occurred since the 1960s through the urbanisation of the suburbs with much stronger growth in recent decades in jobs within the suburbs rather than in the central city. In contrast, urban distress is located within areas of central cities, often also in areas of public housing, where there has been increased concentrations of unemployed and underprivi-leged people who have been left behind in the latest surge of economic growth (Forsyth 1997, HUD 1997).

The search for the ideal size of a neighbourhood and the idea that design can achieve a level of social interaction and sociability is reminis-cent of the 1950s and 1960s neighbourhood planning models used in British and US new towns (Schaffer 1972, Clapson 1998). In these, there was a belief that through planning and design it was possible to 'engineer' the development of 'community', by which was generally meant integrated social relations whereby people in general worked and lived within the same spatial area. Such overlapping relationships, it was assumed, would build trust and strengthen broader 'community' relations, producing 'better' living arrangements than those associated with the inter-war mass housing 'estates' which were just 'places to live' and did not incorporate work or communal space and activities. One of the problems, then as now, is that of the spatial scales chosen by the architects and planners. These did not always correlate with how individuals and families constructed their life patterns. Commuting from one neighbourhood to another for work and friendship defied the ideas of internal balance and continually disrupted the idea that 'communities' were spatially determined (Stacey 1969, Bell and Newby 1982, Cohen 1982). In the revival of the focus upon community planning, there has again been debate over the 'ideal' size. One suggestion has been population units of 30,000 but what about shifting work patterns and the rise of home-based/mobile work enabled by information technology? These trends suggest a lessening of the spatial constraints to social relations rather than the reverse.

An associated movement, also mainly in the USA, has been the growth of the smart growth agenda. Here, the objective has been to create more intelligent use of space and integrated mixed-use developments in new areas and in the redeveloped inner city cores. This combines a concern for brown- and green-field developments based on a more holistic approach. The problem is defined as arising from sprawl – which was seen as being associated with 'rapid suburban growth' which consumes land at a faster rate than the population grows, even as central cities and inner suburbs decline. (New Zealand Smart Growth Network 2000). A move to more compact design thus saves land and reduces infrastructure costs.

The American Urban Land Institute (1996) provides some defining characteristics of smart growth development. These are:

- development that is economically viable and preserves open spaces and natural resources;

- land-use planning which is comprehensive, integrated and regional;

- collaboration of public, private and non-profit sectors on growth and development issues to achieve mutually beneficial outcomes;

- certainty and predictability inherent in the development process;

- infrastructure being maintained and enhanced to serve existing and new residents;

- redevelopment of infill housing, brown-field sites, such as former industrial areas and obsolete buildings, being actively pursued;

- urban centres and neighbourhoods as integral components of a healthy regional economy;

- compact suburban development being integrated into existing commercial areas, new town centres and/or near existing or planned transport facilities;

- development on the urban fringe which integrates a mix of land uses, preserves open space, is fiscally responsible and provides transportation options.

Smart growth thus contains both sustainable and neo-traditional arguments. The former are about more restrained use of green-field sites and the reduction of waste and the latter emphasize holistic development rather than pure house design. In some ways, this reflects the varying emphases of architects and planners with the former more focused on design issues and the latter on the overall linkage of the various aspects of a new or rehabilitated area.

The two models of urban form that emerge are both characterised by a view of the past in which working and social life are seen as closely connected in one place (Urry 2000). For many of today's suburban and urban dwellers, mobility is an integral component of their lives. Access to the private car and its use to construct both social and work lives is a crucial taken-for-granted aspect of life. The huge increases in fuel prices in 2000, as a result of demand outstripping supply and currency falls against the US dollar, led to widespread demonstrations against governments across Europe and other parts of the world and pressure to reduce the cost through tax adjustments. Some see this as a indication of decreasing available energy and the need to plan and live within smaller territorial areas. In contrast to this localising trend is the capacity of people, through technology, to link to the global community. This is also likely to rework social and work relations in ways that may result in different forms of community from those seen within the neo-traditional perspective.

The new urbanists and smart-growth advocates are quite prescriptive in that they see design as the solution to a range of urban and suburban ills (Talen 1999). If the arrangement of the houses with respect to each other and the placement of community resources was executed in an optimal way, sociability and civility would be engendered. This, in turn, would recreate the more enduring aspects of community that new urbanists see as contained within the small towns of American history and the villages of European societies. This ideology again does not embrace sociological research which argues that such a vision is an idealisation of the past and that the reality for many was less positive. Rural life and small towns can contain oppressive practices, limited social and economic opportunities, and resistance to diversity. Sennett (2000:70), commenting on the new urbanism movement in America, suggests:

> The pristine small towns inspired by New Urbanism are world's apart from the everyday disorders of life; these kitschy, pseudo-communities that advertise themselves as antidotes to suburban sprawl provide little home for difference – differences of the kind that lead to conflicts of ethnicity, class or sexual preference.

The emphasis on prescription and the top-down nature of new urbanism and smart growth is seen in the regulatory environments they tend to produce in order to attempt to create the desired lifestyle. This has led some of their critics to characterise their work as 'creeping socialist' as it reflects their lack of a sufficient acknowledgement of the complexities of the contemporary urban world (O'Toole 1998, Dear 2000).

The particular connection being made here with 'sustainability' is one that focuses on aspects of resource use and management. It does not engage with the wider concerns of sustainable development or the idea of partnership and cooperative engagement with the people who are to receive the benefits of planning. Design and development seem to be somewhat top-down and some aspects of this smart growth are about creating high-value rather than necessarily more durable and resource-efficient development that conserves the wider environment. Further, new urbanism and smart growth are both deficient in confronting the issue of social justice. New urbanism explicitly began with a view that American suburbia needed restructuring to provide improved quality of life for middle-class Americans. One consequence of the emphasis upon the residential community has been the growth of the gated community separating social groups and continuing 'the planning and design professions' long involvement in the perpetuation of residential enclaves' (Luymes 1997:200). The smart-growth agenda appears also to be strongly underpinned by development interests representing the property, land development and financial industries in the USA and thus are part of the 'growth machine' that has consistently shaped urban form (Molotoch and Logan 1987).

Summary

The sustainable city has been the theme of this chapter and the rise of this debate has been identified within the literature about urban futures and in the planning practices adopted across many countries in the 1990s. The debate has many dimensions and thus the aspects introduced into urban development become significant. The original formulation in, for example, the Brundtland Report in 1987 clearly linked together environmental and social concerns. Sustainable development requires economic, social and environmental change for it to be successfully achieved. Since 1987, selected aspects rather than the whole of the Report have been incorporated into policy. The argument of this chapter has been that to achieve sustainable cities there is a need to engage not only with the debate about social justice – about inclusion and exclusion and the enabling of full participation by all citizens – but also with that about environmental and ecological systems.

Further Reading

Sustainability and Cities

Becker, E. and Jahn, T., eds, 1999, *Sustainability and the Social Sciences: A Cross-Disciplinary Approach to Integrating Environmental Considerations into Theoretical Reorientation*. London: Zed Books. The book is the outcome of a UNESCO project to develop 'a cross disciplinary approach to integrating environmental consideration into theoretical reorientation'. Chapter 1 debates the question of the definition and understanding of sustainability within the social sciences. Other chapters of value are 4, 14 by Redclift and 10 by Eichler.

MacNaghten, P. and Urry, J., 1998, *Contested Natures*. London: Sage. Chapter 7, 'Sustaining Nature', pp. 212–48, draws on a variety of British data to debate the question of what is understood by sustainability.

Polese M. and Stren, R., 2000, *The Social Sustainability of Cities*. Toronto: University of Toronto Press. Chapter 1, 'Understanding the New Socio-cultural Dynamics of Cities: Comparative Urban Policy in a Global Context'. pp. 3–38. This book is a collection of chapters focusing on a range of cities from across the world which were part of a UNESCO study examining social sustainability and cities. Cities included were: Montreal, Toronto, Miami, Baltimore, Geneva, Rotterdam, Sao Paulo, San Salvador, Nairobi, and Cape Town.

Satterthwaite, D., ed., 1999, *The Earthscan Reader in Sustainable Cities*. London: Earthscan Publications. The whole of this book is an excellent cross-disciplinary analysis of sustainable cities: part 2 links sustainable development and cities; part 3 investigates different sectoral programmes (for example, health, transport, and so on) and sustainable development goals for cities; part 4 looks at city-level action, including Agenda 21-based activity, and the final section looks at sustainable development for cities within a regional and national context.

UNCHS. 1996a, *An Urbanizing World: Global Report on Human Settlements*, Oxford: Oxford University Press.

UNCHS. 2001a, *Cities in a Globalizing World*. Report prepared by UNCHS for Habitat plus 5 in New York, June 2001. London: Earthscan Publications Ltd.

UNCHS. 2001b, *The State of the World's Cities Report 2001*. Nairobi: UNCHS.

These three reports provide excellent data and examples of city development strategies from around the world and include both detailed case material and overview articles.

Web sites

Sustainability debates

http://www.unesco.org/most
http://susdev.eurofound.ie/
http://www.unchs.org/istanbul+5/
http://www.ea.gov.au/esd/
http://www.unesco.org/science/wcs/index.htm
http://www.un.org/
http://www.un.org/databases/
http://www.sustainabledevelopment.org/blp
http://www.bestpractices.org
http://www.soci.canterbury.ac.nz/suphome.htm

Smart growth

http://www.smartgrowth.org/
http://www.sprawlwatch.org/frames.html
http://www.livablecommunities.gov/

New urbanism

http://www.cnu.org/

10

Reflections

The exploration of the transformation of cities began with the recognition that we are now entering a world dominated, more than at any other time in our history, by the urban condition. Over half of the world's population now live in cities. These cities are, however, diverse and increasingly so despite the forces of globalisation, seen by some analysts, to create conditions of growing similarity. The world of the global urban condition is one of paradoxes. At one level, there is the greater degree of interdependence flowing from a global information and economic system and access to a common set of cultural experiences through the power of the global media. At another level, there still persist strong local attachments and unique places where people fashion their sense of identity. Place thus does not disappear off the agenda as we move into the new millennium, it does, however, take on new attributes. The other paradox lies in the arguments about control. One view is that the new information systems and technologies provide a way of opening out opportunities to seek to acquire knowledge, of empowering people who can now access what information they want, when they want it, twenty-four hours a day, whereas others see these as new aspects of control. The new information systems on the World Wide Web are also mostly open systems where there are no hierarchies and authenticated places for knowledge. It's a huge supermarket where people can sample and select, mix and match and be informed or confused. It opens out the possibilities of more varied pathways to learning and challenges the traditional cannons and organisation of knowledge. It's a librarian's worst nightmare as there is no classification according to rules. Or is it? Is this the hype or the reality? There is the growth of a digital divide separating those with access to the information world and those denied it often through lack of basic services and economic resources. At the Habitat 2 meeting in 1996, a dialogue was held on *Cities, Communication and the Media in an Information Society* (UNCHS 1996b), which stressed the empowering nature of the new technologies. The delegate from Tanzania pointed out, after much enthusiastic discussion about the new possibilities of the global information age, that for his country and his community power and clean water were still basic requirements that they did not have and so participation in this new world was limited. This draws our attention to the continuing need to address the basic infrastructure elements of urban life if we are to eradicate poverty and increase opportunities (Polese 2000).

A further unresolved question is whether the transfer of 'power' which an open knowledge system provides is more of an illusion than a reality; is it part of a more general shift from collective forms of activity and provision to more individual ones which may be potentially alienating and lead to the growth of social dislocation?

The other significant shift in our knowledge has come through the belief that we are now able to see and understand events as they happen. The global world is now at our fingertips and thus no longer a mystery to us. We have been everywhere, often via television, film and the computer but, nonetheless, we have a sense that we have a first-hand 'real' account; there are no new places to be explored. We have even been inside the human body and scrutinised it minutely with the aid of advanced camera and digital technology. The camera lens and the production team often mediate the experience. It is a packaged and controlled experience rather than one we control ourselves. This is a further paradox of control; we have the power over the switch or the cursor; we can turn on our television and computer and see the 'world as it is' but in the end we do not necessarily control what we see. So our image and knowledge of the global city and its everyday life are obtained through snapshots and glimpses; our knowledge is made up of a collage of images, some from 'real' life and some from fictionalised accounts from the soaps and the sitcoms. The streets of Los Angeles and Bangkok, of Sao Paulo and London, are known to us via the media and we are subject to its interpretative lens as we try and make sense of a changing world.

How does this shift in knowledge and perception, and the increasingly global nature of the world impact upon life within, and our interpretation of, the city? Understanding this change requires a historical context, thus the roots of urbanisation were our starting point. However, the emphasis in this text has been upon the last one hundred years of the twentieth century and the urban transformations that have occurred in its final decades.

The 'great transformation' of economic, political, intellectual and spatial life that occurred around 200 years ago in Western Europe ushered in the 'modern world' (Giddens 1998). It was a transformation that reworked understandings of time and space. The clock replaced the seasons; work became regulated according to time and was located in industrial buildings. This necessitated creating living environments close to the new sites of production thus forming the industrial cities. These were the new urban phenomena and soon became, in the 'developed

world,' the main location for human settlement. They began as disorgan-
ised spaces, except where they were planned by aristocrats (as in the
Swedish industrial settlements) or by the utopian socialists (for example,
Saltaire, Bourneville, Port Sunlight, New Lanark in the UK). As the problems of unregulated growth became apparent, a struggle ensued around
order and control of development. Planning emerged as a separate urban
activity with its own sets of ideals and prescriptions for city life and its
own professional group of advocates and administrators dedicated to
bring order out of the apparent chaos of industrial cities. Zoning, regulatory authorities and legal systems were largely the instruments of control
utilised and a strong functional separation of space was attempted especially around the place of work and residence.

Sociology, as a formal discipline, arose as a set of explanations for the
rise of the modern world, thus the city and its structure and life has been
one of the central interests of the discipline. The analysis provided by
urban analysts of the industrial/modern city was explored in Chapter 2.
There have been two streams of urban analysis, the first focuses more
upon structures, economic processes and state linkages and forms the
basis of the analysis in Chapter 2. It is a mix of American and European
thought. Amongst this, the work of the Chicago School in the 1920s and
1930s was particularly influential and informed much of thinking about
the city in urban analysis – the 'bulls eye' model of concentric zones being
repeated in the majority of urban texts and courses for decades, so creating a clear sense in the minds of most observers and many groups of
students that the city grows out from the centre as a result of invasion,
succession and domination and the operations of the land market. The
work of the Chicago School leant itself to quantification and, through the
latter part of the twentieth century, more sophisticated methods of measurement became used as computer technology enabled the manipulation
of large data sets, culminating in the rise of GIS (Geographical Information Systems) as an integral part of contemporary urban analysis within
the policy and research worlds. The Chicago School was deficient in its
attention to politics, power and human agency, so alternative theory,
drawing more from European traditions, developed. Critiques from the
1960s to the 1980s saw the emergence of a focus upon urban managers
and the access to, and allocation of, urban resources such as land, housing,
work, and social and community provisions by the local and central state
and their agents as central issues for analysis. This work reflected a
growing critique of modernist administrative bureaucratic control and
re-allocation procedures to ensure social equity under predominantly
social democratic political regimes. In the 1970s, neo-Marxist structuralist
analysis began to flourish, focusing upon the process of capital accumulation, both national and international, wherein the urban became a reflec-

tion of these broad economic imperatives facilitated by a client state according them legitimacy.

The challenge to the conceptions evolving from the modernist urban project is addressed in the debates arising out of globalisation and post-modernity. These are about the extent of change and how we might understand that change. They are, in various ways, attempts to answer the question of what, if anything, is now different. Dear (2000) argues that the roots of a postmodern urban analysis lie in a rejection of the dominant 1970s' Marxist structuralism, the influence of the post-structuralist writers, such as Foucault and the emergence of the postmodern critique from philosophy, feminism and post-colonialism. To that should be added environmentalism and the challenge to the boundary between the natural and the social worlds that was a product of the enlightenment view that people could, through science and technology, control the natural world and bend it to their purposes. The limitations of this view are now becoming increasingly apparent as we recognise the impacts of global warming and climate change, ozone depletion, waste disposal of toxic substances, the long-term degradation of parts of the eco-system and the future shape, size and distribution of the population. The latter part of the book has therefore highlighted the challenge between the need for collective responses to both global and urban problems and the continuing pressures towards individualism arising from the consumerism of the present system of wealth creation and distribution.

One response to the postmodern challenge has been to return to the more humanistic tradition concerned with the meaning of urban life. This is a tradition more grounded in urban ethnographies and qualitative research and devoted to showing what everyday life in the city was like and how individuals and social groups developed their sense of place and meaning. This work thus sought to understand the impact of urban change upon communal and interpersonal relations. It is the arena of debate about the nature of community, micro-level relations and everyday life within the houses and homes that we 'construct' and occupy.

The postmodern debate at its most extreme leads to a relativising of experience, all is reduced to our own set of knowledge, what we see is all there is to see, what we personally experience is all that is authentic. This leads to a somewhat anarchical view of the world. It also eliminates the 'social' from consideration. For Baudrillard, all that is left for the individual is a form of individual resistance to the excess of the postmodern world of simlucra and seduction (Dodd 1999). Do we thus become couch potatoes before our screens or do we become empowered social actors? Does the access to knowledge, in the seemingly open environment of the twenty-first century, truly empower us or does it merely confuse our understanding of what is real and what is imagined – of what has changed and what has in fact stayed the same? Is the globalisation of everything in fact a massive sham and media circus, which takes away, rather than encourages, our agency as social actors?

Reflecting on both globalisation and the city at the beginning of the twenty-first century necessitates looking closely at the origins of our theories of the city. The discussion of demographic and migratory change in Chapter 2 drew attention to the fact that growth is increasingly a feature of Africa and Asia rather than the nations considered to be at the core of the global system. The cities of New York, London and Tokyo, in the year 2000, were seen as at the apex of the global system. Will this persist? Do they have the continuing capacity to capture and hold the attributes of power and control within the global system? So far they have done well. The data available show, that they have continued their domination through acquiring the new forms of significance; they are key nodes in the flow of information and financial capital. Will this persist or will the new knowledge and communication systems eventually wrest control from such physically located 'places' to more dispersed sites? This raises the question of the future 'digital' city where relations may increasingly be virtual. However, as the Amsterdam and Christchurch experience show, there is a continuing importance, even where the new technologies are used, of interpersonal relations. In may of course not be cities that are virtual but homes and work places. There is evidence of increasing amounts of home-based work and a growing debate about the likely impact this could have upon urban form. One future-scenario workshop I attended recently had all of us working from our virtual offices and no work in the centre of the city. Instead, it was entirely turned over to be a place of recreation, leisure and heritage buildings. In such scenarios, there is often little attention placed on how such restructuring will be achieved without a radical reworking of economic relationships.

The dominance of Western European and North American experience in past urban theory is another source of increasing unease as greater attention is now being given to the variety of expressions of urbanisation that are found around the world. The hegemony of western-based theory is increasingly being challenged (King 1996, 2000; Jacobs 1996; Perkins and Thorns 2000a). The rise of the Los Angeles School of urban analysis in the USA (Davis 1991, Cenzatti 1993, Soja 2000) and the view that Los Angeles is the quintessential postmodern city is a valuable corrective to the view that all cities are like Chicago and grew from the centre outwards. Los Angeles 'breaks the mold' and is a dispersed, multi-centre, multi-ethnic urban area with a proliferation of both information workers and, at the same time, 'minimum-wage, part-time service industry jobs [for example, fast-food outlets] and a massive informal sector' (Dear 2000:15). Los Angeles is, however, deeply connected to American culture and society through its history and traditions, which is not the case for all cities around the world.

Colonial cities, for example, were products of 'other places' and were implanted into the local setting by people who came and ordered the society in ways which were often alien to the local indigenous people. The results are different from either Europe or North America. Australia and Aotearoa/New Zealand are interesting in that they are the products of a British colonial tradition but have been influenced in different ways. Both countries have cities with dispersed populations and have, for the past one hundred or so years, been mostly focused upon the question of urban growth. Major differences emerge, however, from the differing migratory streams in the two countries and in the relationships that developed with their indigenous peoples.

Auckland, for example, is largely a Polynesian and British city – as these are the predominant elements in the population mix and cultural heritage. This shows itself in the governance institutions of the city, based on British models, and in the cultural landscape and visual appearance that increasingly reflects its varied heritage. In contrast, Melbourne is a much more multicultural city with a more diverse set of European, and more recently, Asian people migrating and influencing local social institutions, urban design and the cultural landscape (Collins 1988, Watson and Gibson 1995). What this shows is that the patterns of migration and the historical, political and cultural context help to explain differences of urban form between post-colonial and the modern or postmodern cities of Europe and North America. Further, it suggests that we should be somewhat sceptical about claims to universalism and theories that do not sufficiently recognise difference.

In drawing the threads together, what stands out is that transformation and change have been central to the urban experience of the past one hundred years. Change has always been part of the human condition and times without change are probably a rarity. Questions then focus on the speed and complexity of the change rather than change per se. The period from 1980 to 2000 is considered, by some, to have been a time of such rapid change that it has created a totally new set of conditions and experiences. Others see the changes as the latest phase in an unfolding story. In earlier discussions, we observed that globalisation had been part of the European experience since at least the fifteenth century when explorers discovered and established trading relations with other lands. Even before then, there were migrations and movements of people. There is the amazing story, that we now understand as a result of archaeological and other data, of the Polynesian migrations from the Northern Pacific, down through the Philippines into what is now known as Polynesia, and eventually, about a thousand years ago, to Aotearoa/New Zealand.

Urban analysis needs to recognise, therefore, change and continuity. It needs to acknowledge the importance of particular places and local configurations of natural and social factors and to understand the complexity of everyday life, so distancing itself from both structural over-determination and the extremes of postmodern relativism. The course for cities in the next decades is, as always, hard to plot with any certainty. Urban analysis has not been especially good in the past at predicting the future. With current anxiety about scientific prediction, it would be a brave person who would forecast the future. However, some issues are likely to be central to the urban agenda. The first of these is the question of growth and 'sustainability'. The recognition of the finiteness of the global ecology and its impact upon the future of cities is a key concern on the global and local political agenda. The language of sustainability has permeated the thinking of governments and local communities. The consequences of embracing this wider concept, drawing together the ecological, bio-physical, social and economic aspects of development into a single pro-gramme are still not fully appreciated. At the centre of this new agenda is the unresolved tension between those who see it as possible to solve the environmental challenges to urban development through technical, bio-physical and design solutions and those who see the solution lying in more extensive social change. Unless environmental issues are solved within a framework that also addresses issues of social justice, it's diffi-cult to see how lasting change can be affected. People who are excluded, who are without the basic necessities of life, and who are constantly being made aware of their deprivation are unlikely to embrace changes which continue to reinforce their marginalised position.

The second issue is the need to recognise and preserve the diversity within and between cities. Allied to this is a rejection of an urban project based around the assumption that what happens in one part of the world will necessarily occur in another. This is something to be explored rather than assumed. More research is needed which explores the multiple and complementary pathways of urban change that are emerging. This will, in turn, allow a greater appreciation of both the causal and contingent factors which are shaping the cities of the new millennium.

The third issue is the challenge posed to our understanding of urban change by the shifts in population levels and migration paths. On the basis of current population predictions, there will be areas of the world characterised by growth whereas others, especially Western Europe, will experience decline. On current fertility rates, many European countries face long-term decline in their population. How will this change their urban patterns? Will cities also decline, and will the issues of decline, surplus infrastructure and social provision replace those of growth? Will the mayors of many towns be like the mayor of an Italian town in a recent

BBC documentary, and spend their evenings in the bars trying to persuade their young men that it is time to marry and have children to keep the local community alive? There are also the consequences of ageing. This again poses new problems for the cities. Do they have the right mix of housing, modes of transport, support services and forms of social provision? What will a city with a declining number of children be like as a place to live? Will this create new social stresses and strains? In other parts of the world, the pressures of growth will continue and the issues of infrastructure cost, environmental degradation and the creation of wealth-generating opportunities will be crucial. To achieve 'sustainable development' in these cases will require not just local but also global action and recognition of issues of redistribution and debt.

The final issue will be that of the place of the 'social'. In much of the most recent postmodernist analysis, there has been a tendency to reduce the social component of the analysis to the individual. This is part of a wider refocusing upon personal experiences as the centre of life as opposed to collective experiences. In part, this reflects the growth of the information age in which many activities are disaggregated and conducted by individuals on their own, and not necessarily in relation to others. The power of the new technology allows both greater control, through increased possibilities of surveillance, and greater freedom through opening out the ways that people can gain knowledge and experience. One scenario is that this creates an urban world of isolated, home-centred, somewhat disembodied individuals and a decline in communal institutions and activities. This is the cyber city of remote connections in which we shop on the Internet, entertain ourselves through computers and television, diagnose and treat ourselves with the aid of virtual medics and live out our relationships in virtual reality. To most of us, this appears rather futuristic and unrealistic. The extent of erosion in the 'social', however, is shown in the increasing attention directed towards identifying and strengthening 'social capital' and capacity building and community formation.

The one thing that is certain is that we live in a world of complexity and increasing uncertainty with respect to the path of future urban change. Research and critical reflection upon our urban practice as researchers and citizens of the global world is a crucial task if we are to improve our understanding of the urban world that is unfolding.

Bibliography

Aasen, C.T. 1992. 'The Urban Sustainability Question. New Zealand Cities, Culture and Planning', Keynote Address to New Zealand Planning Institute 1992 Annual Conference. *Planning Quarterly* **106**, 15–19.

Abrams, C. 1967. *The City is the Frontier*. New York: Harper & Row.

Abrams, P. 1968. *The Origins of British Sociology, 1834–1914: An Essay with Selected Papers*. Chicago: University of Chicago Press.

Abramsson, M., L.-E. Borgegard and U. Fransson. 2000. 'Housing Careers – Some Empirical Evidence of a Complex Concept. Paper presented to the ENHR Conference, Gavle, Sweden, 2000.

Aglietta, M. 1979. *A Theory of Capitalist Regulation*. London: New Left Books.

Alexander, I. 1998. 'Community Action and Urban Sustainability: Hope for the Millenium?' *Urban Policy and Research* **16**, 107–16.

Allen, I.R., (ed.). 1977. *New Towns and the Suburban Dream: Ideology and Utopia in Planning and Development*. London: Kennikat Press.

Allison, R. 1990. '*Re*-designing Women'. *Broadsheet* **175**, 12–13.

Allmendinger, P. and H. Thomas. 1998. *Urban Planning and the British New Right*. London: Routledge.

American Urban Land Institute. 1996. Material from their website:www.demographia.com/db-adb-uli.htm

Amin, A. (ed.). 1994. *Post-Fordism: A Reader*. Oxford: Blackwell.

Anderson, I. 2001. 'Pathways through Homelessness: Towards a Dynamic Analysis'. Paper presented to the Managing Housing and Social Change: Building Social Cohesion, Accommodating Diversity Conference, City University of Hong Kong, 2001.

Andrieu, M. 1999. Population Growth: Facing the Challenge. *The OECD Observer* **217–18**, 29–31.

Angotti, T. 1993. *Metropolis 2000: Planning, Poverty, and Politics*. London: Routledge.

Armstrong, N. 1992. 'Homeworking and Gender Relations'. In *The Gender Factor* (ed.) S. Olsson. Palmerston North: The Dunmore Press.

Armstrong, W. 1980. 'Land, Class, Colonialism: The Origins of Dominion Capitalism'. In *New Zealand and the World* (ed.) W.E. Willmott. Christchurch: University of Canterbury.

Ashton, H. 2000. 'St.Albans Website'. Unpublished B.A. Hons. paper, Department of Sociology, University of Canterbury.

Auckland et al. 2001. *Quality of Life in New Zealand's Six Largest Cities: Findings from Monitoring Social, Economic and Environmental Conditions in Auckland, Christchurch, Manukau, North Shore, Waitakere and Wellington* = Te pai me te oranga o te oho i roto o ngaa rohe nunui, e ono, o Aotearoa. Project commissioned by the Councils of Auckland City. Auckland, NZ: Auckland City Council, Christchurch City Council, Manukau City Council, Waitakere City Council, North Shore City Council, Wellington City Council.

Australian Institute of Family Studies. 1996. *Australian Life Course Survey*. Melbourne: Australian Institute of Family Studies.

Badcock, B.A. 1989. 'Homeownership and the Accumulation of Real Wealth'. *Society and Space* **7**, 61–77.

——. 2000. 'Home Ownership and the Illusion of Egalitarianism'. In *European Housing in Australia* (ed.) P. Troy. Cambridge: Cambridge University Press.

Ball, M. 1982. 'Housing Provision and the Economic Crisis'. *Capital and Class* **7**, 66–77.

236

Banks, J.A. 1954. *Prosperity and Parenthood: A Study of Family Planning among the Middle Classes*. London: Routledge.

Basset, K. and J. Short. 1980. *Housing and Residential Structure: Alternative Approaches*. London: Routledge and Kegan.

Baudrillard, J. 1988. *Jean Baudrillard: Selected Writings* (ed.) M. Poster. Cambridge: Polity Press.

——. 1998. *The Consumer Society: Myths and Structures*. London: Sage.

Bauman, Z. 1992. *Intimations of Postmodernity*. London: Routledge.

——. 1998. *Work, Consumerism and the New Poor*. Buckingham: Open University Press.

Beauregard, R.A. 1990. 'Trajectories of Neighbourhood Change: The Case of Gentrification'. *Environment and Planning A* **22**, 855–74.

Beck, U. 1992. *The Risk Society: Towards a New Modernity*. London: Sage.

——. 2000. 'Living Your Own Life in a Runaway World: Individualisation, Globalisation and Politics'. In *On the Edge: Living with Global Capitalism* (eds) W. Hutton and A. Giddens. London: Random House.

Beck, U., A. Giddens and S. Lash. 1994. *Reflexive Modernization: Politics, Tradition and Aesthetics in the Modern Social Order*. Cambridge: Polity Press.

Becker, E. and T. Jahn, (eds). 1999. *Sustainability and the Social Sciences: A Cross-Disciplinary Approach to Integrating Environmental Considerations into Theoretical Reorientation*. London: Zed Books.

Becker, E., T. Jahn and I. Stiess. 1999. 'Exploring Uncommon Ground: Sustainability and the Social Sciences'. In *Sustainability and the Social Sciences* (eds) E. Becker and T. Jahn. London: Zed Books.

Bedford, R. and I. Pool. 1997. 'Population Change: From Dynamics and Structures to Policies: Background Paper'. Paper presented to the Population Conference, Wellington, 1997.

Bell, D. 1997. *Consuming Geographies: We Are Where We Eat*. London: Routledge.

Berger, B. 1960. *Working-class Suburb*. Berkeley, California: University of California Press.

Berman, M. 1982. *All that is Solid Melts into Air: The Experience of Modernity*. New York: Simon and Schuster.

Berner, E. and R. Korff. 1995. 'Globalisation and Local Resistance: The Creation of Localities in Manila and Bangkok'. *International Journal of Urban and Regional Research* **19**, 208–22.

Berry, B.J.L. and J.D.K. Kasarda. 1977. *Contemporary Urban Ecology*. New York: Macmillan Publishing Co.

Berry, M. 1983. 'The Australian City in History: Critique and Renewal'. In *Urban Political Economy: The Australian Case* (eds) L. Sandercock and M. Berry. Sydney: George Allen and Unwin.

——. 1984. 'Urbanisation and Accumulation: Australia's First Long Boom Revisited'. In *Conflict and Development* (ed.) P. Williams. Sydney: George Allen and Unwin.

Best, S. 1989. 'The Commodification of Reality and the Reality of Commodification: Jean Baudrillard and Post-modernism. *Current Perspectives in Social Theory* **19**, 23–51.

Bhatti, M. and A. Church. 2000. 'The Hoover in the Garden: Gender, Leisure and Homemaking in Late Modernity'. Paper presented to the ENHR Conference, Gavle, Sweden, 2000.

Blair, T.L. 1974. *The International Urban Crisis*. St. Albans: Granada.

Blakely, E.J. and M.G. Snyder. 1997. *Fortress America: Gated Communities in the United States*. Washngton D.C.: Brookings Institution Press.

Blanc, M. 1998. 'Social Integration and Exclusion in France: Some Introductory Remarks from a Social Transaction Perspective'. *Housing Studies* **13**, 781–92.

Blowers, A. and K. Pain. 1999. 'The Unsustainable City?' In *Unruly Cities? Order/Disorder* (eds) S. Pile, C. Brook and G. Mooney. London: Routledge.

Bluestone, B. and B. Harrison. 1986. *The Great American Job Machine: The Proliferation of Low-Wage Employment in the U.S. Economy*. Washington D.C.: United States Congressional Joint Committee.

Blyth, S.A. 1999. 'Shifting to a Sustainable City? Participation in Wellington Our City – Our Future Strategy'. Unpublished MA Thesis: Massey University.

Boston, J., P. Dalziel and S. St John. 1999. *Redesigning the Welfare State in New Zealand: Problems, Policies, Prospects.* Auckland: Oxford University Press.

Bott, E. 1957. *Family and Social Network: Roles, Norms, and External Relationships in Ordinary Urban Families.* London: Tavistock Publications.

Bourdieu, P. 1984. *Distinction: A Social Critique of the Judgement of Taste.* Cambridge, Mass.: Harvard University Press.

Bourne, L.S. 1998. 'Reurbanization, Uneven Urban Development, and the Debate on New Urban Forms'. *Urban Geography* **17**, 690–713.

Boyer, R. 1988. *The Search for Labour Market Flexibility: The European Economies in Transition.* Oxford: Clarendon Press.

Britton, S.G. 1991. 'Recent Trends in the Internationalisation of the New Zealand Economy'. *Australian Geographical Studies* **29**, 3–25.

Britton, S.G., R.B. Le Heron and E. Pawson. 1992. *Changing Places in New Zealand: A Geography of Restructuring.* Christchurch: The Society.

Brodie, J. 1996. 'New State Forms, New Political Spaces'. In *States against Markets: The Limits of Globalisation* (eds) R. Boyer and D. Drache. London: Routledge.

Browne, A. and R. Reeves. 1999. 'Population Zero', *The Press.* Christchurch.

Bulmer, M. 1984. *The Chicago School of Sociology: Institutionlization, Diversity, and the Rise of Sociological Research.* Chicago: University of Chicago Press.

Burchardt, T., Julian Le Grand and David Piachaud. 1999. 'Social Exclusion in Britain 1991–1995'. *Social Policy and Administration* **33**, 227–44.

Burgers, J. 1996. 'No Polarisation in Dutch Cities? Inequality in a Corporatist Country'. *Urban Studies* **33**, 99–105.

Burgess, E.W. 1967. 'The Growth of the City'. In *The City* (eds) R.E. Park, E.W. Burgess and R.D. McKenzie. Chicago: Chicago University Press.

Burgess, E.W. and D. Bogue, (eds). 1964. *Contribution to Urban Sociology.* Chicago: Chicago University Press.

Burgess, J. and C.M. Harrison. 1998. 'Environmental Communication and the Cultural Politics of Environmental Citizenship'. *Environment and Planning A* **30**, 1445–60.

Burke, T. 1988. 'Public Housing and the Community'. In *New Houses for Old* (ed.) R. Howe. Melbourne: Ministry of Housing and Construction.

Byrne, D. 1999. *Social Exclusion.* Buckingham: Open University.

Calasanti, T.M. and A. Bonanno. 1989. 'The Social Creation of Dependency. Dependency Ratios, and the Elderly in the United States: A Critical Analysis'. *Social Science and Medicine* **23**, 1229–36.

Caldeira, T.P.R. 1996. 'Building up Walls: The New Pattern of Spatial Segregation in Sao Paulo'. *International Social Science Journal* **48**, 55–66.

Calthorpe, P. 1993. *The Next American Metropolis: Ecology, Community, and the American Dream.* New York: Princeton Architectural Press.

Calthorpe, P. and W.B. Fulton. *c.* 2001. *The Regional City: Planning for the End of Sprawl.* Washington D.C.: Island Press.

Cameron, J. 1997. *Without Issue: New Zealanders who Choose not to have Children.* Christchurch: Canterbury University Press.

Campbell, C. 1995. 'The Sociology of Consumption'. In *Acknowledging Consumption: A Review of New Studies* (ed.) D. Miller. London: Routledge.

Carson, R. 1962. *The 'Silent Spring'.* London: Hamish Hamilton.

Carter, H. 1983. *An Introduction to Urban Historical Geography.* London: Edward Arnold.

Castells, M. 1976. 'Is There an Urban Sociology?' In *Urban Sociology: Critical Essays* (ed.) C.G. Pickvance. London: Tavistock.

——. 1977a. 'Towards a Political Urban Sociology'. In *Captive Cities* (ed.) M. Harloe. London: Wiley.

——. 1977b. *The Urban Question.* London: Edward Arnold.

——. 1983. *The City and the Grassroots.* London: Edward Arnold.

——. 1996. *The Rise of the Network Society.* Cambridge, Mass.: Blackwell Publishers.

——. 1997. *The Power of Identity.* Cambridge, Mass.: Blackwell Publishers.

——. 1998. *Information Age: Economy, Society, and Culture; vol.3.* Malden, Mass.: Blackwell Publishers.

Castles, F.G. 1985. *The Working Class and Welfare: Reflections on the Political Development of the Welfare State in Australia and New Zealand 1890–1980.* Wellington: Allen & Unwin.

Castles, S. 1997. 'Asia-Pacific Migration and the Emerging Civil Societies'. *Asian Migrant* **10**, 41–8.

Castles, S. and G.K. Kosack. 1973. *Immigrant Workers and Class Structure in Western Europe.* London: Oxford University Press.

Caudrey, A. 1986. 'Mozart's New Tune'. *New Society.* 31 January, 177–8.

Celso, D. and J. Klink. 1999. 'Working Together for Urban Revitalization and Social Inclusion: The Approach in Santo Andre, Sao Paulo, Brazil'. In Research Community for the Habitat Agenda: Linking Research and Policy for the Sustainability of Human Settlements. International Conference Geneva, July 6–8 1998 M.L.C. Cagli, (ed.). Rome: CERFE Group.

Cenzatti, M. 1993. *Los Angeles and the LA School: Postmodernism and Urban Studies.* Los Angeles: Los Angeles Forum for Architecture and Urban Design.

Chand, S.K. and A. Jaeger. 1996. *Aging and Populations and Public Pension Schemes: Occasional Paper No.147.* Washington D.C.: International Monetary Fund.

Clapson, M. 1998. *Invincible Green Suburbs, Brave New Towns: Social Change and Urban Dispersal in Postwar England.* New York: Manchester University Press.

Clarke, C., C. Peach and S. Vertovec (eds). 1990. *South Asian Overseas: Migration and Ethnicity.* Cambridge: Cambridge University Press.

Cockburn, C. 1977. *The Local State: Management of Cities and People.* London: Pluto Press.

Cohen, A.P., (ed.). 1982. *Belonging-Identity and Social Organisation in British Rural Cultures.* Manchester: Manchester University Press.

Coleman, A. and King's College, University of London, Design Disadvantagement Team. 1985. *Utopia on Trial: Vision and Reality in Planned Housing.* London: Shipman.

Collins, J. 1988. *Migrant Hands in a Distant Land.* Sydney: Pluto Press.

Comte, A. 1876. *The Course of Positive Philosophy.* London: George Bell and Sons.

Congress for New Urbanism. 1996. 'The Congress for New Urbanism'. Internet: http://www.cnu.org/

Cooke, P. 1989. *Localities: The Changing Face of Urban Britain.* London: Unwin Hyman.

Corrigan, P. 1997. *The Sociology of Consumption: An Introduction.* London: Sage.

Craig, J.L. 1998. *Environmental Drivers and Relationships with Urban Environments: Urban Sustainability in New Zealand.* Report of a workshop sponsored by the Royal Society of New Zealand, the New Zealand National Commission for UNESCO, and the Parliamentary Commissioner for the Environment. The Royal Society of New Zealand: Miscellaneous Series 53.

Cresswell, R. 1974. *The New Town Goal of Self-Containment: Milton Keynes.* Milton Keynes: Milton Keynes Development Corporation.

Crompton, R. 1996. 'Consumption and Class Analysis'. In *Consumption Matters* (eds) S. Edgell, K. Hetherington and A. Warde. Oxford: Blackwell Publishers.

——. 1998. *Class and Stratification: An Introduction to Current Debates.* Cambridge: Polity Press.

——. 2000. *Renewing Class Analysis.* Malden, Mass.: Blackwell.

Culhane, D. and M. Fried. 1988. 'Paths in Homelessness: A View from the Street'. In *Affordable Housing and the Homeless* (ed.) J. Friedrichs. Berlin: Walter de Gruyter.

Cullingworth, J.B. 1972. *Town and Country Planning in Britain.* London: Allen and Unwin.

Curtin, P. 1997. 'Africa and Global Patterns in Migration'. In *Global History and Migration* (ed.) G. Wang. Boulder: Westview Press.

Da Silva, A.A. 2000. 'Sao Paulo and the Challenges for Social Sustainability: The Case of an Urban Housing Policy'. In *The Social Sustainability of Cities: Diversity and the Management of Change* (eds) M. Polese and R. Stren. Toronto: University of Toronto Press.

Daly, G. 1996a. 'Migrants and Gate Keepers: The Links between Immigration and Homelessness in Western Europe'. *Cities* **13**, 11–23.

——. 1996b. *Homeless: Policies, Strategies, and Lives on the Street*. London: Routledge.

Damer, S. 1974. 'Wine Alley: The Sociology of a Dreadful Enclosure'. *Sociological Review* **22**, 221–48.

——. 1990. *Glasgow; Going for a Song*. London: Lawrence and Wishart.

Davis, D. 2001. 'The Non-Economic Consequences of Chinese Urban Housing Reforms'. Paper presented to the Managing Housing and Social Change: Building Social Cohesion, Accommodating Diversity Conference, City University of Hong Kong, 2001.

Davis, K. 1973. *Cities: Their Origin, Growth and Human Impact*. San Francisco: W.H. Freeman and Company.

Davis, M. 1991. *City of Quartz: Excavating the Future in Los Angeles*. London: Verso.

——. 1995. 'Fortress Los Angeles: The Militarization of Urban Space'. In *Metropolis* (ed.) P. Kasinitz. Los Angeles: Macmillan.

De Bruin, A. and A. Dupuis. 1995. *The Implications of Housing Policy for Women in Non-nuclear Families*. Paper presented to the 18th Conference of the New Zealand Geographical Society, University of Canterbury, Christchurch.

De Swaan, J. Manor, E. Oyen and E.P. Reis. 2000. 'Elite Perceptions of the Poor: Reflections for a Comparative Research Project'. *Current Sociology* **48**, 43–54.

Dear, M. 1992. 'Understanding and Overcoming the NIMBY Syndrome'. *Journal of the American Planning Association* **58**, 288–300.

——. 2000. *The Postmodern Urban Condition*. Oxford: Blackwell.

Dear, M.J. and J.R. Wolch. 1987. *Landscapes of Despair: From Deinstitutionalisation to Homelessness*. Cambridge: Polity Press.

Debord, G. 1983. *Society of the Spectacle*. Detroit: Black and Red.

Dempsey, K. 1990. *Smalltown*. Melbourne: Oxford University Press.

Dennis, N. 1968. 'The Popularity of the Neighbourhood Community Idea'. In *Readings in Urban Sociology* (ed.) R.E. Pahl. Oxford: Pergamon.

Denoon, D. 1983. *Settler Capitalism: The Dynamics of Dependent Development in the Southern Hemisphere*. Oxford: Clarendon Press.

Department of Housing and Urban Development. (HUD). 1997. *State of the Nation's Cities*. Washington: HUD.

Dickens, P. 2000. 'Society, Space and the Biotic Level: An Urban and Rural Sociology for the New Millenium'. *Sociology: A Journal of the British Sociological Association* **34**, 147–64.

Dieleman, F. and S. Musterd. 1992. *The Randstad: A Research and Policy Laboratory*. Dordrecht: Kluwer Academic Publishers.

Ditch, J., A. Lewis and S. Wilcox. 2001. *Social Housing, Tenure and Housing Allowances: An International Review*. University of York.

Dobriner, W. (ed.). 1958. *The Suburban Community*. New York: Pitmans.

Dobriner, W. 1963. *Class in Suburbia*. New Jersey: Prentice Hall Inc.

Dodd, N. 1999. *Social Theory and Modernity*. Cambridge: Polity Press.

Dolgon, C. 1999. 'Soulless Cities: Ann Arbor, The Cutting Edge of Discipline: Postfordism, Postmodernism, and the New Bourgeoisie'. *Antipode* **31**, 129–62.

Duany, A., E. Plater-Zyberk, A. Krieger and W.R. Lennertz. 1992. *Andres Duany and Elizabeth Plater-Zyberk: Towns and Town-making Principles*. New York: Rizzoli.

Duffy, M. 1994. 'Suburbia's New Cathedrals'. *The Independent Australia's National Quality Monthly*, March 28–33. Surrey Hills, NSW.

Duncan, N. 1996. *Body Space: Destabilising Geographies of Gender and Sexuality*. London: Routledge.

Duncan, S. and M. Goodwin. 1988. *The Local State and Uneven Development: Behind the Local Government Crisis*. Cambridge: Polity Press.

Dunleavy, P. 1979. 'The Urban Basis of Political Alignment: Social Class, Domestic Property Ownership, and State Intervention in Consumption Process'. *British Journal of Political Science* **9**, 409–43.

——. 1980. *Urban Political Analysis: The Politics of Collective Consumption*. London: Macmillan – now Palgrave Macmillan.

Dupuis, A. 1992. 'Financial Gains from Owner-Occupation. The New Zealand Case 1970–1988'. *Housing Studies* **7.1**, 27–44.

Dupuis, A. and D.C. Thorns. 1996. 'Meanings of Home for Older Home Owners'. *Housing Studies* **11**, 485–501.

——. 1998. 'Home, Home Ownership and the Search for Ontological Security'. *The Sociological Review* **46**, 24–47.

Durkheim, E. 1960. *The Division of Labour in Society*. New York: Macmillan.

Dyos, H.J. 1954. 'The Growth of a Pre-Victorian Suburb, South London 1580–1836'. *Town Planning* **25**, 53–78.

Eade, J., (ed.). 1997. *Living the Global City: Globalization as a local process*. London: Routledge.

Edgell, S., K. Hetherington and A. Warde, (eds). 1996. *Consumption Matters: The Production and Experience of Consumption*. Oxford: Blackwell Publishers.

Ehrlich, P.R. 1968. *The Population Bomb*. New York: Ballantine Books.

Eichler, M. 1999. 'Sustainability from a Feminist Sociological Perspective: A Framework for Disciplinary Reorientation'. In *Sustainability and the Social Sciences: A Cross-Disciplinary Approach to Integrating Environmental Considerations into Theoretical Reorientation* (eds) E. Becker and T. Jahn. London: Zed Books.

Ellen, W. 1993. *Zambia Peri-Urban Self-Help Project*. Report prepared for the Overseas Development Administration, London, October 1993.

Elliot, B. and D. Macrone. 1982. *The City Patterns of Domination and Conflict*. London: Macmillan – now Palgrave Macmillan.

Encyclopedia of Life Support Systems. (EOLSS). 1997. *Global Crisis Sustainable Development*. London: EOLSS Publishers Co Ltd.

Engels, F. 1971. *The Condition of the Working Class in England:* Translated and edited by W.O. Henderson and W.H. Chaloner (2nd edn). Oxford: Blackwell.

Fainstein, S.S. and S. Campbell, (eds). 1996. *Readings in Urban Theory*. Cambridge, Mass.: Blackwell Publishers.

Farnsworth, C. 1998, October. Design. In *Professional Builder* **63**, 11.

Featherstone, M. 1991. *Consumer Culture and Post Modernism*. London: Sage.

——. 1993. 'Global and Local Cultures'. In *Mapping the Futures: Local Cultures, Global Change* (eds) J. Bird, B. Curtis, T. Putnam, G. Robertson and L. Tickner. London: Routledge.

Findlay, A.M., H. Jones and G.M. Davidson. 1998. 'Migration Transition or Migration Transformation in the Asian Dragon Economies?' *International Journal of Urban and Regional Research* **22**, 643–63.

Fine, B. 1995. 'From Political Economy to Consumption'. In *Acknowledging Consumption: A Review of New Studies* (ed.) D. Miller. London: Routledge.

Firat, A.F. and N. Dholakia. 1998. *Consuming People: From Political Economy to Theaters of Consumption* (Consumer Research and Policy Series). London; New York: Routledge.

Fischer, C.S. 1984. *The Urban Experience*. Jovanovich, Florida: Harcourt & Brace.

Fitzpatrick, T. 1997. 'A Tale of Tall Cities'. *The Guardian On-Line*, 6 February 1997.

Fogelsong, R. 1996. 'Planning the Capitalist City'. In *Readings in Planning Theory* (eds) S. Campbell and S.S. Fainstein. Oxford: Blackwell.

——. 1999. 'Walt Disney World and Orlando: Deregulation as a Strategy for Tourism'. In *The Tourist City* (eds) D.R. Judd and S.S. Fainstein. New Haven: Yale University Press.

Forester, J. 1999. *The Deliberative Practitioner: Encourging Participatory Planning Processes*. Cambridge, Mass.: MIT Press.

Forrest, R. and A. Murie. 1995. *Housing and Family Wealth: Comparative International Perspectives*. London: Routledge.

Forsyth, A. 1997. 'Five Images of a Suburb: Perspectives on a New Urban Development'. *Journal of the American Planning Association* **63**, 45–60.

Frank, A. 1981. *Capitalism and Underdevelopment in Latin America*. Harmondsworth: Penguin.

Frankel, B. 1994. 'Class, Environmental and Social Movements'. In *The Polity Reader in Social Theory*. Oxford: Blackwell.

Friedan, B. 1963. *The Feminine Mystique*. London: Gollancz.

Friedman, J. 1995. 'Where Do We Stand: A Decade of World City Research'. In *World Cities in a World System* (eds) P. Knox and P. Taylor. Cambridge: Cambridge University Press.

Frisken, F., L.S. Bourne, G. Gad and R.A. Murdie. 2000. 'Governance and Social Sustainability: The Toronto Experience'. In *The Social Sustainability of Cities: Diversity and the Management of Change* (eds) M. Polese and R. Stren. Toronto: University of Toronto Press.

Froebel, F., J. Heinrichs and D. Kreye. 1980. *The New International Division of Labour*. Cambridge: Cambridge University Press.

Game, A. 1991. *Undoing the Social: Towards a Deconstructive Sociology*. Toronto: University of
Toronto Press.

Gans, H.J. 1962. *The Urban Villagers: Group and Class in the Life of Italian Americans*. New York:
Free Press of Glencoe.

——. 1967. *The Levittowners*. New York: Vintage.

——. 1972. *People and Plans*. Harmondsworth: Penguin.

Garreau, S. 1991. *Edge City: Life on the New Frontier*. New York: Doubleday.

Gatt, L., (Project manager). 2001. *Quality of Life in New Zealand's Six Largest Cities*. Auckland
City Council, Christchurch City Council, Manakau City Council, North Shore City
Council, Waitakere City Council, Wellington City Council.

Geddes, P. 1949. *Cities in Evolution*. London: Williams & Norgate.

Gibson, K. and S. Watson. 1994. *Metropolis Now: Planning and the Urban in Contemporary
Australia*. Leichhardt: Pluto Press.

Giddens, A. 1987. *Sociology, a Brief but Critical Introduction*. San Diego: Harcourt Brace
Jovanovich.

——. 1998. 'Runaway World': Reith Lectures.

——. 1998. *The Third Way: The Renewal of Social Democracy*. Malden, Mass.: Polity Press.

——. 2001. *The Global Third Way Debate*. Cambridge: Polity Press.

Giddens, A. and W. Hutton. 2000. 'In Conversation'. In *On the Edge: Living with Global Capitalism* (eds) W. Hutton and A. Giddens. London: Random House.

Gilloch, G. and W. Benjamin. 1996. *Myth and Metropolis: Walter Benjamin and the City*. Cambridge: Polity Press.

Gilroy, R. 2000. '"But could it be different?" Developing a New Paradigm of Home and
Neighbourhood'. Paper presented to the ENHR Conference, Gavle, Sweden, 2000.

Gilroy, R. and R. Woods. 1994. 'Housing Women'. London, New York: Routledge.

Glass, R. 1955. Urban Sociology. *Current Sociology* **4**, 5–19.

Godfrey, B.J. 1999. 'Revisiting Rio de Janeiro and Sao Paulo'. *The Geographical Review* **89**,
94–121.

Goodman, R. 1972. *After the Planners*. Harmondsworth: Penguin.

Gordon, P. and H.W.R. Richardson. 1997. 'Are Compact Cities a Desirable Planning Goal?'
Journal of the American Planning Association **63**, 95–106.

Gorz, A. 1982. *Farewell to the Working Class: An Essay on Post-industrial Socialism*. London:
Pluto.

Gotham, K.F. 1998. 'Blind Faith in the Free Market: Urban Poverty, Residential Segregation,
and Federal Housing Retrenchment, 1970–1995'. *Sociological Inquiry* **68**, 1–31.

Gottdiener, M. 1997. *The Theming of America: Dreams, Visions and Commercial Spaces*. Boulder,
Colorado: Westview Press.

Gouldner, A.W. 1979. *The Future of Intellectuals and the Rise of the New Class: A frame of
Reference, Theses, Conjectures, Arguments, and an Historical Perspective on the Role of Intel-
lectuals and Intelligentsia in the International Class Contest of the Modern Era*. New York:
Seabury Press.

Graham, S. 1997. 'Telecommunications and the Future of Cities: Debunking the Myths'.
Cities **14**, 21–9.

——. 1998. 'Spaces of Surveillant Simulation: New Technologies, Digital Representations,
and Material Geographies. *Environment and Planning D: Society and Space* **16**, 483–504.

——. 1999. 'Global Grids of Glass: On Global Cities, Telecommunications and Planetary
Urban Networks'. *Urban Studies* **36**, 929–49.

Greed, C.H. 1999. 'Introducing Social Town Planning'. In *Social Town Planning* (ed.) C.H.
Greed. London: Routledge.

Gurney, C. 1999. 'Pride and Prejudice: Discourses of Normalisation in Public and Private
Accounts of Home Ownership'. *Housing Studies* **14**, 163–83.

Haar, P. 2000. 'A Self-help Approach to Remote Area Housing, St Paul's Village, Moa Island, Torres Strait, 1986–92'. In *Settlement: A History of Australian Indigenous Housing* (ed.) P. Read. Canberra: Aboriginal Studies Press.

Haggstrom, C. 2000. 'The Teenage Room as Practice in Modern Living'. Paper presented to the ENHR Conference, Gavle, Sweden, 2000.

Hall, P. 1993. 'Forces Shaping Urban Europe'. *Urban Studies* **30**, 883–98.

——. 1997. 'The Future of the Metropolis and its Form'. *Regional Studies* **31**, 211–20.

Hall, R.D., D.C. Thorns and W.E. Willmott. 1984. 'Community, Class and Kinship-bases for Collective Action within Localities. *Environment and Planning, D, Space and Society* **2**, 201–16.

Hamid, T. and M. Foud. 1993. *The Incidence of Poverty in Developing Countries; An ILO Compendium of Data*. A World Employment Programme Study. Geneva: International Labour Office.

Hamnett, C. 1991. 'The Blind Men and the Elephant: The Explanation of Gentrification'. Transactions of the Institute of British Geographers, **16**, **2**, 173–89.

——. 1999. *Winners and Losers: Home Ownership in Modern Britain*. London: UCL Press.

Hamnett, C., M. Harmer and P. Williams. 1991. *Safe as Houses. Housing Inheritance in Britain*. London: Paul Chapman.

Harloe, M. 1977. *Captive Cities*. London: Wiley.

Harvey, D. 1973. *Social Justice and the City*. London: Edward Arnold.

——. 1981. 'The Urban Process under Capitalism: A Framework for Analysis'. In *Urbanization and Urban Planning in Capitalist Society* (eds) M. Dear and A.J. Scott. London: Methuen.

——. 1989. *The Urban Experience*. Oxford: Basil Blackwell.

——. 1990. *The Condition of Postmodernity: An Enquiry into the Origins of Cultural Change*. Oxford: Blackwell.

Hawley, A. 1950. *Human Ecology: A Theory of Community Structure*. New York: Ronald Press.

Hayden, D. 1980. 'What Would a Non-Sexist City be Like?' *Signs: Journal of Women in Culture and Society* **5**, 169–87.

Hazeldine, T. 1998. *Taking New Zealand Seriously: The Economics of Decency*. Auckland: Harper Collins.

Healey, P. 1998. 'Collaborative Planning in a Stakeholder Society'. *Town Planning Review* **69**, 1–21.

Held, D., A. McGrew, D. Goldblatt and J. Perraton. 1999. *Global Transformations: Politics, Economics and Culture*. Cambridge: Polity Press.

Henderson, J. 1989. *The Globalisation of High Technology Production: Society, Space and Semi-conductors in the Restructuring of the Modern World*. London: Routledge.

Higgins, J. 1999. 'From Welfare to Workfare'. In *Redesigning the Welfare State in New Zealand* (eds) J. Boston, P. Dalziel and S. St.John. Auckland: Oxford University Press.

Hill, R.C. and J.R. Feagin. 1987. 'Detroit and Houston: Two Cities in Global Perspective'. In *The Capitalist City* (eds) M.P. Smith and J.R. Feagin. Oxford: Basil Blackwell Ltd.

Hillery, G. 1955. 'Definitions of Community; Areas of Agreement'. *Rural Sociology* **20**, 111–23.

Hillier, J. and P. McManus. 1994. 'Pull up the Drawbridge: Fortress Mentality in the Suburbs'. In *Metropolis Now* (eds) K. Gibson and S. Watson. Leichhardt, NSW: Pluto Press Australia Ltd.

Hirano, K. 2000. 'Transnational Flows of People and International Exchanges: Phenomena and Activities'. In *Globalism, Regionalism and Nationalism: Asia in Search of its Role in the Twenty-First Century* (ed.) Y. Yamamoto. Oxford: Blackwell.

Hirano, K., S. Castles and P. Brownlee. 2000. 'Towards a Sociology of Asian Settlement: Focus on Japan'. *Asian and Pacific Migration Journal* **9**, 243–53.

Hirst, P. and G. Thompson. 1996. *Globalization in Question: The International Economy and the Possibilities of Governance* Cambridge: Polity Press.

Hoch, C. 1986. 'Homeless in the United States'. *Housing Studies* **1**, 228–40.

Holton, R.J. 1998. *Globalization and the Nation State*. London: Macmillan Press – now Palgrave Macmillan.

Hong, S.W. 1996. 'Seoul: A Global City in a Nation of Rapid Growth'. In *Emerging World Cities in Pacific Asia* (eds) F.-C. Lo and Y.-M. Yeung. Tokyo: United Nations University Press.

Hopkins, J. and J. Riley. 1998. *Blokes and Sheds*. Auckland: Harper Collins.

Howard, E. 1898. *Tomorrow*, later republished as, 1902, *Garden Cities of To-morrow*. Cambridge, Mass.: M.I.T. Press.

Hoyt, H. 1939. *The Structure and Growth of Residential Neighbourhoods in American Cities*. Washington D.C.: U.S. Government Printing Office.

Hughes, P. 2000. *The Contribution of the Resource Management Act 1991 to Sustainability: A Report Card after 8 Years*. Wellington: Office of the Parliamentary Commissioner for the Environment.

Hutton, W. and A. Giddens. 2000. *On the Edge: Living with Global Capitalism*. London: Jonathan Cape.

Huxley, M. 1994. 'Panoptica: Utilitarianism and Land-use Control'. In *Metropolis Now* (eds) K. Gibson and S. Watson. Leichhardt, NSW: Pluto Press.

Institute for Social-Ecological Research (ISOE). 1997. *Sustainability as a Concept of the Social Sciences*. Frankfurt-am Main: ISOE.

International Longevity Centre. 1996. *Decline of Fertility and Population Aging in East Asia*. Tokyo: ILC.

Jacobs, J. 1996. *The Edge of Empire: Postcolonialism and the City*. London: Routledge.

Jaques, R. 1999. Co-housing – The New Suburbia? *Build*, 56–8.

Jarvis, V. and S. Prais. 1988. 'Two Nations of Shopkeepers: Training for Retailing in France and Britain'. Discussion Paper No. 40. London: National Institute of Economic and Social Research.

Jencks, C. 1984. *The Language of Post-Modern Architecture*. New York: Rizzoli.

Jessop, B. 1990. 'Regulation Theories in Retrospect and Prospect'. *Economy and Society*, **19**, 2, 153–216.

Jessop, B. and N.-L. Sum. 1999. 'An Entreprenurial City in Action: Emerging Strategies for (Inter-)Urban Competition in Hong Kong'. Paper presented to The Future of Chinese Cities: A Research Agenda for the 21st Century Conference, Shanghai, 1999.

Jessop, B. and University of Essex. Dept. of Government. 1989. *Thatcherism: The British Road to Post-Fordism?* Essex Papers in Politics and Government; no. 68. Colchester [England]: Dept. of Government, University of Essex.

Johnson, B. 1999. 'Is Atlanta's 'New Urbanism' the End of Suburban Sprawl? *National Real Estate Investor* **41**, 5.

Johnson, L. 1994b. 'Colonising the Suburban Frontier: Placemaking on Melbourne's Urban Fringe'. In *Metropolis Now: Planning and the Urban in Contemporary Australia* (eds) K. Gibson and S. Watson. Leichhardt, NSW: Pluto Press.

Johnson, L. (ed.). 1994a. *Suburban Dreaming*. Deakin: Deakin University Press.

Johnson, R.J. 1973. *Urban Residential Patterns*. London: G. Belland Sons Ltd.

Joseph Rowntree Foundation. 1995. *Income and Wealth Findings, United Kingdom*. York.

Judd, D.R. 1999. 'Constructing the Tourist Bubble'. In *The Tourist City* (eds) D.R. Judd and S.S. Fainstein. New Haven: Yale University.

Judd, D.R. and S.S. Fainstein. 1999. *The Tourist City*. New Haven: Yale University Press.

Katz, P. 1994. *The New Urbanism: Toward an Architecture of Community*. New York: McGraw-Hill Inc.

Keat, R. and J. Urry. 1975. *Social Theory as Science*. London: Routledge & Kegan Paul.

Kellet, J.R. 1969. *The Impact of Railways on Victorian Cities*. London: Routledge & Paul.

Kelsey, J. 1997. *The New Zealand Experiment: A World Model for Structural Adjustment*. Auckland: Auckland University Press.

Kemeny, J. 1977. 'A Political Sociology of Home Ownership in Australia'. *Australia and New Zealand Journal of Sociology* **13**, 47–52.

——. 1978. *Home-ownership and Privitization in Capitalist Societies: A Cross-cultural Perspective*. University of Queensland: International Sociological Association, AN2 Branch, University of Queensland.

——. 1981. *The Myth of Home Ownership*. London: Routledge and Kegan Paul.

Kendig, H. 1979. *New Life for Old Suburbs*. Sydney: George Allen and Unwin.

Kennett, P. 1994. 'Exclusion, post-Fordism and the "New Europe"'. In *A New Europe? Eco-*

nomic Restructuring and Social Exclusion (eds) P. Brown and R. Crompton. London: UCL Press.

Kerr, S. 1997. 'Resource Management as Politics: The Slow Shuffle towards a Dissertation Proposal'. Paper presented to the Lincoln University Postgraduate Student Research Conference, Department of Human and Leisure Sciences, Lincoln University, 1997.

Kesteloot, C. 2000. 'Brussells: Post-Fordist Polarization in a Fordist Spatial Canvas'. In *Globalizing Cities: A New Spatial Order?* (eds) P. Marcuse and R. van Kempen. Oxford: Blackwell.

Khondker, H.H. 2000. 'Globalization: Against Reductionism and Linearity'. *Development and Society* **29**, 17–33.

Kidokoro, T. 1995. 'Planning and Development Control Systems of Mega-Cities in Southeast Asia'. *Regional Development Studies* **1**, 171–81.

Kilmartin, L. and D. Thorns. 1978. *Cities Unlimited.* Sydney: George Allen and Unwin.

Kilmartin, L., D.C. Thorns and T. Burke. 1985. *Social Theory and the Australian City.* Sydney: Allen and Unwin.

Kim, K.S. and N. Gallent. 1998. 'Regulating Industrial Growth in the South Korean Capital'. *Cities* **15**, 1–11.

King, A. (ed.). 1996. *Re-Presenting the City.* Basingstoke: Macmillan – now Palgrave Macmillan.

King, A.D. 1976. *Colonial Urban Development: Culture, Social Power and Environment.* London: Routledge and Kegan Paul.

——. 2000. 'Cities: Contradictory Utopias'. In *Global Futures: Shaping Globalization* (ed.) J. Nederveen Pieterse. London: Zed Books.

Kleinman, M. 1999. 'Housing and Regeneration: The problem or the Solution'. *National Institute Economic Review.* **170**, 78–86.

Knox, P. 1991. 'The Restless Urban Landscape'. *Annals of American Geographers* **81**, 181–209.

——. 1993. *The Restless Urban Landscape.* Engelwood Cliffs, New Jersey: Prentice Hall.

——. 1996. 'Globalization and the World City Hypothesis'. In *Scottish Geographical Magazine.* **112**, 124–6.

Knox, P.L. and P.J. Taylor (eds). 1995. *World Cities in a World System.* Cambridge: Cambridge University Press.

Kumar, K. 1995. *From Post-Industrial to Post-Modern Society: New Theories of the Contemporary World.* Oxford: Blackwell.

Lamberg-Karlovsky, C.C. and M. Lamberg-Karlovsky. 1973. 'An Early City in Iran'. In *Cities: Their Origin, Growth and Human Impact* (ed.) K. Davis. San Fransisco: W.H. Freeman and Company.

Laquian, A.A. 1996. 'The Multi-ethnic and Multicultural City: An Asian Perspective'. *International Science Journal* **147**, 43–53.

Larner, W. 1998. 'Hitching a Ride on the Tiger's Back: Globalisation and Spatial Imaginaries in New Zealand'. *Environment and Planning D: Society and Space* **16**, 599–614.

Lash, S. 1999. *Another Modernity, A Different Rationality.* Oxford: Blackwell.

Lash, S. and J. Urry. 1987. *The End of Organised Capitalism.* Madison, Wisconsin: University of Wisconsin Press.

Lash, S. and J.U. Urry. 1994. *Economies of Signs and Space.* London: Sage.

Latour, B. 1993. *We Have Never Been Modern.* Cambridge, Mass.: Harvard University Press.

Le Heron, R. and E. Pawson, (eds). 1996. *Changing Places in New Zealand.* Auckland: Longmans.

Lee, J., R. Forrest and W.K. Tam. 2001. 'Comparing East Asian Home Ownership: Market, State and Institutions'. Paper presented to the Managing Housing and Social Change: Building Social Cohesion, Accommodating Diversity City University of Hong Kong, 2001.

Lee, P. 1999. 'Where are the Socially Excluded? Continuing Debates in the Identification of Poor Neighbourhoods'. *Regional Studies* **33**, 483–86.

Lee, P. and A. Murie. 1994. *Social Exclusion Review: A Report of the Scottish Office.* The University of Birmingham.

Lemon, J. 1984. 'Toronto Among North American Cities'. In *Forging a Consensus* (ed.) V.L. Russell. Toronto: University of Toronto Press.

——. 1985. *Toronto Since 1918*. Toronto: James Lorimer and Co.

Levine, M.V. 2000. 'A Third-World City in the First World: Social Exclusion, Racial Inequality, and Sustainable Development in Baltimore, Maryland'. In *The Social Sustainability of Cities: Diversity and the Management of Change* (eds) M. Polese and R. Stren. Toronto: University of Toronto Press.

Levitas, R. 1998. *The Inclusive Society?: Social Exclusion and New Labour*. Basingstoke: Macmillan – now Palgrave Macmillan.

Lewis, G. 1998. 'Capital of Desire: Bangkok as a Regional Media Metropolis'. *Social Semiotics* **8**, 239–54.

Ley, D. and R. Cybriwsky. 1974. 'Urban Graffiti as Territorial Markers'. *Annals of the Association of American Geographers* **64**, 491–505.

Logan, J.R. 2000. 'Still A Global City: The Racial and Ethnic Segmentation of New York'. In *Globalizing Cities: A New Spatial Order?* (eds) P. Marcuse and R. van Kempen. Oxford: Blackwell.

Logan, J.R. and H.L. Molotch. 1987. *Urban Fortunes: The Political Economy of Place*. Berkeley, California: University of California Press.

Longcore, T.R. and P.W. Rees. 1996. 'Information Technology and Downtown Restructuring: The Case of New York City's Financial District'. *Urban Geography* **17**, 354–72.

Longhurst, B. and M. Savage. 1996. 'Social class, Consumption and the Influence of Bourdieu: Some Critical Issues. In *Consumption Matters* (eds) S. Edgell, K. Hetherington and A. Warde. Oxford: Blackwell.

Loomis, W.F. 1973. 'Rickets'. In *Cities: Their Origin, Growth and Human Impact* (ed.) K. Davis. San Fransisco: W.H. Freeman and Company.

Low, N. 1999. *Planning for Social and Ecological Sustainability*. Research School of Social Sciences, Australian National University.

Lowe, S. 1986. *Urban Social Movements: The City after Castells*. London: Macmillan – now Palgrave Macmillan.

Luke, T.W. 1995. 'Sustainable Development as a Power/Knowledge System: The Problem of 'Governmentability'. In *Greening Environmental Policy: The Politics of a Sustainable Future* (eds) F. Fischer and M. Black. New York: St. Martins Press – now Palgrave Macmillan.

Lunday, J.D. 1996. Towards a More Sustainable Urban Form. *Planning Quarterly: Journal of the NZ Planning Institute, Inc.* **123**, 20–3.

Luymes, D. 1997. 'The Fortification of Suburbia: Investigating the Rise of Enclave Communities. *Landscape and Urban Planning* **39**, 187–203.

Lynch, K. 1960. *The Image of the City*. Cambridge, Mass.: MIT Press.

Lyon, D. 1994. *Postmodernity*. Buckingham: Open University Press.

Lyotard, J.F. 1984. *The Postmodern Condition: A Report on Knowledge*. Minneapolis: University of Minnesota Press.

MacNaghten, P. and J. Urry. 1995. 'Towards a Sociology of Nature'. *Sociology* **29**, 203–20.

——. 1998. *Contested Natures*. London: Sage Publications.

MacNeish, R.S. 1964. 'The Origins of New World Civilization'. In *Cities: Their Origin, Growth, and Human Impact* (ed.) K. Davis, (Intro.). Berkeley: University of California.

Mann, M. 1990. *The Macmillan Student Encyclopaedia of the Social Sciences*. London: Macmillan Press – now Palgrave Macmillan.

Marcus Cooper, C. 1995. *House as a Mirror of Self*. Berkeley: Conari Press.

Marcuse, P. 1989. Dual City: A Muddy Metaphor for a Quartered City. *International Journal of Urban and Regional Research* **13**, 697–708.

——. 1995. 'Not Chaos, but Walls: Postmodernism and the Partitioned City'. In *Postmodern Cities and Spaces* (eds) S. Watson and K. Gibson. Oxford: Blackwell.

Marcuse, P. 2000. 'The Language of Globalization'. *Monthly Review*. **52**, 1–4. Website: www.monthlyreview.org/700marc.htm

Marcuse, P. and R. van Kempen. 2000. *Globalizing Cities: A New Spatial Order?* Malden Mass.: Blackwell.

Marsh, A. 2001. 'Housing Policy and the Social Exclusion Agenda'. Paper presented to the Managing Housing and Social Change: Building Social Cohesion, Accommodating Diversity Conference, City University of Hong Kong, 2001.

Marsh, A. and D. Mullins. 1998. 'The Social Exclusion Perspective and Housing Studies: Origins, Applications and Limitations'. *Housing Studies* **13**, 749–60.

Massey, D. 1984. *Spatial Divisions of Labour: Social Structures and the Geographies of Production.* London: Macmillan – now Palgrave Macmillan.

——. 1994. *Space, Place and Gender.* Cambridge: Polity Press.

——. 1995. 'Places and Their Pasts'. *History Workshop Journal* **39**, 182–92.

——. 1995. *Spatial Divisions of Labour: Social Structures and the Geographies of Production,* 2nd edn. London: Macmillan – now Palgrave Macmillan.

Massey, D.S. and A.B. Gross. 1994. 'Migration, Segregation, and the Geographic Concentration of Poverty'. *American Sociological Review* **59**, 425–45.

Matthew, J. 1992. 'Homeless'. In *Newsweek,* 6 April 1992.

McDermott, W. 1973. 'Air Pollution and Public Health'. In *Cities: Their Origin, Growth and Human Impact* (ed.) K. Davis. San Francisco: W.H. Freeman and Company.

McDowell, L. 1989. 'Gender Divisions'. In *The Changing Social Structure* (eds) C. Hamnett, L. McDowell and P. Sarre. London: Sage.

——. 1997. *Capital Culture: Gender at Work in the City.* Malden, Mass.: Blackwell Publishers.

——. 1999. *Gender, Identity and Place: Understanding Feminist Geographies.* Oxford: Polity Press.

McKenzie, R. 1933. *The Metropolitan Community.* New York: McGraw-Hill.

McKenzie, S. 1980. 'Women's Place–Women's Space'. *Area* **12**, 547–9.

Mellor, J.R. 1977. *Urban Sociology in an Urbanized Society.* London: Routledge & Kegan Paul.

Memon, A. and B. Gleeson. 1995. 'Towards a New Planning Paradigm: Reflections on the NZ RMA'. *Environment and Planning B* **22**, 109–24.

Memon, P.A. and H.C. Perkins. 2000. *Environmental Planning and Management in New Zealand.* Palmerston North: Dunmore Press.

Mennell, S. 1985. *All Manners of Food: Eating and Taste in England and France from the Middle Ages to the Present.* Oxford: Blackwell.

Merklen, D. 2001. *Urban Development Projects: Neighbourhood, State and Ngos.*: UNESCO.

Miller, D., P. Jackson, N. Thrift, B. Holbrook and M. Rowlands. 1999. *Shopping, Place, Identity.* London: Routledge.

Mills, C.W. 1956. *The Sociological Imagination.* Harmondsworth: Penguin.

Mitchell, G. 2000. 'The Industry that Time Forgot'. In *A History of European Housing in Australia* (ed.) P. Troy. Cambridge: Cambridge University Press.

Molotch, H. and J. Logan. 1987. *Urban Fortunes: The Political Economy of Place.* Berkeley, Ca.: University of California Press.

Mort, F. 1996. *Cultures of Consumption: Masculinities and Social Space in Late Twentieth-Century Britain.* London: Routledge.

Mowbray, M. and L. Bryson. 1981. 'Community the Spray-on Solution'. *Australian Journal of Social Issues.* **16**, 255–67.

Mullins, P. 1977. 'The Social Base, Stake and Urban Effects of a Brisbane Urban Social Movement'. *The Australian and New Zealand Journal of Sociology* **13**, 29–35.

——. 1981a. 'Theoretical Perspectives on Australian Urbanization: Material Components in the Reproduction of Australian Labour Power. *Australian and New Zealand Journal of Sociology* **17**, 65–76.

——. 1981b. Theoretical Perspectives on Australian Urbanization: Social Components in the Reproduction of Australian Labour Power. *Australia and New Zealand Journal of Sociology* **17**, 35–43.

——. 1987. 'Community and Urban Social Movements'. *Sociological Review* **35**, 347–69.

——. 1999. 'International Tourism and the Cities of Southeast Asia'. In *The Tourist City* (eds) D.R. Judd and S.S. Fainstein. New Haven: Yale University Press.

Murie, A. and R. Forrest. 1988. *Selling the Welfare State: the Privatisation of Public Housing.* London: Routledge.

Murphy, L. 1994. *Understanding Tenant Protest: Research Themes and Issues.* Proceedings of the Housing Research Conference, Wellington: Ministry of Housing.

National Association of Home Builders. 1999. 'NAHB's Statement of Policy On Smart Growth'.

Newman, O. 1972. *Defensible Space.* New York: Macmillan.

Newman, P. 1992. 'The Compact City: An Australian Perspective'. *Built Environment* **18**, 285–300.

Newman, P. and J. Kenworthy. 1999. *Sustainability and Cities: Overcoming Automobile Dependence*. Washington D.C.: Island Press.

New Zealand Smart Growth Network. 2000. *Smart Growth: Intelligent Development in a New Century*. Rotorua.

Nilsen, R.D. 2000. 'Children in the Houses: Preliminary Results from a Study with Girls and Boys'. Paper presented to the ENHR Conference, Gavle, Sweden, 2000.

Oakley, A. 1974. *The Sociology of Housework*. London: M. Robertson.

O'Connor, J. 1973. *The Fiscal Crisis of the State*. New York: St Martin's Press.

Offe, C. 1975. The Theory of the Capitalist State and the Problem of Policy Formation. In *Stress and Contradiction in Modern Capitalism* (ed.) L.N. Lindberg, et al. London: Lexington Books.

O'Loughlin, J. and J. Friedrichs. 1996. 'Polarization in Post-Industrial Societies: Social and Economic Roots and Consequences'. In *Social Polarization in Post-Industrial Metropolises* (eds) J. O'Loughlin and J. Friedrichs. New York: Walter de Gruyter.

Organisation for Economic Co-Operation and Development (OECD). 1996. 'Innovative Policies for Sustainable Urban Development: The Ecological City'. Paris: Organisation for Economic Co-Operation and Development.

OECD. 2000. *Economic Outlook*: December.

Organisation for Economic Co-operation and Development. 1998. 'Territorial Development. Integrating Distressed Urban Areas'. Paris: Organisation for Economic Co-Operation and Development.

O'Toole, R. 1998, 'April. Uninventing the Automobile'. *Across the Board*. **35**, 4.

Owens, S.E. and P. Rickaby. 1992. 'Settlements and Energy Revisited'. *Built Environment* **18**, 247–52.

Page, S.J. 1996. 'City Profile: Wellington'. *Cities* **13**, 125–34.

Pahl, R.E. 1975. *Whose City?* (2nd edn). Harmondsworth: Penguin.

——. 1977. 'Managers, Technical Experts and the State: Forms of Mediation, Manipulation and Dominance in Urban and Regional Development. In *Captive Cities* (ed.) M. Harloe. London: Wiley.

Park, R.E. 1952. *Human Communities: The City and Human Ecology*. Glencoe: The Free Press.

Parliamentary Commissioner for the Environment. 1998. *The Cities and Their People: New Zealand's Urban Environment*. Wellington: Parliamentary Commissioner for the Environment.

Parnwell, M.J.G. and L. Wongsuphasawat. 1997. 'Between the Global and the Local: Extented Metropolitanisation and Industrial Decision-making in Thailand. *Third World Planning Review* **19**, 119–38.

Pawley, M. 1978. *Home Ownership*. London: Architectural Press.

Pearson, D. 1994. 'Community'. In *New Zealand Society* (eds) P. Spoonley, D. Pearson and I. Shirley. Palmerston North: Dunmore Press.

Pearson, D.G. and D.C. Thorns. 1983. *Eclipse of Equality: Social stratification in New Zealand*. Sydney, NSW: Allen and Unwin.

Perkins, H.C. 1988a. 'Bulldozers in the Southern Part of Heaven, Defending Place Against Rapid Growth, Part 1: Local Residents' Interpretations of Rapid Urban Growth in a Free-standing Service-class Town. *Environment and Planning A* **20**, 285–308.

——. 1988b. 'Bulldozers in the Southern Part of Heaven, Defending Place Against Rapid Growth, Part 2: The Alliance Strikes Back. *Environment and Planning A* **20**, 435–56.

Perkins, H.C., D.C. Thorns and A. Winstanley. 1999. *The Study of Home from a Social Scientific Perspective: An Annotated Bibliography*. Christchurch: House and Home Project, University of Canterbury and Lincoln University.

Perkins, H.C., P.A. Memon, S.R. Swaffield and L. Gelfand, (eds). 1993. *Environmental Planning in New Zealand*. Palmerston North: Dunmore Press.

Perkins, H.C. and D.C. Thorns. 1999. 'House and Home and Their Interaction with Changes in New Zealand's Urban System, Households and Family Structures'. *Housing, Theory and Society* **16**, 124–35.

——. 2000a. 'Making a Home: Housing, Lifestyle and Social Interaction'. Paper presented to the ENHR Conference, Gavle, Sweden, 2000.

——. 2000b. 'Place Promotion and Urban and Regional Planning in New Zealand'. In *Environmental Planning and Management in New Zealand* (eds) A. Memon and H.C. Perkins. Palmerston North: Dunmore Press.

——. 2000c. 'Urban Sustainability and City Planning'. In *Environmental Planning and Management in New Zealand* (eds) A. Memon and H.C. Perkins. Palmerston North: Dunmore Press.

——. 2001a. 'Gazing or Performing? Reflections on Urry's Tourist Gaze in the Context of Contemporary Experience in the Antipodes'. *International Sociology* **16**, 185–204.

——. 2001b. 'Houses, Homes and New Zealanders' Everyday Lives'. In *Sociology of Everyday Life in New Zealand* (ed.) C. Bell. Palmerston North: Dunmore Press.

——. 2001c. 'A Decade On: Reflections on the Resource Management Act 1991 and the Practice of Urban Planning: New Zealand'. *Environment and Planning B. Planning and Design* **28**, 639–54.

Perkins, H.C., D.C. Thorns, A. Winstanley and B. Newton. 2002. *The Study of 'Home' from a Social Scientific Perspective: An Annotated Bibliography* (University of Canterbury and Lincoln University, House and Home Project). Christchurch: University of Canterbury and Lincoln University.

Pickvance, C.G., (ed.). 1976. *Urban Sociology: Critical Essays*. London: Tavistock.

Pirenne, H. 1956. *Medieval Cities: Their origins and the revival of trade*. Garden City, New York: Doubleday.

Planning Commission. 1993. *Report of the Expert Group on the Estimation of Proportion and Number of the Poor*. New Delhi: Government of India.

Polese, M. 2000. 'Learning from Each Other: Policy Choices and the Social Sustainability of Cities'. In *The Social Sustainability of Cities: Diversity and the Management of Change* (eds) M. Polese and R. Stren. Toronto: University of Toronto Press.

Polese, M. and R. Stren. 2000. *The Social Sustainability of Cities: Diversity and the Management of Change*. Toronto: University of Toronto Press.

Potts, L. 1990. *The World Labour Market: A History of Migration*. London: Zed Books.

Poulantzas, N. 1978. *State, Power, Socialism*. London: New Left Books.

Power, A. 1993. *Hovels to High Rise: State Housing in Europe since 1850*. London: Routledge.

Pratt, G. 1982. 'Class Analysis and Urban Domestic Property: A Critical Examination'. *International Journal of Urban and Regional Research* **6**, 481–502.

Pusey, M. 1991. *Economic Rationalism in Canberra: A Nation Building State Changes its Mind*. Cambridge: Cambridge University Press.

Putnam, R.D. 1995. 'Bowling Alone: America's Declining Social Capital'. *Journal of Democracy* **6**, 65–78.

Quigley, J.M., S. Raphael and S. Smolensky. 2000. 'Homeless in California, Homeless in America'. *Review of Economics and Statistics*.

Quinti, G. 1999. Exclusion sociale et pauvreté: vers des nouveaux modèles de mesure et d'évaluations. In *Research Community for the Habitat Agenda: Linking Research and Policy for the Sustainability of Human Settlements*. International Conference Geneva, July 6–8 1998 (ed.) M.L.C. Cagli. Rome: CERFE Group.

Rakodi, C. 1997. *The Urban Challenge in Africa: Growth and Management of its Large Cities*. Tokyo: United Nations University.

Read, P. (ed.). 2000. *Settlement: A History of Australian Aboriginal Indigenous Housing*. Canberra, Aboriginal Studies Press.

Redfield, R. 1960. *The Little Community Peasant Society and Culture*. Chicago: University of Chicago Press.

Rees, W.E. 1999. 'Achieving Sustainability: Reform or Transformation'. In *Sustainable Cities* (ed.) D. Satterthwaite. London: Earthscan Publications Ltd.

Rex, J. and R. Moore. 1967 (reprint 1974). *Race, Community, and Conflict: A Study of Sparkbrook*. London: Oxford University Press for the Institute of Race Relations.

Ribeiro, L.C.d.Q. and L.C. Do Lago. 1995. 'Restructuring in Large Brazilian Cities: The Centre/Periphery Model. *International Journal of Urban and Regional Research* **19**, 369–82.

Riesman, D. 1961. *The Lonely Crowd*. New Haven: Yale University.

Rimmer, P.J., (ed.). 1997. *Pacific Rim Development: Integration and Globalisation in the Asia-Pacific Economy*. Canberra: Allen and Unwin.

Ritzer, G. 1998. *The McDonaldization Thesis: Explorations and Extensions*. London: Sage Publications.

Robertson, R. 1992. *Globalization: Social Theory and Global Cultures*. London: Sage Publications.

Robertson, R. and H.H. Khondker. 1998. 'Discourses of Globalization'. *International Sociology* **13**, 25–40.

Roelofs, J. 1999. Building and Designing with Nature: Urban Design. In *The Earthscan Reader in Sustainable Cities* (ed.) D. Satterthwaite. London: Earthscan Publications Ltd.

Rojeck, C. and J. Urry. 1997. *Touring Cultures: Transformations of Travel and Theory*. London: Routledge.

Rose, D.A. 1990. 'A Feminist Perspective on Employment, Restructuring and Gentrification: The Case of Montreal'. In *The Power of Geography* (eds) J. Wolch and M. Dear. Boston: Unwin Hyman.

Rossi, P.H. 1956. *Why Families Move: A Study in the Social Psychology of Urban Residential Mobility*. New York: The Free Press.

Rothstein, M. 1998, 4 February. 'Offices Plugged in and Ready to Go'. In *New York Times*.

Ruud, M.E. 2000. 'Youth and Housing. Preferences, Options and Limitations'. Paper presented to the ENHR Conference, Gavle, Sweden, 2000.

Saegert, S. 1980. 'Masculine Cities and Feminine Suburbs: Polarised Ideas, Contradictory Realities'. *Signs* **5**, supplement 596–611.

Sandercock, L. 1976. *Cities for Sale: Property, Politics and Urban Planning in Australia*. London: Heinemann.

Sandercock, L., (ed.). 1997. *The Political Economics of New Zealand*. Auckland: Oxford University Press.

Sandercock, L. 1998. *Making the Invisible Visible: A Multicultural Planning History*. Berkeley: University of California Press.

Sangregorio, I.-L. 2000. *Collaborative Housing in Sweden*. Sweden: Byggforkningsradet (The Swedish Council for Building Research).

Sassen, S. 1991. *The Global City: New York, London, Tokyo*. Princeton, NJ: Princeton University Press.

——. 1994. *Cities in a World Economy*. Thousand Oaks: Pine Forge Press.

——. 1996. 'Rebuilding the Global City: Economy, Ethnicity and Space'. In *Re-Presenting the City* (ed.) A.D. King. Basingstoke: Macmillan – now Palgrave Macmillan.

——. 1999. 'Global Financial Centers'. *Foreign Affairs* **78**, 75–87.

Satterthwaite, D. 1999. *The Earthscan Reader in Sustainable Cities*. London: Earthscan publications.

Saunders, P. 1981. *Social Theory and the Urban Question*. London: Hutchinson.

——. 1986. *Social Theory and the Urban Question, (2nd edn)*. London: Hutchinson.

——. 1990a. *A Nation of Homeowners*. London: Unwin Hyman.

——. 1990b. *Social Class and Stratification*. London: Routledge.

Saunders, P. and P. Williams. 1989. 'The Constitution of Home: Towards a Research Agenda'. *Housing Studies* **3**, 81–93.

Savage, M. and A. Warde. 1993. *Urban Sociology, Capitalism and Modernity*. London: Macmillan Press – now Palgrave Macmillan.

Saville-Smith, K. 2000. 'Positioning Women and Children in New Zealand's Urban Life'. In *Environmental Planning and Management in New Zealand* (eds) P.A. Memon and H.C. Perkins. Palmerston North: Dunmore Press.

Schaffer, F. 1972. *The New Town Story*. London: Granada Publishing Limited.

Schmalenbach, H. 1961. 'The Sociological Category of Communion'. In *Theories of Society-Foundations of Modern Sociology* (eds) T. Parsons, E. Shils, K. Naegele and J. Pitts. New York: Free Press.

Schmidt, J.D. 1998. 'Globalisation and Inequality in Urban South-east Asia'. *Third World Planning Review* **20**, 127–45.

Schollmann, A., H.C. Perkins and K. Moore. 2000. 'Intersecting Global and Local Influences in Urban Place Promotion: The Case of Christchurch, New Zealand'. *Environment and Planning A.* **32**, 55–76.

Scholte, J.A. 2000. *Globalization: A Critical Introduction.* Basingstoke: Macmillan Press – now Palgrave Macmillan.

Schuman, T. 1991. A Framework for Existence: Toward a Non-heroic Architecture. *Journal of Architectural and Planning Research* **8**, 4–8.

Searle, G. and M. Bounds. 1999. 'State Powers, State Land and Competition for Global Entertainment: The Case of Sydney'. *International Journal of Urban and Regional Research* **23**, 165–72.

Seeley, J.R., R.A. Sim and E.W. Loosley. 1956. *Crestwood Heights.* New York: Basic Books.

Seidman, S. 1994. *Contested Knowledge: Social Theory in the Postmodern Era.* Oxford: Blackwell.

Sennett, R. 2000. 'Street and Office: Two Sources of Identity'. In *On the Edge: Living with Global Capitalism* (eds) W. Hutton and A. Giddens. London: Random House.

Sexton, R. 1995. *Parallel Utopias: The Sea Ranch, California; Seaside, Florida.* Vancouver: Rain Coast Books.

Shanghai Pudong New Area Press and Information Office. 1998. *Shanghai Basic Facts: Pudong New Area.* Beijing China: Intercontinental Press.

Shields, R. 1992. *Lifestyle Shopping and the Subject of Consumption.* London: Routledge.

——. 1996. 'Social Spatialization and the Built Environment: The West Edmonton Mall'. In *Geography and Identity: Living and Exploring Geopolitics of Identity* (ed.) D. Crow. Washington D.C.: Maisonneuve Press.

Silverstone, R., (ed.). 1997. *Visions of Suburbia.* Routledge, London.

Simmel, C. 1969. 'The Metropolis and Mental Life'. In *Classic Essays on the Culture of Cities* (ed.) R. Sennet. New York: Appleton Century Crofts.

Simmel, G. 1971. 'The Metropolis and Mental Life'. In *Georg. Simmel* (ed.) D. Levine. Chicago: University of Chicago Press.

Simmie, J. 1974. *Citizens in Conflict.* London: Hutchinson.

——. 1981. *Power, Property and Corporatism: The Political Sociology of Planning.* London: Macmillan – now Palgrave Macmillan.

Sivanandan, A. 1990. *Communities of Resistance: Writings on Black Struggles for Socialism.* London: Verso.

Sjoberg, G. 1960. *The Preindustrial City, Past and Present.* Glencoe, Illinois: The Free Press.

——. 1973. 'The Origin and Evolution of Cities'. In *Cities: Their Origin, Growth and Human Impact* (ed.) K. Davis. San Fransisco: W.H. Freeman and Company.

Skinner, B.F. 1976. *Walden Two.* New York: Macmillan.

Smart, A. 2001. 'Housing and Regulation Theory: Domestic Demand and Global Financialization'. Paper presented to the Mananging Housing and Social Change: Building Social Cohesion, Accommodating Diversity Conference, City University of Hong Kong, 2001.

Smith, M.P. 1980. *The City and Social Theory.* Oxford: Basil Blackwell.

Smith, M.P. and J.R. Feagin. 1987. *The Capitalist City: Global Restructuring and Community Politics.* Oxford: Basil Blackwell.

Smith, N. 1987. 'Of Yuppies and Housing: Gentrification, Social Restructuring, and the Urban Dream'. *Environment and Planning D Society and Space* **15**, 151–72.

——. 1996. 'After Tompkins Square Park: Degentrification and the Revanchist City'. In *Re-Presenting the City* (ed.) A. King. Basingstoke: Macmillan – now Palgrave Macmillan.

Smith, N. and P. Williams. 1986. *Gentrification of the City.* London: Allen and Unwin.

Soja, E. 1993. 'Postmodern Cities': Transcript of Conference Address. Paper presented to the Postmodern Cities Conference, University of Sydney, 1993.

Soja, E.W. 1989. *Postmodern Geographies: The Reassertion of Space in Critical Social Theory.* London: Verso.

——. 2000. *Postmetropolis: Critical Studies of Cities and Regions.* Oxford: Blackwell Publishers.

Soler, J. 1989. 'The Incredible Document Known as the Mazengarb Report'. *Sites* **19**, 22–32.

Somerville, P. 1992. 'Homelessness and the Meaning of Home: Rooflessness or Rootlessness? *International Journal of Urban and Regional Research* **16**, 529–39.

Somerville, P. 1998. 'Explanations of Social Exclusion: Where does Housing Fit in?' *Housing Studies* **13**, 761–80.

Sorkin, M. 1992. *Variations on a Theme Park: The New American City and the End of Public Space.* New York: Hill & Wang.

Southworth, M. 1997. 'Walkable Suburbs? An Evaluation of Neotraditional Communities at the Urban Edge'. *Journal of the American Planning Association* **63**, 28–44.

Southworth, M. and B. Parthasarathy. 1997. 'The Suburban Public Realm II: Eurourbanism, New Urbanism and the Implications for Urban Design in the Amercan Metropolis'. *Journal of Urban Design* **2**, 9–33.

Spearitt, P. 1994. 'I shop therefore I am'. In *Suburban Dreaming* (ed.) L. Johnson. Geelong, Victoria: Deakin University Press.

Stacey, J. 1990. *Brave New Families: Stories of Domestic Upheaval in Late Twentieth Century America.* New York: Basic Books.

——. 1996. *In the Name of the Family: Rethinking Family Values in the Postmodern Age.* Boston: Beacon Press.

Stacey, M. 1969. 'The Myth of Community Studies'. *British Journal of Sociology* **20**, 134–47.

Steuteville, R. 1998. 'Sustainable Development Meets New Urbanism'. *Business: Emmaus* **20**, 22–8.

Storper, M. and A.J. Scott. 1989. 'The Geographical Foundations and Social Regulation of Flexible Production Complexes'. In *The Power of Geography: How Territory Shapes Social Life* (eds) M. Dear and J. Wolch. Boston: Unwin Hyman.

Strauss, A.L. 1961. *Images of the American City.* New York: The Free Press.

Stren, R., R. White and J. Whitney. 1992. *Sustainable Cities: Urbanization and the Environment in International Perspective.* Boulder, Colorado: Westview Press.

Stretton, H. 1970. *Ideas for Australian Cities.* Melbourne: Georgian House.

——. 1974. *Housing and Government.* Sydney: ABC Publishing.

Suttles, G.D. 1972. *The Social Construction of Communities.* Chicago: University of Chicago Press.

Talen, E. 1999. 'Sense of Community and Neighbourhood Form: An Assessment of the Social Doctrine of New Urbanism'. *Urban Studies* **36**, 1361–79.

The Economist. 1998. 'Sao Paulo: Brazil's Troubled Megalopolis'. *The Economist*, 23 May, 1998, 41.

The International Institute for the Urban Environment. 1998. *Indicators for Sustainable Urban Development.* Nickerstteg, The Netherlands: The International Institute for the Urban Environment.

Therborn, G. 2000. 'Globalisations: Dimensions, Historical Waves, Regional Effects, Normative Governance'. *International Sociology* **15**, 151–79.

Thomas, K. 2000. 'Entering the She Zone'. *Middle East.* **298**, 27–8.

Thorns, D. 1992. *Fragmenting Societies? A Comparative Analysis of Regional and Urban Development.* London: Routledge.

——. 1995. 'Housing Wealth and Inheritance: The New Zealand Experience'. In *Housing and Family Wealth* (eds) R. Forrest and A. Murie. London: Routledge.

Thorns, D. and C. Sedgwick. 1997. *Understanding Aotearoa.* Palmerston North: Dunmore Press.

Thorns, D.C. 1997. 'Global Meets the Local, Tourism and the Representation of the City'. *Urban Affairs Review.* **33**, 189–208.

——. 1972. *Suburbia.* London: McGibbon and Kee.

——. 1993. 'Toronto in the 1980s: A Post-Modern or Post Fordist City?' Paper presented to the Postmodern Cities Conference Proceedings, Department of Urban and Regional Planning, The University of Sydney, 1993.

Thorns, D.C. 1998. 'Intergenerational Conflict and the Debate over Welfare Reform'. In *Politics, Policy and Practice: Essays in Honour of Bill Willmott* (eds) R. Du Plessis and G. Fougere. Christchurch: Department of Sociology, University of Canterbury.

Thrift, N. 1996. *Spatial Formations.* London: Sage.

Timms, D.W.G. 1971. *The Urban Mosaic.* Cambridge: Cambridge University Press.

Toennies, F. 1956. *Community and Society* (Trans. C.P. Loomis). Michigan: Michigan State University Press.

Townsend, M. 2000. 'Building the Future from the Fragments: Women's Views on 21st-Century Housing and Neighbourhoods'. Paper presented to the ENHR Conference, Gavle, Sweden, 2000.

Townsend, P. 1979. *Poverty in the United Kingdom*. Harmondsworth: Penguin.

——. 1993. *The International Analysis of Poverty*. New York: Harvester/Wheatsheaf.

Tsenkova, S. 2001. 'Housing and Social Change: The Case of Riga'. Paper presented to the Managing Housing and Social Change: Building Social Cohesion, Accommodating Diversity Conference, City University of Hong Kong, 2001.

Tyner, J.A. 2000. 'Global Cities and Circuits of Global Labor: The Case of Manila, Philippines'. *The Professional Geographer* **52**, 61–74.

United Nations Educational, Scientific, and Cultural Organisation (UNESCO). 2000. *Science for the Twenty-first Century*. Proceedings of the World Congress of Science. Paris: UNESCO.

United Nations Centre for Human Settlements (UNCHS). 1996a. *An Urbanizing World: Global Report on Human Settlements*. Oxford: Oxford University Press.

UNCHS. 1996b. *Cities, Communication and the Media in an Information Society*. Habitat 2 Dialogues. Nairobi: UNCHS.

——. 2001a. *Cities in a Globalizing World: Global Report on Human Settlements 2001*. London: Earthscan Publications Ltd.

——. 2001b. *The State of the World's Cities Report 2001*. Nairobi: UNCHS(H).

——. 2001c. 'A Tale of Two Cities: Dicken's London'. In *The State of the World Cities Report 2001* (ed.) UNCHS. Nairobi: UNCHS(H).

——. 2001d. 'A Tale of Two Cities: Riis's New York'. In *The State of the World's Cities Report 2001* (ed.) UNCHS. Nairobi: UNCHS(H).

United Nations International Crime and Justice Research Institute (UNCRI). 1995. *Criminal Victimisation of the Developing World*. Rome: UNCRI.

United Nations Population Division. 2000. *World Population Prospects: The 1998 Revision*. New York: United Nations Publications.

Urban Task Force and Rogers. R.G. 1999. *Final Report of the Urban Task Force*. Chaired by Lord Rogers of Riverside. London: Spon.

Urry, J. 1981. 'Localities, Regions and Social Class'. *International Journal of Urban and Regional Research* **5**, 455–74.

——. 1991. *The Tourist Gaze*. London: Sage.

——. 1995. *Consuming Places*. London: Routledge.

——. 2000. *Sociology beyond Societies: Mobilities for the 21st Century*. London: Routledge.

Valentine, G. 1991. 'Women's Fear and the Design of Public Space'. *Built Environment* **16**, 288–303.

Valentine, G. 1999. 'Eating in: Home, Consumption and Identity'. *Sociological Review* **47**, 491–525.

Veblen, T. 1934. *The Theory of the Leisure Class? An Economic Study of Institutions*. New York: The Modern Library.

Wachter, S. 2000. 'Housing Policy in the U.S'. Paper presented to the ENHR Conference, Gavle, Sweden, 2000.

Walker, A. 1982. 'Dependency and Old Age'. *Social Policy Administration* **16**, 115–35.

——. 1990. 'The Economic 'Burden' of Ageing and the Prospect of Generational Conflict'. *Ageing and Society* **10**, 377–90.

Wall, G. 1997. 'Sustainable Tourism – Unsustainable Development'. In *Tourism Development and Growth: The Challenge of Sustainability* (eds) S. Wahab and J.P. Pigram. London: Routledge.

Wallerstein, I.M. 1974. *The Modern World-System: Capitalist Agriculture and the Origins of the European World Economy in the Sixteenth Century*. New York: Academic Press.

——. 1979. *The Capitalist World Economy: Essays*. Cambridge: Cambridge University Press.

——. 1998. *Utopistics, or, Historical Choices of the Twenty-first Century*. New York: New Press.

——. 2000. 'Globalization or the Age of Transition? A Long-Term View of the Trajectory of the World System'. *International Sociology* **15**, 249–65.

Walton, J. 1987. 'Urban Protest and the Global Political Economy'. In *The Capitalist City* (eds) M.P. Smith and J.R. Feagin. Oxford: Basil Blackwell Ltd.

Wang, G., (ed.). 1997. *Global History and Migration*. Boulder: Westview Press.

Warde, A. 1991. 'Gentrification and Consumption: Issues of Class and Gender'. *Environment and Planning D, Society and Space* **9**, 223–32.

——. 1996. 'Afterword: The Future of the Sociology of Consumption'. In *Consumption Matters* (eds) S. Edgell, K. Hetherington and A. Warde. Oxford: Blackwell.

Waters, M. 1995. *Globalization*. London: Routledge.

Watson, S. and H. Austerberry. 1986. *Housing and Homelessness: A Feminist Perspective*. London: Routledge.

Watson, S. and K. Gibson, (eds). 1995. *Postmodern Cities and Spaces*. Oxford: Blackwell.

Weber, A.F. 1889. *The Growth of Cities in the Nineteenth Century*. New York: Macmillan.

Weber, M. 1921. *The City*. New York: The Free Press.

Whitehead, C.M.E. 2000. 'From Homelessness to Rooflessness: Shifting Priorities in a Privatised Economy'. Paper presented to the ENHR Conference, Gavle, Sweden, 2000.

Wild, R. 1981. *Australian Community Studies and Beyond*. Sydney: Allen and Unwin.

Williams, P. 1978. 'Urban Managerialism: A Concept of Relevance?' *AREA* **10**, 236–40.

——. 2001. 'Home Ownership and Changing Housing and Mortgage Markets: The New Economic Realities'. Paper presented to the Managing Housing and Social Change: Building Social Cohesion, Accommodating Diversity City University of Hong Kong, 2001.

Willmott, P.R.H. 1992. *Urban Trends 1*. London: Policy Studies Institute.

Wilson, E. 1992. *The Sphinx in the City: Urban life, the Control of Disorder and Women*. Berkeley: University of California.

Winter, I. 1994. *The Radical Home Owner*. Melbourne: Gordon and Breach Publishers.

Wirth, L. 1938. 'Urbanism as a Way of Life'. *American Journal of Sociology* **44**, 1–24.

Wood, D. 1993. 'Sustainable Development in the Third World: Paradox or Panacea. *The Indian Geographical Journal* **68**, 6–20.

Wood, D. and R. Beck. 1990. 'Do's and Dont's: Family Rules, Rooms, and their Relationships. *Children's Environments Quarterly* **7**, 2–14.

World Bank. 1996. *Liveable Cities for the 21st century*, Washington: World Bank.

World Commission on Environment and Development (WCED). 1987. *Our Common Future*. Oxford: Oxford University Press.

Yates, J. 2000. 'Housing Implications of Social, Spatial and Structural Change'. Paper presented to the ENHR Conference, Gavle, Sweden, 2000.

Yates, J. and C. Whitehead. 1998. 'In Defense of Greater Agnosticism. A Response to Galster's Comparing Demand-side and Supply-side Housing Policies. *Housing Studies* **13**, 415–23.

Yeung, Y.-M. 1996. 'An Asian Perspective on the Global City'. *International Social Science Journal* **48**, 25–31.

——. 1997. 'Geography in the Age of Mega-cities. *International Social Science Journal* **49**, 91–104.

Young, I.M. 1997. *Intersecting Voices: Dilemmas of Gender, Political Philosophy and Policy*. Princeton, New Jersey: Princeton University Press.

Young, M. and P.W. Willmott. 1958. *Family and Kinship in East London*. Glencoe, Illinois: The Free Press.

Zorbaugh, H.N. 1929. *The Gold Coast and the Slum*. Chicago: University of Chicago Press.

Zukin, S. 1982. *Loft Living: Culture and Capital in Urban Change*. New Brunswick, New Jersey: Rutgers University Press.

——. 1991. *Landscapes of Power: From Detroit to Disneyland*. Berkeley: University of California Press.

——. 1995. *The Culture of Cities*. Cambridge, Mass.: Blackwells.

Index